I0123756

Social movements and Ireland

MANCHESTER
1824

Manchester University Press

edited by Linda Connolly and Niamh Hourigan

SOCIAL MOVEMENTS AND IRELAND

Manchester University Press

Copyright © Manchester University Press 2006

While copyright in the volume as a whole is vested in Manchester University Press, copyright in individual chapters belongs to their respective authors, and no chapter may be reproduced wholly or in part without the express permission in writing of both author and publisher.

Published by Manchester University Press
Altrincham Street, Manchester M1 7JA, UK
www.manchesteruniversitypress.co.uk

British Library Cataloguing-in-Publication Data is available

Library of Congress Cataloging-in-Publication Data is available

ISBN 978 0 7190 7243 7 paperback

First published by Manchester University Press 2006

This edition first published 2016

The publisher has no responsibility for the persistence or accuracy of URLs for any external or third-party internet websites referred to in this book, and does not guarantee that any content on such websites is, or will remain, accurate or appropriate.

Printed by Lightning Source

Contents

Foreword • Mario Diani

It was a great pleasure – and a great honour – to be invited to Cork in 1998, to give the opening address to the International Sociological Association conference, out of which the volume you are about to read has ultimately emerged. It is even a greater pleasure – and a greater honour – to be asked to write this foreword. There are many reasons why readers should find *Social movements and Ireland* of interest. Here are mine, starting with the most obvious one: this book fills a huge gap in European social movement scholarship. It does so by providing a broad and encompassing account of a range of social movements in a country which has not been at the core of social movement analysts' concerns over the last few decades. This is not to say, of course, that they have not paid attention to collective action based in Ireland. Irish nationalism has, in particular, attracted huge interest and inspired top class scholarship (just think, among many other possible examples, of Cynthia Irvin's study of 'Militant Nationalism' in the Basque Country and Ireland, or of Robert White's analyses of collective violence dynamics in Northern Ireland). All in all, however, it is fair to say that Ireland is not the first country that springs to mind when social movement analysis is mentioned. There are many reasons for this, among which I would probably include the small size of the Irish academic community and the relative peripheral location of the country – at least until it rebranded itself as a 'Celtic tiger'. Whatever the case, the collection assembled by Linda Connolly and Niamh Hourigan does a great job at explaining to social movement scholars worldwide why we should care about Ireland.

However, providing new empirical information on a national case which was previously relatively undocumented is by no means the greatest contribution of this volume. Instead, there are at least three theoretical reasons why we should look at social movements – in particular, new social movements – in Ireland. The first has to do with the fact that, by usual theoretical criteria, Ireland should have been a most unlikely location for those types of collective action. At least until the recent dramatic economic transformation, factors such as the dominant presence of the Catholic church, the persistence of rural society, the ailing economy, and the weakness of the new middle class should all have conjured to make new politics and new social movements a largely inconspicuous phenomenon. And yet, although they do not provide systematic quantitative evidence on the different movements analysed, virtually all the chapters collected here consistently point to a significant role of new social movements in Irish society. One of the most intriguing aspects of this book has precisely to do with the relationship between the movements and their environment, in particular, their cultural environment. It is fitting, therefore, that the title refers to *Social movements **and** Ireland,* rather than **in Ireland,** as most titles would probably read.

Another positive associated with this book is its contribution to a better understanding of the concept of new social movements and its heuristic power. As Alberto Melucci noted a long time ago, both critics and advocates of NSM theory often rely on a misleading view of movements as unified objects to which specific empirical properties should be attached. Accordingly, they tend to reify the idea of the new social movement in specific empirical instances of collective action. Endless – and largely pointless – discussions of whether a certain movement (be it of the women's rather than environmental or civil rights type) be actually a good example of a "new social movement" almost inevitably result. While being firmly rooted in the new social movements theoretical tradition, the contributors to this book manage quite successfully to stay away from those deficiencies. Instead, they illustrate how that particular theoretical perspective can be conveniently applied to a broader range of cases, including nationalism and movements which developed well before the 1960s.

The third reason why I found *Social movements and Ireland* a stimulating and thought-provoking reading has to do with its authors' relationship to the globalization debate and, most directly, to the blossoming literature on what is increasingly identified as the 'global justice movement'. The years which separate 1998, when most of the contributors met in Cork at the ISA conference I have already mentioned, from 2006, have not been just routine years. In 1999, the 'battle of Seattle' drew worldwide attention to the emergence of a new political actor, mobilised in the global arena, on behalf of an agenda that creatively merged typical postmaterialist issues and concerns with issues of inequality and material deprivation. This led many analysts – including myself – to regard the 'new social movements' approach as unable to capture the restructuring of contemporary conflicts which was taking place. Through their careful application of the new social movement perspective to the Irish case, the contributors to this book suggest otherwise. They convincingly warn us against the risk of dismissing that theoretical apparatus in its entirety.

Linda Connolly and Niamh Hourigan have showed considerable resolve – not to mention intellectual finesse – in carrying on this project over the years. I deeply appreciate the opportunity to commend them and their fellow authors for this achievement.

Mario Diani
Trento

Acknowledgements

The genesis of this book was an international conference on social movements, held at University College Cork in 1998, which was organised by Linda Connolly in cooperation with the International Sociological Association (social movements section). Linda thanks all those who contributed to this conference, in particular: Mario Diani, Klaus Eder and Linda Cardinal.

We wish to thank all the authors involved in this book for their cooperation, efficiency and congeniality.

Tony Mason at Manchester University Press also must be thanked for his patience with us and for his enthusiasm for this project, and indeed other Irish sociological projects. Thanks are also due to Derek Speirs for granting us permission to publish his 'Reclaim the Night' photograph on the cover, and to Gloria Greenwood for indexing the book.

We would like to acknowledge the support of the Faculty of Arts UCC for its assistance in funding the publication of this text.

On a personal level, each of us wishes to thank individuals: Linda especially thanks Andy for his support. Niamh expresses her thanks to her partner Derrick Amrein for his continuing support and love during a very busy period.

And, finally, the two people we wish to thank most of all are our two sons – Benjamin (born 22 November 2004) and Curtis (born 17 August 2004) – each of whom managed to create something not unlike a social movement while we were completing this text.

Linda Connolly and Niamh Hourigan
Cork

Abbreviations

AIM	Action, Information, Motivation
CHLR	Campaign for Homosexual Law Reform
CRM	Civil Rights Movement
EEC	European Economic Community
EU	European Union
FNT	Feachtas Náisúinta Telifíse
GATS	General Agreement on Trade and Services
GLF	Gay Liberation Front
IGRM	Irish Gay Rights Movement
IWLM	Irish Women's Liberation Movement
IWU	Irish Women United
LETS	Local Exchange Trading Scheme
NAFTA	North American Free Trade Agreement
NGF	National Gay Federation
NGO	non-governmental organisation
NICRA	Northern Ireland Civil Rights Association
NSM	New Social Movement
NWP	National Women's Party
OSM	old social movement
PLAC	Pro-Life Amendment Campaign
RAR	Residents Against Racism
REP	Rural Environmental Protection Scheme
RMT	Resource Mobilisation Theory
RTE	Radio Telifís Éireann
RUC	Royal Ulster Constabulary
SLM	Sexual Liberation Movement
SMI	Social Movement Industry
SMO	Social Movement Organisation
TnaG	Teilifis na Gaeilge
WEF	World Economic Forum
WTO	World Trade Organisation

Notes on contributors

LINDA CONNOLLY is a Senior Lecturer in the Department of Sociology at University College Cork.

LAURENCE COX is a Lecturer in the Department of Sociology at the National University of Ireland, Maynooth.

NIAMH HOURIGAN is a Lecturer in the Department of Sociology at University College Cork.

ALANA LENTIN is a political sociologist, writer and anti-racist activist.

GERARD MULLALLY is a Lecturer in the Department of Sociology at University College Cork.

LOUISE RYAN is a Senior Researcher at Middlesex University.

PAUL RYAN lectures in the Department of Social Sciences at the Dublin Institute of Technology.

JIM SMYTH is a Senior Lecturer in the Department of Sociology at Queens' University Belfast.

HILARY TOVEY is a Senior Lecturer in the Department of Sociology at Trinity College Dublin.

Introduction • *Linda Connolly and Niamh Hourigan*

THE term 'new social movement' is used to describe movements which have come to prominence since the 1960s (Nash 2000: 102), a decade that marked the emergence of a whole range of 'new' protests as citizens took to the streets and protested against the prevailing goals and orientation of Western societies. Dramatically, the students at Berkeley embroiled the campus in turmoil over the issues of free speech and civil rights; a conflict over administrative regulations at a small university outside Paris escalated into the May revolts and brought France to the edge of collapse; and student protests in Berlin again gave the city the appearance of a war zone.

The most prominent of the 'new' social movements to emerge in the 1960s were the women' s, peace, civil rights and student movements. Although these movements mobilised around a diversity of issues, their participants shared common concerns – a demand for more political participation; a critique of centralised and bureaucratised apparatuses; and scepticism about a singular conception of 'progress' that stresses economic growth while ignoring its negative side effects (Diani 1992: 9). These movements demonstrated ideological, tactical and organisational similarities which set them apart from other, more conventional, forms of politics. They also demonstrated a significant degree of similarity cross-nationally – second-wave feminism, for example, mobilised liberal and radical organisations simultaneously in several countries. The term 'new social movements' (NSMs) was coined to conceptualise the clusters of movement activity that were emerging and interacting on a large scale throughout this period.

NSM theory developed initially in Europe to help explain why a host of movements that emerged in the 1960s and 1970s did not seem to fit the model of Marxian class conflict that had been the dominant model in much social movement theory. The 'newness' of the putatively new social movements is said to consist of such factors as a greater emphasis on group, or collective, identity, values and lifestyles, and a tendency to emerge more from middle- than working-class constituencies. The emergence of the Green Party in Germany with its emphasis on environmental and peace issues, feminism and alternative non-consumerist lifestyles is often portrayed as representing a synthesis of the NSMs, which are aimed at a broad, general, social liberation.

Although the student movement began to dissipate within a few years, it marked the beginning of a broader wave of collective action that affected virtually all advanced industrial democracies in subsequent decades. The general public began to develop widespread political interest beyond traditional economic and class concerns and addressed a 'new' range of social problems, cultural and quality of life issues that had resulted from the aftermath of the modernisation process set in motion after the Second World War. A new style of collective action and politics emerged as organised groups of citizens shifted from traditional methods of interest representation and party politics to a more participatory and expressive political style in the domain of, primarily, civil society.

NSMs have become a permanent feature of modern democracies globally. Many commentators believe that social movements are key agents for bringing about change in societies. *Social Movements and Ireland* draws on cutting-edge research and empirical work to address the development of a range of NSMs that emerged in the Irish and in the international context in the period from the 1960s to the present, as well as some movements with an older history. This volume grew out of an international conference on social movements that was organised in co-operation with the International Sociological Association's social movements section, and held at University College, Cork, in 1998.[1] Although this conference incorporated contributions from several countries, it was evident that a collection which brought together the papers on Irish social movements was particularly timely and long overdue. In agreement with Olesen (2005), current debates about globalisation and civil society often give the mistaken impression that social action is basically detached from the local and the national. However, by focusing on Ireland, several chapters demonstrate how social movements should be theorised in relation to globalisation in a more complex manner (see especially the chapters by Mullally, Tovey and Cox). Furthermore, the sociology of Ireland is generally obscured in mainstream European accounts of social and political change – despite the fact that quality research produced on Irish politics, culture and society has been published internationally for some decades. Ireland tends to be ignored as opposed to critically integrated as a challenging case study in mainstream social theory/comparative accounts of NSMs (most likely because of its distinctive circumstances as a former colony of Britain as well as its unique political, economic and social trajectory when compared to the rest of Europe, throughout the course of the twentieth century).

Yet, it is a particularly interesting case study for social movements theorists. In particular, the analysis of social movements in Northern Ireland challenges the liberal political stance of much social movement theorising. Apart from engaging in political lobbying and consensus-based politics, organised conflict and violence can also be directed at the State by social movements – while state-sponsored violence can be directed at social movements. Social movements in Northern Ireland can also be studied in greater depth in relation to theories of nationalism and postcolonialism. Additionally, it is often inaccurately assumed that NSMs could not and did not flourish in societies 'like Ireland' (a country with a small, predominantly rural, population on the periphery of Western Europe) either before or after the 1960s, because of the social and political dominance of the Catholic Church and it's close relationship with the State. However, although the social and political power of the Catholic Church in Irish culture and society was undoubtedly considerable for much of the twentieth century, this served as a catalyst as well as a constraint for the emergence of radical social movements from the 1960s onwards.

Linda Connolly demonstrates in chapter 3 how Irish feminists, for example, defiantly advocated the availability and legalisation of contraception in the 1970s and campaigned for abortion in the 1980s in direct opposition to Church teaching. Similarly, as Paul Ryan outlines in chapter 4, the gay and lesbian movement in Ireland successfully campaigned for the decriminalisation of homosexuality, which was also vehemently opposed by the Catholic Church. Social movements in Ireland (including Northern Ireland) have not been adequately integrated in recent accounts of NSMs in Britain either (Byrne 1997, for example) – despite a strong degree of interaction and exchange between some movements in the Irish and British contexts (such as the women' s movement and environmental movements). Lack of attention to Northern Ireland in analysis of *British* social movements is particularly remarkable given the centrality of the most recent phase of conflict apropos the British State, as Jim Smyth argues in chapter 5. A further gap in the mainstream literature has been the neglect, until relatively recently, of political violence and in particular state-sponsored violence in European-based research. In general, movements with a nationalistic, ethnic or religious dimension have been neglected in mainstream analysis, which tends to employ a consensual liberal political framework in the analysis of European movements. In chapter 8, Alana Lentin provides an analysis of Irish Traveller issues; and Niamh Hourigan demonstrates in chapter 6, on Irish language media campaigns, how from the 1960s onwards rapid modernisation and economic development, as well as erupting violence, in Northern Ireland led to a period of massive flux where national cultural ideology and the project of nation-building became subject to profound and intense questioning in the Irish context.

This volume aims to address these and other lacunae by systematically relating international theoretical debates about NSMs, including European and American approaches, to Irish issues and debates. The analysis provided aims to both develop this field further in Ireland and to provide new contributions and perspectives in the arena of British and international social movements theory, based on the Irish experience. At the same time, a distinct account of the development of Irish society and ongoing social change is provided in this text through its focus on substantive questions – gender, civil rights, rural development, consumerism, environmentalism, language, sectarianism, sexuality, war, globalisation, racism, ethnicity and immigration. Social movements analysis has only recently emerged as a field of inquiry in Irish political research, which has tended to focus more on the State and formal politics as the basis of social and cultural change. However, as each chapter in this text demonstrates, social movements have been important agents in the immense social and cultural change Ireland has experienced both in the past and in recent decades. Giugni suggests (1999: xi):

> To understand why and how public displays of protest by relatively powerless social actors may be effective, and what consequences they produce, is of utmost importance, for the history and present of human societies are studded with such public displays. In fact, it has become a common state of affairs to maintain that social movements are crucial actors in the processes of social and political change.

Ireland is no exception to this, as each chapter demonstrates in depth. By the 1960s, a range of nascent protest groups and campaigns were forming in Ireland. For example, the conservationist Irish Georgian Society opposed the destruction of Georgian Dublin; Housing Action emerged to campaign for housing rights both in Dublin and in Derry, where the campaign was a catalyst for the formation of the Northern Ireland Civil Rights Association and culminated in 'Bloody Sunday' – one of the major turning points in the recent phase of conflict in Northern Ireland; a family planning campaign consolidated, which subverted the law by providing contraception illegally and provided an impetus for the women's movement; and anti-war and student protests were staged. In the 1970s, a second wave of feminist activism, that had its origins in the first wave of feminism in the earlier part of the century, was propelled into the public arena and by the 1980s a pro-life movement, environmental movement, gay and lesbian movement and nationalist protest in response to the Hunger Strikes in the Maze Prison in Belfast were all mobilising. In recent years, the anti-war, animal rights, pro-life, men's rights and anti-globalisation movements have also mobilised in Ireland.

Declining membership in political parties and low turnouts in elections and referenda is a recognised problem in Ireland and elsewhere. Crucially, social movements in Ireland can be said to have generated an alternative and more citizen oriented type of politics in civil society in Ireland alongside the established system of political parties and representation. NSMs are often seen to remain intentionally outside the institutional framework of government and as preferring to influence policy through political pressure and the weight of public opinion rather than becoming directly involved in conventional politics. However, as several of the contributions in this volume demonstrate, the delineation between institutional and non-institutional activism is often more fluid in the development of social movements. Movement strategies often target both the State and civil society at the same time. Furthermore, as Ger Mullally demonstrates in chapter 4, movements or movement organisations that start out as autonomous and radical can become mainstreamed and even institutionalised over time.

Movements are often thought to have a direct and straightforward impact on formal institutions and the State by campaigning for changes in the law and in policy, for example. However, in agreement with Crossley (2002: 9), movements also ' ... problematize the ways in which we live our lives and ... call for changes in our habits of thought, action and interpretation'. Accordingly, although movements are associated with episodes of revolution and mass protest in the public imagination, the kinds of changes movements aspire towards and achieve are more often local and cultural in nature. Nevertheless, as chapter 1 demonstrates, various interpretations of the relationship between movements and socio-cultural/regime change exist in the field of movement analysis.

Defining social movements

In general, social movements are hard to define. By nature, they are elusive phenomena with unclear boundaries in time and space. Movements generally mobilise in several different centres (often in both institutional and non-institutional contexts) at the same time and the impact of activism is typically diffuse, pervasive and uneven at the structural and cultural levels. Several definitions exist in the field. For Dahlerup (1986: 2):

> A social movement is a conscious, collective activity to promote social change, representing a protest against the established power structure and against the dominant norms and values. The commitment and active participation of its members or activists constitute the main resource of any social movement.

A social movement is frequently defined as a network of visible organisations. Other definitions focus more on the symbolic and cultural dimensions of movements. Foweraker, for instance, argues there is some agreement that a social movement must be defined not as a group of any kind, but as a 'process' (1995: 23). By conducting internal dialogue, debates and workshops, for example, activism becomes associated with personal development and change at the individual level. Movements may also unleash creativity and powerful symbolism through protest songs, murals and political art.

In view of all this, where can a social movement be said to begin and end? Can certain types of activism, such as short-term or single-issue protests/campaigns, be considered truly part of 'a social movement' – or are they just transient forms of collective action? According to Crossley (2002: 8): 'Part of the "movement" in social movements is a transformation in the habits, including linguistic and basic domestic habits, that shape our everyday lives.' In this broad cultural definition, taking a portion of our household waste to recycling centres, using our cars less or buying an anti-perspirant that does not contain harmful CFCs are small everyday gestures that are very much shaped by the activities of the environmental movement. At the same time, prominent and highly organised protests (such as the dramatic tactics of eco warriors at the Glen of the Downs in Co. Wicklow) and organised campaigns (such as the anti-incinerator campaign in Ringaskiddy, Co. Cork) in recent years, initiatives that tend to lobby the polity and rely heavily on access to the media and established channels of influence, can be also said to encompass 'the environmental movement' in the Irish case. Is the consumer taking his or her waste to the local recycling centre as much a part of the environmental movement as the eco warrior in the Glen of the Downs or the paid worker/lobbyist in the headquarters of Greenpeace?

Each chapter in this volume demonstrates various positions on how to define and research 'social movements'. Some postmodernist scholars even reject the term, arguing that there is no agreed definition of a social movement. In this view, activist networks articulate a confluence of cultural practices and identities that cannot be neatly categorised. Accordingly, rather than adopt a fixed definition it is perhaps helpful, in agreement with Byrne (1997), to think about where social movements might 'fit' in a continuum of political action which stretches from mainstream political parties at one extreme, to promotional interest groups, to social movements and politically inspired riots and civil disobedience at the other. As we look at different movements and theories in detail, throughout this text, the qualitatively different nature of social movements when compared with more mainstream forms of collective political action becomes apparent. In the process, the ongoing quandary of definition in the movement paradigm is further problematised and developed.

Social movements and Ireland: the cultural context

Social movements (including nationalist, labour, suffrage and cultural movements) were fundamental in creating the political conditions and revolution that paved the way for the establishment of the Irish Free State in 1922. However, collective action in civil society became regarded as a relatively marginal form of political expression in the early decades of the Irish State's existence. Catholicism, nationalism and the desire for political stability in the newly formed post-colonial State created an institutional conservatism and authoritarianism in Irish politics and society that persisted for some decades. Despite this history, in common with most Western countries, NSMs began to appear in the 1960s in Ireland, including Northern Ireland. In the Irish Republic, the 1960s was a period of economic modernisation and a general opening up of society to new secular ideas and values, while in the North the late 1960s marked the onset of three decades of violence and conflict – often referred to as 'the Troubles'. In contrast, the 1980s was a period marked by economic recession, high unemployment and emigration in Ireland. However, by the 1990s Ireland again experienced unprecedented economic growth and social change. In the aftermath of 'the Celtic Tiger' boom, lifestyles, consumerism, social values, work, family life, leisure, intimate relations, religious practices and so forth have transformed profoundly in contemporary Ireland. Under the new conditions of modernity in Ireland traditional forms of class identity are said to have 'dissolved': changes in the labour market and in gender relations and family forms allegedly render the institutions of the welfare state unsustainable and inappropriate; globalisation and reflexivity in lifestyle choice and consumption make centralised forms of economic control less workable; while the established political parties and political institutions are said to have lost their legitimacy as a consequence of public apathy and the widespread corruption revealed within the polity in recent tribunals. The changing conditions of modernity also involve democratisation of personal lives in which relationships between lovers, friends, parents and children, for example, are no longer strictly governed by religion, traditional assumptions and expectations. In Northern Ireland, the Belfast Agreement of 1998 marked the beginning of an intricate Peace Process which led to a ceasefire culminating in the recent announcement that the IRA is to decommission its weapons.

How can studies of social movements illuminate all these developments? A range of social movements in Ireland have targeted perceived negative effects of modernisation and social change while attempting to create alternative modernities and sites of resistance. The social movements analysed in this volume relate directly to substantive questions in the social and cultural transformation recently experienced in Ireland – gender (Louise Ryan and Connolly), environmentalism (Mullally), rural life, production and consumer issues (Tovey), sectarianism and political conflict (Smyth), minority language issues (Hourigan), immigration (Lentin), sexuality (Ryan, Paul) and globalisation (Cox). At the same time, a number of theoretical controversies in the field of social movements theory are debated and developed by each author – including for example, the so-called distinction between *new* and *old* movements (Louise Ryan), the question of why certain movements become institutionalised (Mullally), the career of movements repressed by the State (Smyth) and the problem of how to study the consequences and outcomes of movements (Connolly and Hourigan). Overviews of the development of key movements are combined with theoretical analysis, which draws on current frameworks within social movement research internationally, including NSM theory, frame analysis, political opportunity structures and processes, resource mobilisation theory and cultural theoretical perspectives. Each individual chapter also develops methodological questions concerning how to define, study and research social movements in Ireland and elsewhere.

The discussion in this text also reflects on the issue of *activist theorising* (see Cox's chapter). The text makes it clear that many theorists in this field are not just detached observers of social movements – they are in fact proponents of them or, what Eyerman and Jamison (1991) refer to as movement intellectuals. Clearly, we did not adopt a realist, objective position in our approach to social movements in this text. Moreover, it is clear that writing about social movements from the perspective of Ireland generates its own set of positions and critiques of mainstream theorising. The prevailing orientation of mainstream social movements theory is often strongly challenged as a consequence in this volume. Hilary Tovey, for instance, suggests that the association of modernity with industrialisation, urbanisation, science and technology constructed the rural not as a significant location of struggles around modernity's futures but as a backward and residual periphery, passively receiving innovations which always take place elsewhere.

The political orientation of some movements is reflected in several chapters in the standpoint adopted. The gendered nature of social movements theory is notably challenged in this volume. Louise Ryan writes that, with few exceptions, all the leading social movement theorists are men – which is remarkable given the fact that women are so active and dominant in NSMs. The low participation rate of women in the higher echelons of political parties and in governments contrasts with a high level of female participation in social movements. Ryan argues that attention to gender is essential for a thorough and accurate explanation of collective action because the gender-neutral language that characterises much social movement theory obscures the role of gender within the mobilisation, organisation and stratification of movements. Moreover, as both Linda Connolly and Louise Ryan argue, the women's movement is one of the oldest and most persistent movements in the context of Ireland. In agreement with Calhoun (1995), in the nineteenth and early twentieth centuries there were many movements, including the feminist, nationalist, utopian and religious movements, which were very much concerned with lifestyle and identity politics.

The urban as well as the gender bias in the field are also challenged in this text. Niamh Hourigan provides an in-depth assessment of Gaeltacht protest movements in Ireland. And, as indicated above, Hilary Tovey demonstrates that the literature on social movements has had little to say about rural or agrarian collective action. Despite the rich tradition of collective action by small farmers, peasants and farm-workers around the world, including Ireland, social movements with predominantly urban constituencies have received the most attention by scholars as well as the general public. Tovey demonstrates how Ireland offers a rich history of rural social movements which have been generally neglected by students of social movements and collective action: including, the farmers' cooperative movement, the organic movement, movements for rural development, environmental activism, mobilisations against the genetic modification of food, LETS movements, language rights movements, religious and spiritual movements, anti-waste and anti-waste disposal movements, slow food and local food movements, and experiments in sustainable living.

Although this text provides an in-depth account of innovative research, in many respects this volume highlights the need for further research. A key question that arises from the collection is how can factors unique to the Irish case illuminate the comparative study of social movements? More comparative work, further locating Irish movements in the context of globalisation and transnationalism, is required. Some other significant movements also need to be theorised in the case of Ireland. A gap which readers may note in the text is the absence of a specific study of movements of the right and, more specifically, Catholic fundamentalist movements which played a key role in the landmark divorce and abortion referenda and campaigns of the 1980s and 1990s in Ireland. Sociologists have devoted some attention to the activities of Catholic organisations such as PLAC (Pro-Life Amendment Campaign) and SPUC (Society for the Protection of the Unborn Child) (see Inglis 1998; Hug 1999; Connolly 2002; Connolly and O'Toole 2005). Journalist Emily O' Reilly has also written a detailed account of the many and varied organisational forms and tactical strategies used by the Catholic right. However, so far, there has been little scholarship on the politics of the right in Ireland from a social movements perspective. The text's focus on left-oriented movements perhaps reflects the broader influence of social movement theorisation in Europe, which has tended to devote greater attention to NSMs and less attention to fundamentalist organisations. Similarly the growth of men's rights organisations – constituting a men's rights movement? – is a subject that requires more research in the Irish context. Community development is also a major activist sector in Ireland that can be located in the NSMs paradigm. And there is much more that can be done on the question of social movements and Northern Ireland. Consequently, although *Social Movements and Ireland* provides a rich analysis of globalisation, environmentalism, rural society, immigration and ethnicity, sectarianism, gender, sexuality, language and the media in the context of Ireland, essentially this text is a benchmark for the further analysis of a range of social movements.

Note

1 The conference organised by Linda Connolly, incorporated over eighty participants and was addressed by Mario Diani and Klaus Eder. It was the Second Regional Conference on Social Movements and Change with the title: 'Social Movements in Transition: moving towards the millennium?' It was supported by the Department of Sociology, University College, Cork and the International Sociological Association – Social Movements, Collective Action and Social Change Research Committee.

Introduction

Bibliography

Byrne, P., 1997 *Social Movements in Britain* (London: Routledge).

Calhoun, C., 1995 '"New Social Movements" of the Early Nineteenth Century', in Traugott, M. (ed.) *Repertoires and Cycles of Collective Action* (London: Duke University Press), pp. 173–215.

Connolly, L., 2002 *The Irish Women's Movement: From revolution to devolution* (Basingstoke: Palgrave).

Connolly, L. and O'Toole, T., 2005 *Documenting Irish Feminisms: The second wave* (Dublin: Lilliput).

Crossley, N., 2002 *Making Sense of Social Movements* (Buckingham: Open University Press).

Dahlerup, D., 1986 'Is the New Women's Movement Dead? Decline or change of the Danish movement', in Dahlerup, D. (ed.) *The New Women's Movement: Feminism and political power in Europe and the US* (London: Sage), pp. 217–44.

Diani, M., 1992 'The Concept of Social Movement', *Social Review*, 40:1, 1–25.

Eyerman R., and Jamison, A., 1991 *Social Movements: A cognitive approach* (Cambridge: Polity Press).

Foweraker, J., 1995 *Theorizing Social Movements* (London: Pluto Press).

Giugni, M., 1999 'Introduction: social movements and change', in Giugni, M., McAdam, D. and Tilly, C. (eds) *From Contention to Democracy* (Lanham, MD: Rowman & Littlefield).

Hourigan, N., 2003 *Escaping the Global Village: Media, language and protest* (Lanham, MD: Lexington Books).

Hug, C., 1999 *The Politics of Sexual Morality in Ireland* (Basingstoke: Macmillan).

Inglis, T., 1998 *Moral Monopoly: The rise and fall of the Catholic Church* (Dublin: University College Dublin Press).

Nash, K., 2000 *Contemporary Political Sociology: Globalisation, politics and power* (Oxford: Blackwell).

Olesen, T., 2005 'Transnational Publics: new spaces of social movement activism and the problem of global shortsightedness', *Current Sociology*, 53:3, 419–40.

1 · Linda Connolly

Theories of social movements: a review of the field

OVER the last four decades, more and more people have been turning their backs on mainstream politics and parties, and pursuing more unconventional ways of 'making themselves heard' (Byrne 1997). Social scientists have revived the idea of 'social movements' to explain this phenomenon. From the 1960s onwards most Western countries experienced waves of protest in the form of social movements. The most prominent of these were the women's, the environmental, the peace/anti-Vietnam, the civil rights and the student movements. Some of these movements were considered *new* (such as the environmental movement), and others were existing and had mobilised in earlier periods (first-wave feminism, for example). Although these movements mobilised around a diversity of issues, their participants seemed to share common concerns. According to Dieter Rucht (1991:9), chief among these was the quest for more political participation; a critique of centralised and bureaucratised apparatuses; and scepticism about a singular conception of 'progress' that stresses economic growth while ignoring its negative side effects. This chapter reviews the main theoretical perspectives that have developed in the analysis of these movements in the US and Europe and provides a context for understanding the ways in which social movements in Ireland (new and old) are currently being analysed.

Social movements theory has developed in a multifaceted manner in recent decades. The developments of the 1960s prompted a major paradigmatic shift in the field in the US where conventional ideas about 'collective behaviour' were challenged. In the first half of the twentieth century, theorists in the field mainly believed that social movements emerge primarily as collective responses to specific grievances in society. Movements and collective behaviour were considered remove primarily social psychological phenomena. What became termed 'structural strain', for instance, was thought to lead to a disruptive psychological state such as alienation, cognitive dissonance or relative deprivation (Turner

[*11*]

and Killian 1957; Smelser 1962). When this psychological disturbance reaches the aggregate threshold required to produce a social movement/collective action, the causal sequence is complete. Social movements, in this framework, are primarily a collective response to a society in disarray. Movement organisations do not play a prominent role in this model. Too much organisation, especially formal organisation, is considered a symptom of institutionalisation. And eventually bureaucratisation, centralisation and oligarchisation of movement organisations were thought to mark the end of a movement.

In contrast to these traditional *breakdown* perspectives, resource mobilisation theory (RMT) emerged in the 1960s in the US and stressed the more rational and organised character of social movement activities, which was increasingly manifest in the *new* social movements that emerged in this period in the US and elsewhere. The followers of social movements were no longer conceptualised as disparate and alienated masses at the margins of society and politics (Rucht 1991: 9) – on the contrary, the new generation of activists was drawn largely from the educated and middle-class sections of society. In contrast to traditional theories, the conceptual boundary between conventional and unconventional behaviour became blurred and protest was conjectured as a more normal than abnormal phenomenon of social and political life. Ideas of rational choice and the sociology of organisations were explicitly adopted.

There was no corresponding paradigmatic shift in European sociological thought. The notion that there is an axial relationship between social movements and broader social and cultural change has existed since the nineteenth century. However, the central idea that the social movements that emerged in the 1960s are part of an overarching phenomenon of *new social movements* (NSMs) was developed. The relationship between social movements and broader social change is a common point of reference in the NSMs arena. However, despite a degree of homogeneity in the NSMs literature, in reality this perspective became a highly differentiated and complex field. Some analysts promote the idea that NSMs herald a new societal type, they emphasise the parallels to earlier movements or speculate that these groupings will assume the central role of the labour movement and the liberal bourgeois movement in earlier societies (Rucht 1991).

This chapter will discuss the emergence of each of these frameworks and will provide a synopsis of key interventions in this field.

Assumptions of classical approaches to collective behaviour

Classical approaches to collective behaviour in American sociology were underlined by the notion of 'system strain', framed by the Parsonian notion of 'societal integration' (Parsons 1964) – which seemed threatened either by revolutionary agitation or by totalitarian movements. According to Mayer (1995: 171):

Theories of social movements: a review

First in the classical-functionalist approaches, which were dominant in American social movement research until the early 70s, collective behaviour was triggered by societal strain, hence disorganisation, and mediated via social 'uprootedness' and anomie (Smelser, 1962) or via frustration and fear (Gurr, 1970).

Variations of this approach all share the core assumption that individual deprivations, breakdowns of the social order and homogenising ideologies are important preconditions for the emergence of social movements (Mayer 1995: 171). Smelser (1962), for instance, contended that collective behaviour is an irrational and cognitively inadequate response to structural strains emerging from the modernisation of society. Kornhauser (1959) suggested that collective behaviour results from participants' disconnectedness from normal or traditional social relations. According to Ryan (1992: 163), psychology-based explanations of social movement participation include characteristics related to an authoritarian personality (Adorno et al. 1950); feelings of marginality (Lasswell and Blumenstock 1939); isolation (Ernst and Loth 1952); personality peculiarities (Hoffer 1952); some kind of individual pathology (Heberle 1951); and aggressive tendencies (Dollard et al. 1971). In terms of general social theory, analysis of the emergence of social movements was related to mass society and cultural milieu perspectives (Mills 1956; Kornhauser 1959; Riesman 1961; Gusfield 1962); social conflict forces (Dahrendorf 1958); structural change (Smelser 1962); and relative deprivation perceptions (Merton and Kitt 1950; Davies 1962; Gurr 1970).

The category 'social movement' was used to encompass quite a broad number of so-called movements – including fascist, communist and 'emancipatory' movements. The defining feature of the 'aberrant' behaviour considered to characterise movement participation was that it occurs apart from the national consensus and established norms. In this framework, movements do not follow prevailing norms and the social actors who participate in social movements are marginal and alienated members of society. Structures associated with the complex processes of movement formation received little attention in this perspective. The growth and expansion of a movement was attributed more to factors of communication, such as rumour, circular reaction and diffusion, in which homogenising ideologies play an important role (Mayer 1995: 171). Viewing resistance to modernisation/social change as irrational (presumably because modernisation was considered a 'good thing'), classical theorists focused primarily on the micro level of social psychological analysis. The origins of social movements are therefore explained by reference to the same dynamics that account for individual participation in movement activities. In short, answers to micro questions of individual participation and answers to macro questions of movement emergence are sought in the characteristic profile of participants and the presumed regressive psychological functions attendant to participation (Mayer 1995: 172).

While not all theorists had an agreed view of collective behaviour as an irrational response of alienated individuals to change, they all shared an emphasis on the psychological dimensions to breakdown combined with emphasis on the central role of crude modes of communication, volatile goals and the transitory nature of social movements:

> The underlying assumption begins that, if the resistance does not overwhelm modernising elites and institutions are successfully defended, the resistance is bound to fail. Modernisation will eventually provide the blessings of progress to all. (*ibid*)

The political model in which social movements were located in this framework was based on the pluralist ideal of an open polity. Because the pluralist model/view of society takes for granted the rational pursuit of interests through decentralised channels of political access, movements appear as superfluous and irrational. In this view, why would any individual participate in an irrational form of collective action (i.e. a social movement) when established political groupings and interest groups, for example, provide an effective means of political influence? Non-institutional forms of collective action, in this framework, are a matter of marginal groups who lack the cognitive or temporal resources to use established political channels. The political system is presumed to be always receptive with ease of access in the pluralist model. Consequently, social movements were viewed primarily as spontaneous outbursts and were not accorded a long-term capacity to influence social change. The political processes, underlying organisational life of a movement and actual political change did not enter this model's analysis.

Early RMT

RMT emerged in the 1970s as a reaction to the explanatory weaknesses of grievances and deprivation models (Smelser 1962; Gurr 1970) of collective behaviour which did not successfully account for the new wave of social movement activity widely observable in American society. Emerging resource mobilisation theorists took the view that social movements emerge not so much because grievances increase as because there is an increase in *resources* available to an aggrieved population. Fundamentally, it is movement *organisations* that facilitate goal achievement and ensure movement survival. Social movement organisations (SMOs) accumulate and allocate resources. Initially it was thought that individual and organisational decisions to support an SMO are rational choices, based on an evaluation of the costs and benefits of participation. Organisation (especially indigenous organisation) was thus considered a key resource in itself (Zald and McCarthy 1987). The resource mobilisation approach has been fruitful in analysing mobilisation processes and in emphasising that existing organisations and networks not only increase the chance that persons will be confronted with a mobilisation attempt, but also make widespread recruitment possible. Pinard (1971), for instance, showed that an increase in relative deprivation leads only to more protest if a collectivity has a certain degree of organisation, which acts as a catalyst for mass mobilisation.

The resource mobilisation framework became extremely useful for charting the life history of specific movements, for examining the level of societal support for and constraint on movement organising and in connecting social movements to the central political processes of a given society (Ryan 1992: 3). It focuses on the complex ways a movement creates interest and support for its goals. Resources refer to the assets garnered by a movement, and mobilisation refers to the control and use of assets. Mobilisation can be defined in two ways: in terms of the creation and activation of commitment. Mobilisation as activation involves the already committed members in a stage of resurgence and the forms of organisation and activism they undertake. Mobilisation for commitment refers to the actions implemented by the resurgent movement to increase the base of potential participants. Primarily, resource mobilisation was a dynamic perspective that shifted the focus in the US from *why* people join a social movement to *how* they attempt to change their condition and also how movements expanded and grew. Analysis of social movements was directed away from the heavy emphasis on the social psychology of movement participants towards analysis of the ongoing problems and strategic dilemmas of movement leaders.

The strength of the resource mobilisation approach has been in analysing mobilisation processes and in emphasising the role of existing organisations and *networks* in laying the groundwork for social movement formation and continuity. According to one commentator, by the end of the 1980s resource mobilisation accounted for approximately three-quarters of the literature in the field of social movements in the US (McClurg Mueller 1992: 3). Zald and McCarthy (1977, 1979, 1987) were largely responsible for the establishment of resource mobilisation in the field of social movements in the US. They challenged the assumption of a close link between the frustrations or grievances of a collectivity of actors and the growth/decline of movement activity. Other early and influential volumes published include the work of Oberschall (1973), Gamson (1975) and Tilly (1978). Gamson's *Power and Discontent*, published in 1968, emphasised the consequences of the differential distribution of political access and resources for strategies of influence, and Tilly and his colleagues were developing their collective action and strike analysis programme in the early 1970s.

Resource mobilisation stressed the complex problems of mobilisation in relation to the manufacture of discontent, tactical choices and the infrastructure of society and movements. Previous emphasis on structural strain, generalised belief and deprivation largely ignored these ongoing problems and strategic dilemmas within social movements. Many of the practical questions that have concerned social movement leaders by analysing the dynamics and tactics of social movement growth, decline and change were addressed in the resource mobilisation paradigm. The variety of resources (both tangible and intangible) that must be mobilised was related to linkages of social movements to other groups, dependence of movements on external support for success, tactics used by authorities to control or incorporate movements and the relationship of social movements to the State.

In the last three decades, the study of social movements has undergone profound change in the US. It is now closer to political sociology than before, and its concerns are more distant from the analysis of traditional collective behaviour analysis of fads, fashions and panics. The transformation of social movement theory in the US rests upon explicit recognition that the mobilisation of resources for collective action is problematical. Distinctive variants of resource mobilisation have been formulated in recent decades, however. Some analysts focused more directly on the relation of collective action to the underlying broad changes in political structures (Tilly); put more emphasis upon the analysis of the linkages among individuals, the mobilisation of individuals through pre-existing structures, and the micro-situational determinants of participation (Oberschall); and/or focused on the political process aspects of mobilisation, noting how opportunities for social movement action are created by regime weakness and instability, as well as regime support (McAdam).

Although the central theoretical statements of resource mobilisation clearly overlapped by the 1980s, they varied in emphasis. Zald and McCarthy concentrated on the SMO and the movement entrepreneur 'looking outward for resources and reflexively looking at constituents and the authorities for tactics and opportunities' (Zald 1992: 333). Other variants included research into micro mobilisation (McAdam 1988), political opportunities (Perrow 1979), and movement's relationship to the State (Tilly 1984). Theorists' attention to these factors also began to move RMT closer to the analysis of politics and political interaction (Piven and Cloward 1977; McAdam 1982). It was observed, for example, that the discovery of a new tactic sometimes activates a protest cycle or shifts it to a new level of interaction with authorities. As long as the opponent does not know how to respond to the tactic, the protesters' chances of success remain high (Klandermans, Kriesi and Tarrow 1988). Eventually this advantage dissipates because the opponent learns how to react to the new tactic. These authors shifted attention from movements as emergent and unstructured forms of collective action to movements as a form of mass politics. Tilly (1978), for instance, traced the development of a concept of 'repertoires' of collective action and the relation between such repertoires and political crises and regime changes. Piven and Cloward (1977) emphasised the importance of electoral realignments in triggering social movements. And Tarrow (1983) argued that a reform cycle runs parallel to the protest cycle and is thus an indicator of how a government responds to the new protest tactic.

The reassertion of the political is one of the major contributions to the field of social movement study. In contrast to the established 'collective behaviour' theories, resource mobilisation located social movements squarely within the realm of rational political action. Considerable evidence was provided to suggest that changes in the structure of political opportunities are central to the ebb and flow of movement activity. The political opportunity structure refers to the distribution of member support and opposition to the political aims of a given challenging group. Challengers are characteristically excluded from any real participation in institutionalised politics because of strong opposition to movements on the part of most polity members. Lipsky (1970) originally described how communist political systems experienced a 'thaw' or 'a process of retrenchment', and posed two questions. Should it not at least be an open question as to whether the political system experiences such stages as fluctuations? Is it not sensible to assume (*ibid*: 14) that the system will be more or less open to specific groups at different times and different places?

Tarrow (1983) proposed a pattern of 'thaw' and contraction as a standard feature of most liberal democratic regimes. Theorists in the field have extensively studied variations in support and opposition that constitute the evolving structure of political opportunities. Jenkins and Perrow (1977: 263) attributed the success of the farm workers' movement of the 1960s to the altered political environment which originated in economic trends and political realignments that took place quite independently of any 'push' from insurgents. McAdam (1982) attributed the emergence of black protest activity in the 1950s to key political trends – including the expansion of the black vote, its shift to the Democratic Party and post-war competition for influence among emerging Third World nations – which served to enhance the bargaining position of civil rights SMOs. Agencies already sympathetic to the movement were crucial resources in the mobilisation process. Broadly speaking, the political opportunity structure of the 1960s facilitated the emergence of a wide variety of social movements. It is similarly argued that the transformed political opportunity structure of the 1980s (economic recession, etc.) encouraged the mobilisation of successful pro-life and New Right movements, such as the Moral Majority in the US.

A central problem in resource mobilisation became how to account for the growth, maintenance and decline of social movements. Tarrow (1983, 1988, 1989) developed the concept of 'cycles of protest' to analyse the rise and decline of individual movements. Cycles of protest are related to the structure of political opportunity – widespread protest is likely to occur when political conditions reduce the costs of collective action and increase the likelihood of success. For instance, political opportunities exist when elites are divided among themselves or are open to the demands of protesters, allies are available, and resources are plentiful. However, beyond explaining how these factors influence a period of widespread protest, this notion is useful in pointing to changes that occur over the course of a period of limited movement activity. During a peak cycle the social movement sector expands in size, with important consequences for the movements and organisations that comprise it – including the potential for both cooperation and competition among movement organisations and other actors drawn into movement activity.[1] As Tarrow (1989: 23) contends, the political opportunity structure changes once a cycle of protest is under way, because 'early riser' movements provide models of action and evidence of elite vulnerability for movements that emerge later in the cycle. The civil rights movement (CRM) in the US, for example, directly or indirectly generated resources which spawned the growth of numerous other movements in the social movement sector of the 1960s. Social movement theorists need to take into account how the outcomes of one round of collective action affect the resources, organisation and tactics of the next (Snyder and Kelly 1979).[2]

When a cycle of protest wanes (in the case of post-independent Irish society, for example) movements find it more difficult to survive. Piven and Cloward (1977) predict an inevitable decline in 'poor people's movements' when conditions of political opportunity dissipate. However, studies of other kinds of movements reveal that certain types of movement organisation do survive. Rupp and Taylor's (1987) analysis of the women's movement in the years between the passage of suffrage and the 1960s shows that the movement was kept alive 'in the doldrums' by its 'elite-sustained' structure consisting of a small, exclusive, and affluent core of feminist activists. This finding points to the more general proposition that movements with different organisational structures have different capacities to survive 'dry' periods for mobilisation. The formalisation of movement organisations can also facilitate ongoing mobilisation.

A central question of any empirical case study is: where does a movement come from? The core assumption of RMT is that movements do not emerge irrationally. The organisational base of previous waves of activism and existing networks are in fact a crucial element of a movement's emergence. One of the main criticisms of social movements theory is often its 'immaculate conception' view of those social movements which emerged during the 1960s (Turner and Killian 1957). Recent empirical work suggests that the break between the movements of the 1960s and those of the earlier part of the century is not as sharp as previously thought. The work of Verta Taylor has been particularly useful in this area. She suggests (1989: 761) that 'what scholars have taken for "births" were in fact breakthroughs or turning points in movement mobilisation'. Taylor (p. 762) uses the NWP (National Women's Party) case in the US to highlight the processes by which social movements maintain continuity *between* cycles of peak activity. Mizruchi's abeyance process is applied to the case. Abeyance is essentially a holding pattern of a group which continues to mount some type of challenge even in a non-receptive environment. In congruence with the resource mobilisation perspective, political opportunities and an indigenous organisational base are viewed as major factors in the rise and decline of social movements.

Critique of resource mobilisation

For over three decades RMT has emphasised the importance of institutional continuities between conventional social life and collective protest. Piven and Cloward (1995) provided a timely reappraisal of this central posit. While acknowledging that traditional breakdown perspectives incorrectly portrayed movements as 'mindless eruptions lacking either coherence or continuity with organised social life' (*ibid*: 137), Piven and Cloward argue that resource mobilisation analysts commit a reverse error: RMT's emphasis on similarities between conventional and protest behaviour has led analysts to understate the differences and thus to normalise collective protest. Blurring the distinction between normative and non-normative forms of collective action is the most fundamental expression of this tendency. Resource mobilisation analysts are clearly aware that some forms of protest violate established norms and a good deal of research accounts for examples of defiance of normative structures. Piven and Cloward argue that in the course of examining the institutional continuities between permissible and prohibited modes of collective action, they often allow this distinction to disappear. Crucially, it is the theoretical problem that is central to breakdown approaches that resource mobilisation disparage – it is non-normative collective action, such as disorder and rebellion, that traditional approaches sought to explain.

Other problems in the resource mobilisation literature were thought to stem from this normalising tendency. Protest is often treated as more organised than it is, as if conventional modes of formal organisation also typify the organisational forms taken by protest. Some analysts normalise the political impact of collective protest to the extent that the processes of influence mobilised by SMOs seem no different from those set in motion by conventional political activities. Piven and Cloward stress that these criticisms do not detract from the generalisation that institutional arrangements pattern both conventional and unconventional collective action.

Typically, RMT has emphasised the structure and working of social movement organisations. This analysis has led to further criticism, based on its lack of incorporation of issues of meaning and symbolism. Ryan (1992: 4) remarked:

Because resource mobilisation was developed with the intention of replacing analyses of movement participants with an analysis of movement organisations (McCarthy and Zald 1977), it is not surprising that this framework is now being criticised for too much emphasis on structure.

According to Ryan, ideology and symbols (songs, banners and ephemera, for example) are used by social movements as effectual strategies and resources for mobilisation. Ryan's analysis of the women's movement in the US incorporates the impact of ideology and symbolic meaning on social movements and reformulates resource mobilisation's *overemphasis* on structures.

Recent work in the field of resource mobilisation (Zurcher and Snow 1981; Ferree and Miller 1985) provides a context for incorporating the mobilisation effects of emotions, symbols and ideology which were frequently ignored in resource mobilisation studies. In the case of the women's movement, for example, while ideology was used by leaders and activists as a mobilising resource and source of group cohesion during the organising stage, at the same time feminist SMOs comprising the movement experienced intense antagonism over conflicting ideologies (Ryan 1992: 54). Although there were disagreements in mainstream feminist groups, radical autonomous groups experienced the greatest divisions.

Ryan contends that ideology provides the rationale for how people lead their lives: it is a belief system for how things should be (1992: 60). The formation of alternative ideologies is a crucial component for social movement development (Gusfield 1970; Zurcher and Snow 1981; Ferree and Miller 1985). Ideology, in addition, functions in the establishment of a framework for individuals to connect with others through common experiences. The development of a challenging ideology thus provides an alternative worldview uniting diverse individuals into a group with a common interest in changing the existing social order (Ryan 1992: 60). Part of the ambience of social movements is to argue about strongly held feelings and convictions – in fact, this is expected of social activists. The ways in which differences are resolved are problematical and tend to stimulate fragmentation of SMOs. Although feminist SMOs reflected activists' diverse experiences, according to Ryan (1992) the women's movement moved very quickly from introducing new ways of shared exploration to a narrowed view of feminist 'legitimacy'. The movement found itself with competitive models of 'right-thinking'. Self-labelled 'radical' groups argued about what being radical really meant, and labelled the liberal sector 'conservative' since its goals included reform within the *existing* legal, social and cultural structures. None of the feminist organisations in the women's movement espoused dictatorial control, yet emphasis on ideological purity often lent itself to rigid mind-sets. Ryan concludes that ideology in the US women's movement was an important resource for garnering social movement support, but became a negative factor in sustaining commitment, particularly in self-defined radical feminist groups (1992: 64).

This gives rise to the question of how resource mobilisation managed to 'neatly side-step' meaning, symbolism and ideology in explaining social movement activity (Morris and McClurg Mueller 1992).[3] Morris and McClurg Mueller argue that grievances, ideologies, manipulation of symbols through oratory and the written word, media portrayals, consciousness raising and identities should all be taken into account in chaptering a social movement – in short, a social psychology is reaffirmed (see Preface to Morris and McClurg Mueller 1992). From the beginning, critics of resource mobilisation were quick to point out that social movements could not be reduced to business organisations, industries or conventional political behaviour. Attention was given to how social movements generate and are affected by the construction of meaning, consciousness raising, the manipulation of symbols and collective identities, and how a viable conceptual framework of social movements must simultaneously explain *both* the structural and symbolic side of movements. Morris and McClurg Mueller state:

> The attempt to stay within the natural science framework of a utilitarian, instrumental model has become increasingly strained by the social constructionist perspective of many contributors. However, proponents of this perspective have developed a variety of ingenious strategies for posing semiotic questions of meaning within the resource mobilisation paradigm. (*ibid*: 6)

The definition of the actor, the social context within which meanings are developed and transformed, and the cultural content of social movements have as a consequence been addressed.

In conclusion, since the early 1980s critics have pointed to the absence of an account of values, grievances, ideology and collective identity in the resource mobilisation paradigm that was originally conceptualised by Zald, McCarthy and others (see Fireman and Gamson 1979; Zurcher and Snow 1981; Jenkins 1983; Klandermans 1984; Cohen 1985; Ferree and Miller 1985). McAdam (1988) reiterates that what resource mobilisation has recently come to say about broader macro political perspectives has come to dominate theorising in the field of social movements. While this perspective elucidates the broad political factors that give rise to widespread collective action, the dynamics of individual recruitment to activism are negated:

> [T]hese findings serve to remind us that whatever macro factors underlie collective action, it is the micro dynamics of mobilisation and recruitment that produce and sustain a movement ... The macro political roots of movements may vary, but the micro structural dynamics of collective action are likely to look very similar from movement to movement. (*ibid*: 151)

Ferree and Miller (1985) suggested that the lack of analysis of the effects of social individual thought disregards too much of what we know about cognitive structure and social psychological processes in general. However, much work remains to be done on developing a social psychological model complementary to the resource mobilisation framework (see Morris and McClurg Mueller 1992 for a number of papers attempting this). The absence of a plausible account of values, grievances and ideology has been recognised as a problem, even by researchers themselves working within the resource mobilisation framework (Fireman and Gamson 1979; Ferree and Miller 1985; Klandermans 1988). However, the question of incorporating a social psychology in place of incentive terminology has revived fears that this may lead to a re-emergence of traditional pathological models of collective behaviour that were dominant before the 1960s. Social psychology proponents in the resource mobilisation perspective suggest that analysis of participation in terms of cognitive structure and organisational strategies of recruitment, rather than in terms of the specific motives or incentives individuals have for joining movements, reintroduces the old problem of participation in a new and potentially productive manner.

Undoubtedly, the dehumanising assumptions of rational choice are especially problematical in the study of social movements and have led to a neglect of value differences and conflicts. From the outset, RMT was criticised for its excessively rationalist and instrumentalist approach to social movements (Nash 2000: 123). A presupposition of a pseudo-universal human actor without a personal history or a gender, a race or a class position within a societal history blurs the rich creativity and symbolic discourse which are integral to social movements (Ferree 1992: 30). The next section reviews the field of NSMs which directed social movement analysts to ask 'grand questions' about society and the course of transformation within it – in contrast to the painstaking empirical work in RMT which has tended to focus on social movements themselves.

NSM theory

The NSMs' perspective conceptualises SMOs not as means to realising external goals, but *as goals in themselves*. In this perspective, movements represent democratic niches in a society in which autonomous social action creates new *identities* (Klandermans 1989). Analysis of the impact of industrialisation and modernisation on the growth of new social movements suggests that contemporary movements are no longer rooted in the classical labour–capital contradiction. New groups (such as professionals and governmental officials, are identified as potential constituencies) and problems (connected to the shifting boundaries between public, private and social life, and the struggles against old and new forms of domination) are believed to drive NSMs.

RMT has been criticised for taking for granted the very phenomenon that social movement theory should explain – the existence of SMOs (Melucci 1984).[4] In other words, as long as the very existence of movement organisations can be assumed, the rational–instrumental viewpoint can satisfactorily account for the development of social movements. Cohen (1985) described the NSM approach as the 'identity-oriented paradigm' which enables it to accomplish what resource mobilisation has failed to do – that is, it examines the processes through which collective actors create the identity and solidarity they are defending. SMOs are viewed not simply as instruments to change society, but as networks of groups and individuals sharing and adhering to a conflictual culture and a group identity within a general social identity whose interpretation they contest (Melucci 1985). Creating and defending new identities is to its members an end in itself (Klandermans 1989: 9).

Pivotal movements – the peace, women's, environmental and student movements – are considered elements of an overarching phenomenon known as NSMs in this paradigm.[5] According to Klandermans, the dynamics of the four major social movements and the interrelations between them are striking (1991: 19). The NSMs' approach seeks an explanation for the rise of the social movements of the past four decades in the appearance of new grievances and aspirations in Western societies. For Klandermans, the new movements differ from old movements (generally characterised as the labour movement) in three ways – values, action forms and constituency (*ibid*: 26).

1 Values: NSMs do not accept the premises of a society based on economic growth. They have broken with the traditional values of capitalistic society and seek a different relationship to nature, to one's body and sexuality, to work and consumption.
2 Action forms: NSMs make extensive use of unconventional forms of action. They prefer small-scale, decentralised organisations, are anti-hierarchical and favour direct democracy.
3 Constituency: two groups are particularly predisposed to participate in NSMs. The first group involves people who are paying the costs of problems resulting from modernisation, primarily those who have been marginalised by societal developments. Social class or rank cannot define this group, because the problems it confronts are not limited to particular social strata. The second group consists of those who because of more general shifts in values and needs have become particularly sensitive to problems resulting from modernisation. Members of this group are found primarily among the new middle class and among the well-educated young people working in the services sector primarily – what Berger (1991) terms the 'knowledge class'. Brand et al. (1986) state that new social movements recruit primarily from

this category. The values and needs of this constituency determines the dynamics of the NSMs.

Bert Klandermans has provided an excellent analysis of these perspectives, which are reviewed here in detail. NSM theorists seek to identify where these new values, action forms and constituencies come from. The answer has been sought in various sources, but most explanations link the new developments to industrialisation and economic growth. Brand (1982) classified them in theories focusing either on rising demands or on need defence.

According to Klandermans (1991: 27) one group of authors, drawing on Inglehart's theory (1977) of post-material values, ascribes the rise of NSMs to changed values. Inglehart described a silent revolution in Europe – a dramatic change from materialist to post-materialist values. Post-war youth, assured of the satisfaction of material needs, developed non-material needs such as self-actualisation, quality of life concerns and more political influence. Change in other values were also discerned – conventional middle-class values appeared to be eroding; the traditional work ethic was declining; and attitudes towards work and career were changing. Adherents of these new values were coming into conflict with a political–social system that is essentially materialist.

Another strand of this approach describes NSMs as a reaction to the welfare state which has created new entitlement needs with respect to government services. For Klandermans (1991: 28), increased prosperity has caused the demand for scarce goods to grow. Many of these are 'positional goods' (pleasant living surroundings, a car, good education). When used extensively, they become an obstruction to the satisfaction of other needs (traffic jams, suburbs, the devaluation of academic degrees). The general result is increased competition, which in turn increases the grievances that mobilise movements.

NSM theories have also attributed the phenomenon of social movements to an increased strain related to industrialisation and bureaucratisation. These two processes, it is argued, have resulted in a loss of identity, leading to a decline of traditional ties and loyalties. As a consequence, people become receptive to new utopias and new commitments. Young people are considered particularly vulnerable to this. Industrialisation has many negative consequences for the satisfaction of important needs. Self-destructive aspects of Western society (such as the exhaustion of resources, conflicts between industrialised countries, rising economic, social, psychological and ecological costs of production), together with a decreased problem-solving capacity on the part of institutional politics, have generated tremendous social problems. Having become accustomed to new services, for example, people then become dissatisfied with the level at which services are delivered. These dissatisfactions provide the breeding ground for new social movements.

Klandermans (*ibid:* 28) also reviews how other theorists consider the intervention of the State and capitalistic economy into new reaches of life as the chief explanation for the rise of NSMs (Habermas 1973; Melucci 1980, 1981). The State took upon itself the responsibility for the satisfaction of needs which the market economy could no longer meet. The restructuring of the capitalist economy in the wake of recession led to the exclusion of a growing number of unemployed or otherwise disqualified persons. Increasingly the State was given the task of alleviating the consequence of this process of restructuring. This led to the development of a network of regulatory, ministering, supervisory and controlling institutions, and increased the danger of loss of legitimacy. For Klandermans (1991: 28), the significance of NSMs, as Melucci argues, must be determined against the background of these changes: the NSMs fight for the reappropriation of time, of space and of relationships in the individual's daily experience (1980: 219).

There is clearly diversity in the field of NSMs which reflects the complexity and cultural diversity of the research subject. However, according to Niedhart and Rucht (1991: 421) there are three central models:

1 Cultural model: this emphasises the role of NSMs in terms of fundamental conflict over cultural patterns. Touraine (1981), Eder (1982), Nelles (1984), Raschke (1985) and Melucci (1988, 1989), for example, assumed that NSMs indicate a historically relevant struggle, which is typically not centred on the control over economic and/or political power, but focuses on the sphere of cultural reproduction. Problems of self-reflection, collective identity and collective learning processes play an important role in the mobilisation of NSMs.
2 Political model: this places NSMs closer to the realm of politics (Nedelmann 1984), viewing them as the expression of a new political paradigm (Offe 1985). Here the emphasis lies on the distribution of power, state intervention and the side effects of capitalist welfare states (see Kriesi et al. 1995).
3 Integrative model: this pursues a more integrated perspective and interprets NSMs in a broader structural framework which allows for both a historical and a systematic perspective. One variation of this approach is based on a theory of modernisation which combines economic, political and cultural dimensions (Raschke 1985; Rucht 1988; Brand 1987). Another strand, closer to the Marxist heritage, interprets NSMs both as an outcome and as a cata-lyst of the crisis of the Fordist mode of societal regulation (Hirsch and Roth 1986; Roth, 1989).

NSM theorists have asked different questions from those of resource mobilisa-tion theorists. Habermas, Melucci and Touraine, for example,

> each take a step back from the usual battery of questions regarding the dynamics of movement mobilisation and seek to identify both the key move-

ment clusters belonging to any given era and the main structural tensions which these movements form around. (Crossley 2002: 167)

In contrast to political process/opportunity and resource mobilisation perspectives, the importance of *grievances* and *strains* is reaffirmed rather than viewing them as constants in society. In the NSM paradigm, as societies change so too do sources of strain.

Multiorganisational fields and culture

Melucci (1989) argues that macro theories (such as Habermas's theory of the colonisation of the life-world) explain *why* but not *how* movements are formed and maintained. The strength of resource mobilisation is that it deals with the *how* level of analysis by explaining the growth and development of social movements through emphasising the fundamental importance of existing organisations and the availability of resources (such as money, professional expertise and recruitment networks). However, Melucci contends that while RMT tends to explain how social movements emerge and develop, it does not adequately explain *why* and tends to view collective action as data which are merely given.

Both Klandermans (1991) and Diani (1992) have assessed the question of achieving a synthesis between the European and American approaches to social movements. Klandermans aptly notes that the weaknesses of one appears to be the other's strength (1991: 29). Similarly to Melucci, Klandermans argues that the NSMs field focuses on the structural origins of strain and neglects the *how* of mobilisation, while resource mobilisation does not elaborate on *why* demand (grievances and strain) will appear if there is some supply of SMOs. In short, NSM theory seems to argue that social movements materialise automatically if some demands (grievances) exist – while RMT negates grievances. The main deficit of both approaches is that neither school demonstrates that social problems are not solely objectively given. A social problem does not inevitably generate a social movement. Resource mobilisation recognised this insofar as it postulated that resources play a significant role in the generation of social movements, but it also left several important questions unanswered. Furthermore, it assumed a direct relationship between objective circumstances and individual behaviour, and it did not take into account mediating or framing processes through which people *attribute meaning* to events and interpret situations.

Klandermans suggests that scholars of social movements have increasingly become aware of two principles:

1 What determines the individual's behaviour is not so much reality *per se* as reality but how the individual perceives and interprets it.

2 SMOs themselves play an important role in generating and diffusing meanings and interpretations.

These principles were applied not only in the case of grievances but also in relation to resources, political opportunities and outcomes of collective action.
Scholars in the past fifteen years or so have proposed a number of concepts for
analysing both the ways in which people attribute meaning and define situations
and the way in which SMOs help create and mobilise such meanings. Several
authors have criticised both the RMT and NSM approaches for not fully
explaining the role of *grievance interpretation* (Ferree and Miller 1985; Morris
and McClurg Mueller 1992). Resource mobilisation has a tendency to see a
direct link between objective circumstances and individual behaviour without
taking into account the intervening processes of defining and interpreting the
individual's situation (Klandermans 1989: 9):

> One's interpretations, rather than reality itself, guide political actions. The
> definition of the situation can make an obnoxious situation justifiable in the
> eyes of the victim. If authorities are perceived to be legitimate, coercion is not
> defined as oppression, but as legal enforcement of the law. According to schol-
> ars who emphasise the role of grievance interpretation, the crucial variables in
> movement mobilisation are not anger or frustration but the belief that one's
> interests are common interests, as well as the perception of injustice – that is,
> the belief that these interests are legitimate yet are not being met.

In this critique, the NSM approach also neglects grievance interpretation,
despite its consideration for identity formation. It assumes that the emergence
of contemporary social movements is related to the negative impact of modernisation and industrialisation on the political, social and ecological environment,
but how structural changes are transformed into grievances is not explained.

The development of constructionist approaches as well as syntheses of RMT
and NSMs theory has generated four key concepts in the field of social movements:

1 sponsorship of ideological packages (Gamson 1988, 1992);
2 consensus mobilisation (Klandermans 1984, 1989, 1991);
3 frame alignment (Snow and Bedford 1988, 1992);
4 collective identity (Melucci 1988, 1989).

Gamson's notion of 'sponsorship of ideological packages' concerns public
discourse. At any particular moment in a given society, one political theme will
be represented by several ideological packages. In addition, each political theme
generates a set of packages and counter packages. An ideological package is
constructed around a few core ideas and symbols. Because the mass media play
such a central role in modern societies, social movements are increasingly

involved in a symbolic struggle over meaning and interpretation. Gamson asserts that unless we examine media discourse and investigate how this discourse changes over time we will not be able to understand the formation and activation of the mobilisation potential of social movements. Social movements must compete with representatives of the *official* position, opponents to their cause and competitive organisations who and which also want a voice in the public debate/arena.

Consensus mobilisation refers to attempts to disseminate the views of a social actor throughout various sectors of the population. Klandermans (1988) distinguishes consensus mobilisation from consensus formation. The former is a deliberate attempt by a social actor to create consensus among a subset of the population – the latter concerns the unplanned convergence of meaning in social networks and subcultures. Consensus mobilisation is necessary at each stage of a campaign but its nature differs according to which stage the mobilisation process has reached. Klandermans suggests there are four steps in the process of mobilisation:

1 formation of mobilisation potential;
2 formation and activation of recruitment networks;
3 arousal of the motivation to participate;
4 the removal of barriers to participation.

In forming mobilisation potential, movement organisations must win attitudinal and ideological support. In the forming and activating of recruitment networks, they must increase the probability that in the case of people who *belong* to the movement their mobilisation potential will be reached. In the forming/activating of recruitment networks, they must favourably influence the decision of people who are reached by a mobilisation attempt. In removing barriers they must increase the probability that people who are motivated will eventually participate.

One further distinction between the two is the context of the formation of mobilisation potential in a society and consensus mobilisation in the context of action mobilisation. The first refers to the generation of a set of individuals with a predisposition to participate in a social movement, the second to the legitimation of concrete goals and means of action. Thus the two forms of consensus mobilisation have different time frames – formation of mobilisation potential is a long-term problem and action mobilisation is a short-term matter. The target audiences differ as well. The formation of mobilisation potential means the creation of commitment. In this case the audience is very broad – usually a social category of people who share some characteristic related to the movement's cause. Action mobilisation means the activation of commitment; thus it restricts itself to people who already *belong* to the mobilisation potential of a

movement organisation. The two different processes involve different requirements for communication channels – the formation of mobilisation potential
requires channels with a relatively high impact, but usually employs long-term
strategies. Action mobilisation on the other hand is bound to short-term strategies but can confine itself primarily to limited forms of persuasion. They also
involve different arguments – legitimating the existence of the movement versus
legitimating its strategy. Gamson (1988) and Klandermans (1989) stressed that
SMOs are not the only sources of information in a society, and are often not
even the most credible sources of information. In almost every mobilisation
campaign SMOs must compete with other (sometimes opposing) sources of
information.

The concept of frame alignment attempts to explain mobilisation at the level
of the individual participant and micro mobilisation. Nash writes (2000: 123):

> According to Snow and his associates, it is through 'frames' that social actors
> define grievances, forge collective identities and create, interpret, and trans-
> form opportunities in order to bring about social movements. A 'frame' works
> because it 'simplifies "the world out there" by selectively punctuating and
> encoding objects, situations, events experiences and sequences of actions in
> one's present or past environment' (Snow and Benford 1992: 137).

Snow and Benford (1988, 1992) describe how the cognitive frame of individuals
and the ideological frame of a movement organisation are brought together.
Social movements frame (i.e. assign meaning to and interpret) relevant events
and conditions in ways that are intended to mobilise potential adherents and
constituents, garner bystander support and demobilise antagonists. In mobilisation campaigns there is an attempt to connect the interpretations of
individuals with those of movement organisations so that they are congruent or
complementary. According to Klandermans (1991: 33), Snow and Benford
break down the process of frame alignment into four distinct activities that a
movement will find more or less relevant, depending on the degree of similarity
between the two frames of reference:

1 frame bridging – which involves the linkage of two or more ideologically
  congruent but, structurally unconnected frames regarding a particular issue
  or problems;
2 frame amplification – which refers to the clarification and invigoration of an
  interpretative frame that bears on a particular issue, problem or set of events;
3 frame extension – which involves the expansion of the boundaries of a movement's primary framework so as to encompass interests or points of view that
  are incidental to its primary objectives but of considerable salience to potential adherents;
4 frame transformation – which refers to the re-definition of activities, events

and biographies that are already meaningful from the standpoint of some primary framework, such that they are now seen by the participants to be quite something else.

Clearly, going from frame bridging to frame transformation, the four activities are progressively complex. Consequently, the more of those activities a movement organisation must engage in, the less complicated the task will be. In elaborating the notion of frame alignment, Snow and his colleagues have tried to formulate answers to the questions: what are the key determinants of the differential success of movement framing efforts, and which characteristics of an organisation and its frame of reference contribute to its ability to persuade?

Melucci's concept of collective identity localises the process of the construction of meaning completely within the groups of participants that constitute a social movement. In his view the formation of a collective identity is *the* central task of a social movement. A movement that has developed a collective identity has defined itself as a group and it has also defined its view of the social environment, the participants' shared goals and their shared opinions about the possibilities of and constraints on collective action. According to Melucci (1984, 1989), the formation of a collective identity is not only instrumental for successful collective action – it is a goal in itself. The key point is that if a movement succeeds in creating a new collective identity the participants will integrate that new identity in their everyday lives. Groups experimenting with new lifestyles are themselves a challenge to the dominant culture. Melucci objects to the other three concepts elucidated above because he contends that they take for granted what they must explain – the existence of collective actors. In other words, the sponsorship of ideological packages and the mobilisation of consensus and frame alignment presuppose the existence of a collective identity.

All these perspectives share the view that NSM and resource mobilisation approaches neglect the processes and mechanisms that transform structural factors into collective action. These processes – the social construction of protest – proceed not in a vacuum but in interaction among social actors. Klanderman's argument, detailed above, is that all of these interactions occur in the context of the movement organisation's *multi-organisational field* – the set of organisations in the organisation's environment. It is there that grievances are interpreted, means and opportunities are defined, opponents are appointed, strategies are chosen and justified, and outcomes are evaluated. Interpretations and evaluations are as a rule controversial, and each of the various actors may challenge the interpretations of others. As an SMO competes to influence public opinion or the opinion of its constituency, its multi-organisational field determines its relative significance as an individual actor.

Klandermans (1992) proposed to employ the concept of a multi-organisational field in theories of social movements (the model was originally formulated by Curtis and Zurcher 1973). In exploring and analysing the social construction of protest, other scholars (Diani, for example) have become increasingly interested in networks of groups and organisations, which serve as carriers of the cognitive processes involved in these constructions. As a result, a much more dynamic model is currently emerging in the social movement literature, and movement groups and organisations are now seen as elements in changing configurations. Moreover, it is argued that cooperation, opposition and competition for resources and opportunities within the multi-organisational field share *episodes of protest.*

Conclusion

Diani argues (1992: 11) that social movement actors are engaged primarily in political and/or cultural conflicts aimed at promoting or opposing social change either at the systemic *or* at the non-systemic level. He identifies three basic components of social movements:

1 networks of relations between a plurality of actors;
2 a shared collective identity;
3 engagement in conflictual issues.

The NSM approach, which has dominated the field in Europe, places specific emphasis on conflict as a core element of a social movement. Touraine (1981), for example, connects the emergence of a social movement directly with the dominant conflict in a given society. Resource mobilisation, on the other hand, tends to relate the emergence of a social movement to public action and the political process. It focuses on the conditions that facilitate or constrain the occurrence of collective action and offers a very interesting account of *how* movements work at the meso level of sociological analysis. Networks link SMOs and underpin the distribution of resources for action (including information, expertise, material resources) which create the necessary preconditions for mobilisation. RMT emphasises political opportunities and an indigenous organisational base as major factors in the rise and decline of social movements. The availability of *resources* and an *existing network* of SMOs plays a central role in the generation of a social movement. Grievances are present in the rise and decline of social movements, but are peripheral to resources and organisational structures. The respective success of SMOs in attracting media attention, executing campaigns, accessing resources and recruiting members, and how such factors influence the size and shape of the movement, are central to this framework.

The present situation is that movements are becoming defined and studied in a variety of ways. The new approach attempts to transcend the barriers that still often divide European and North American perspectives on social movements, and also those that divide recent approaches from the older 'collective behaviour' approach (see Crossley 2002, for example). Although there are clear weaknesses in both the NSM and the RMT model, to paraphrase Crossley (*ibid*: 147), we should use them to open issues up but not allow them to close those issues down. In addition, recent work has called for a return to the questions raised by classical collective behaviour theorists in the field who emphasised the cognitive and the psychological dimensions of mobilisation. Naomi Klein's account (1999) of the anti-globalisation movement provided a journalistic account of some even newer movements that have emerged in recent years. Social movements are therefore more prevalent than ever in contemporary societies and remain a core concern for social theory. In the chapters that follow, the extent to which all these theories in the field have informed the study and analysis of social movements in Ireland is addressed.

Notes

1 Zald and McCarthy (1977) define the social movement sector (SMS) as consisting of all social movement industries (SMIs) in a society. An SMO, in their terminology, includes all social movement organisations oriented towards the same general goal(s). Tarrow (1989: 16) defines a social movement more specifically as 'the configuration of individuals and groups willing to engage in disruptive action against others to achieve collective goals'.

2 One of the outcomes that may result is the growth of a countermovement. Depending on its strength, a countermovement may severely limit the strategic and tactical options of the original movement, while at the same time increasing the movement's resources as supporters are alerted to threats from the opposition. The pro-choice movement, for instance, is somewhat unusual in that it has provoked one of the most vigorous and lasting countermovements in the history of reform movements.

3 In 1988 a conference was held in Michigan to discuss the issue of a social psychology of resource mobilisation. The proceedings of this conference were published in 1992 (Morris and McClurg Mueller 1992).

4 See Melucci's analysis (1989) of collective action centred on signs and symbols. He contends that in complex societies contemporary movements operate as signs in the sense that they translate their actions into symbolic challenges to the dominant codes. In other words, collective action is a form. Power resides in the codes that order the circulation of information. Melucci's central point is there are some issues which cannot be solved in the institutional sphere. These issues are confronted in the production of signs and social relations.

5 As a result, specialists usually have only selective knowledge of the field. In comparison to the sub-disciplines of science, for example, which are coordinated at national and international levels and have established institutes and journals, the field of social movements has been uncoordinated and underdeveloped until recent initiatives (see Kriesi et al. 1995).

Bibliography

Adorno, T.W., Levinson, D.J. and Sanford, R.N., 1950 *The Authoritarian Personality* (New York, Harper & Row).

Bagguley, P., 1992 'Social Change, the Middle Class and the Emergence of "New Social Movements": a critical analysis', *Sociological Review*, 40:1, 26–48.

Berger, P.L., 1991 *The Capitalist Revolution: Fifty propositions about prosperity, equality, and liberty* (New York: Basic Books [1986]).

Blumer, H., 1971 'Social Problems as Collective Behaviour', *Social Problems*, 18:3, 298–306.

Brand, K.W., 1987 'Kontinuitat und Diskontinuitat in den neuen sozialen Bewegungen', in Roth, R. and Rucht, D. (eds), *Neue soziale Bewegungen in der Bundrepublik Deutschland* (Frankfurt and New York: Campus).

Brand, K.W., Busser, D. and Rucht, D., 1986 *Neue Soziale Beregungen in West Europa und den USA* (Frankfurt: Ein Internationaler Vergleich and New York: Campus).

Byrne, P., 1997 *Social Movements in Britain* (London: Routledge)

Cohen, J.L., 1985 'Strategy and Identity: new theoretical paradigms and contemporary social movements', *Social Research*, 52:4, 663–716.

Cohen, J.L., 1996 'Mobilisation, Politics and Civil Society: Alain Touraine and social movements', in Clark, J. and Diani, M. (eds), *Alain Touraine* (London: Falmer Press), pp. 173–204.

Cohen, J.L. and Arato, A., 1992 *Civil Society and Political Theory* (Cambridge, MA: MIT Press).

Crossley, N., 2002 *Making Sense of Social Movements* (Manchester: Manchester University Press).

Curtis, R.L. and Zurcher, L.A., 1973 'Stable Resources of Project Movement: the multiorganizational field', *Social Forces*, 52, 53–60.

Dahrendorf, R., 1958 'Toward a Theory of Social Conflict', *Journal of Conflict Resolution*, 2:2, 170–83.

Dalton, R.J and Kuchler, M. (eds), 1990 *Challenging the Political Order: New social and political movements in Western democracies* (Cambridge: Polity Press).

Davies, J.C., 1962 'Toward a Theory of Revolution', *American Sociological Review*, 27:1, 5–19.

Della Porta, D. and Diani, M., 1999 *Social Movements: An introduction* (London: Blackwell).

Diani, M., 1992 ' The Concept of Social Movement', *Sociological Review*, 40:1, 1–25.

Dollard, J., Doob, L. Miller, N. Mowrer, O. and Sears, R., 1971 'Frustration and Agression: definitions', in Davies, J.C. (ed.), *When Men Revolt and Why: A reader in political violence and revolution* (New York, Free Press), pp. 166–80.

Eder, K., 1982 ' A New Social Movement?', *Telos*, 52, 5–20.

Eder, K., 1996 *The Social Construction of Nature* (London: Sage).

Enrst, M. and Loth, D., 1952 *Report on the American Communist* (New York: Holte, Rinehart & Winston).

Evans, R.R., 1973 (ed.), *Social Movements: A reader and source book* (Chicago, IL: Rand–Mcnally).

Fernandez, R.M and McAdam, D., 1989 'Multiorganizational Fields and Recruitment to Social Movements', in Klandermans, B. (ed.), *Organizing for Change: Social movement organizations in Europe and the United States* (Greenwich, CT: JAI Press), pp. 315–40.

Ferree, M.M., 1992 'The Political Context of Rationality: rational choice theory and resource mobilisation', in Morris, A.D. and McClurg Mueller, C. (eds), *Frontiers in Social Movement Theory* (New Haven, CT: Yale University Press), pp. 29–52.

Ferree, M.M. and Hess, B.B., 1985 *Controversy and Coalition: The new feminist movement* (Boston, MA: Twayne).

Ferree, M.M. and Miller, F.D., 1985 'Mobilisation and Meaning: toward an integration of social psychological and resource perspectives on social movements', *Sociological Inquiry*, 55:1, 38–61.

Fireman, B. and Gamson, W., 1979 'Utilitarian Logic in the Resource Mobilization Perspective', in Zald, M.N. and McCarthy, J.D. (eds.), *The Dynamics of Social Movements* (Cambridge, MA: Winthrop Publishers), pp. 8–44.

Foweraker, J., 1995 *Theorizing Social Movements* (London: Pluto).

Friedman, D. and McAdam, D., 1992 'Collective Identity and Activism: networks, choices and the life of a social movement', in Morris and McClurg Mueller (eds), *Frontiers in Social Movement Theory*, pp. 156–73.

Gamson, W.A., 1968 *Power and Discontent* (Homewood, IL: Dorsey Press).

Gamson, W.A., 1975 *The Strategy of Social Protest* (Homewood, IL: Dorsey Press).

Gamson, W.A., 1980 'Understanding the Careers of Challenging Groups: a commentary on Goldstone', *American Journal of Sociology*, 85:5, 1043–60.

Gamson, W.A., 1988 'Political Discourse and Collective Action', in Klandermans, Kriesi and Tarrow (eds), *From Structure to Action: Social movement participation across cultures*, pp. 219–44.

Gamson, W.A., 1992 'The Social Psychology of Collective Action', in Morris and McClurg Mueller (eds), *Frontiers in Social Movement Theory*, pp. 53–76.

Gerlach, L.P. and Hine, V., 1970 *People, Power, Challenge: Movements of social transformation* (Indianapolis, IN: Bobbs-Merrill).

Giugni, M., 1999 'How Social Movements Matter: past research, present problems, future developments', in Giugni, M., McAdam, D. and Tilly, C. (eds), *How Social Movements Matter* (Minneapolis: University of Minnesota Press), pp. xiii–xxxiii.

Gurr, T.R., 1970 *Why Men Rebel* (Princeton, NJ: Princeton University Press).

Gusfield, J.R., 1962 'Mass Society and Extremist Politics', *American Sociological Review*, 27:1, 19–30.

Habermas, J., 1973 *Theory and Practice* (Boston, MA: Beacon Press).

Habermas, J., 1996 *Between Facts and Norms* (Cambridge: Polity Press).

Heberle, R., 1951 *Social Movements* (New York: Appleton–Century–Crofts).

Hirsch, J. and Roth, R., 1986 *Das neue Gesicht des Kapitalismus: Vom Fordismus zum Post-Fordismus* (Hamburg: VSA).

Hoffer, E., 1951 *The True Believer* (New York: Harper & Row).

Inglehart, R., 1977 *The Silent Revolution: Changing values and political style among Western publics* (Princeton, NJ: Princeton University Press).

Inglehart, R., 1981 'Post-Materialism in an Environment of Insecurity', *American Political Science Review*, 75:4, 880–900.

Jenkins, J.C., 1983 'Resource Mobilisation Theory and the Study of Social Movements', *Annual American Review of Sociology*, 9, 527–53.

Jenkins, J.C., 1985 *The Politics of Insurgency: The farm workers' movement in the 1960s* (New York: Columbia University Press).

Jenkins, J.C. and Eckert, C.M., 1986 'Channelling Black Insurgency: elite patronage and professional social movement organisations in the development of the black movement', *American Sociological Review*, 51 (December), 812–29.

Jenkins, J.C. and Perrow, C., 1977 'Insurgency of the Powerless: farm workers' movements (1946–1972)', *American Sociological Review*, 42, 249–68.

Johnston, H. and Klandermans, B. (eds), 1995 *Social Movements and Culture* (London: UCL Press).

Kitschelt, H., 1986 'Political Opportunity Structures and Political Protest: anti-nculear movements in four democracies', *British Journal of Political Science*, 16:1, 57–85.

Kitschelt, H., 1991 'Resource Mobilisation Theory: a critique', in Rucht, D. (ed.), *Research on Social Movements: The state of the art in Western Europe and the USA* (Boulder, CO: Westview Press), pp. 323–47.

Klandermans, B., 1984 'Mobilisation and Participation: social–psychological explanations of resource mobilisation theory', *American Sociological Review*, 49, 583–600.

Klandermans, B., 1988 'The Formation and Mobilisation of Consensus', in Klandermans, Kriesi, and Tarrow (eds), *From Structure to Action: Social movement participation across cultures*, pp. 173–95.

Klandermans, B., 1989 'Introduction: social movement organizations and the study of social movements', in Klandermans, B. (ed.), *Organizing for Change: Social movement organizations in Europe and the United States* (Greenwich, CT: JAI Press), pp. 1–17.

Klandermans, B., 1991 'New Social Movements and Resource Mobilisation: the European and the American approach revisited', in Rucht, D. (ed.), *Research on Social Movements: The state of the art in Western Europe and the USA* (Boulder, CO: Westview Press), pp. 17–44.

Klandermans, B., 1992 'The Social Construction of Protest and Multiorganizational Fields' in Morris and McClurg Mueller (eds), *Frontiers in Social Movement Theory*, pp. 77–103.

Klandermans, B. and Tarrow, S., 1988 'Mobilisation into social movements: synthesising European and American approaches', in Klandermans, Kriesi and Tarrow (eds), *From Structure to Action: Social movement participation across cultures*, pp. 1–38.

Klandermans, B., Kriesi, H. and Tarrow, S. (eds), 1988 *From Structure to Action: Social movement participation across cultures* (Greenwich, CT: JAI Press).

Klein, N., 1999 *No Logo* (London: Flamingo).

Kornhauser, W., 1959 *The Politics of Mass Society* (New York: Free Press).

Kriesberg, L. (ed.), 1978 *Research in Social Movements, Conflicts and Change: An annual compilation of research* (Greenwich, Connecticut: JAI Press).

Kriesi, H. and Tarrow, S. (eds), 1988 *Movement Participation Across Cultures* (Greenwich, CT: JAI Press).

Kriesi, H., Koopmans, R., Dyvendak, J.W., Sellem, J. and Giugni, M. (eds), 1995 *New Social Movements in Western Europe: A comparative analysis* (London: UCL Press).

Lasswell, H. and Blumenstock, D., 1939 *World Revolutionary Propaganda* (New York: Alfred A. Knopf).

Lipsky, M., 1970 *Protest in City Politics* (Chicago, IL: Rand–McNally).

Lofland, J., 1979 'White-Hot Mobilisation: strategies of a millenarian movement', in Zald, M.N. and McCarthy, J.D. (eds), *The Dynamics of Social Movements* (Cambridge, MA: Winthrop Publishers), pp. 157–66.

Lyman, S.M. (ed.), 1995 *Social Movements: Critiques, concepts, case-studies* (London: Macmillan).

McAdam, D., 1982 *Political Process and the Development of Black Insurgency 1930–1970* (Chicago, IL: University of Chicago Press).

McAdam, D., 1983 'Tactical Innovation and the Pace of Insurgency', *American Sociological Review*, 48:6, 735–54.

McAdam, D., 1986 'Recruitment to High-Risk Activism: the case of freedom summer', *American Journal of Sociology*, 92, 64–90.

McAdam, D., 1988 *Freedom Summer: The idealists revisited* (New York: Oxford University Press).

McCarthy, J.D. and Zald, M.N., 1977 'Resource Mobilisation and Social Movements: a partial theory', *American Journal of Sociology*, 82:6, 1212–41.

McClurg Mueller, C., 1987 *Consciousness, Political Opportunity and Public Policy* (Philadelphia, PA: Temple University Press).

McClurg Mueller, C., 'Building Social Movement Theory', in Morris and McClurg Mueller (eds), *Frontiers in Social Movement Theory*, pp. 3–26.

Mayer, M., 1991 'Social Movement Research and Social Movement Practice: the US pattern', in Rucht, D. (ed.), *Research on Social Movements: The state of the art in Western Europe and the USA* (Boulder, CO: Westview Press), pp. 47–120.

Mayer, M., 1995 'Social-Movement Research in the United States: a European perspective', in Lyman (ed.), *Social Movements: Critiques, concepts, case-studies*.

Melucci, A., 1980 'The New Social Movements: a theoretical approach', *Social Science Information*, 19, 199–226.

Melucci, A., 1981 'Ten Hypotheses for the Analysis of New Movements', in Pinto, D. (ed.), *Contemporary Italian Sociology* (Cambridge: Cambridge University Press), pp. 173–94.

Melucci, A., 1984 'An End to Social Movements?' *Social Science Information*, 24, 199–226.

Melucci, A.,1985 'The Symbolic Challenge of Contemporary Movements', *Social Research*, 52:4, 789–816.

Melucci, A., 1988 'Getting Involved: identity and mobilisation in social movements', in Klandermans, Kriesi and Tarrow (eds), *From Structure to Action: Social movement participation across cultures*, pp. 329–47.

Melucci, A., 1989 *Nomads of the Present: Social movements and individual needs in contemporary society* (London: Hutchinson).

Melucci, A., 1996 *The Playing Self: Person and meaning in the planetary society* (Cambridge: Cambridge University Press).

Merton, R.K. and Kitt, A.S., 1950 'Contributions to the Theory of Reference Group Behaviour', in Merton, R.K. and Lazarsfeld, P.F. (eds), *Continuities in Social Research: Studies in the scope and method of the American soldier* (Glenco, IL: Free Press).

Mills, C.W., 1956 *The Power Elite* (New York, Oxford University Press).

Morris, A.D. and McClurg Mueller, C. (eds), 1992 *Frontiers in Social Movement Theory* (New Haven, CT: Yale University Press).

Molotch, H., 1979 'Media and Movements', in Zald, M.N. and McCarthy, J.D. (eds), *The Dynamics of Social Movements: Resource mobilisation, social control, and tactics* (Cambridge, MA: Winthrop), pp. 71–93.

Mottl, T.L., 1980 'The Analysis of Countermovements', *Social Problems*, 27:5, 620–34.

Nash, K., 2000 *Contemporary Political Sociology* (London: Blackwell).

Nedelmann, B. 1984 'New Political Movements and Changes in Processes of Interest Mediation', *Social Science Information*, 23:6, 1029–48.

Neidhardt, F. and Rucht, D., 1991 'The Analysis of Social Movements: the state of the art and some perspectives for future research', in Rucht, D. (ed.), *Research on Social Movements: The state of the art in Western Europe and the USA*, pp. 420–64.

Nelles, W. 1984 'Kollektive Identitat und politiches Handeln in neuen sozialen Bewegungen', *Politische Vierteljahresschrift*, 25, 424–40.

Oberschall, A., 1973 *Social Conflict and Social Movements* (Englewood Cliffs, NJ: Prentice-Hall).

Oberschall, A., 1978 'The Decline of the 1960s' Social Movements', in Kriesberg, L. (ed.), *Research in Social Movements, Conflicts and Change: An annual compilation of research* (Greenwich, CT: JAI Press), pp. 257–89.

Offe, C., 1985 'New Social Movements: challenging the boundaries of institutional politics', *Social Research*, 52, 817–68.

Offe, C., 1990 'Reflections on the Institutional Self-Transformation of Movement Politics: a tentative stage model', in Dalton, R.J. and Kuchler, M. (eds), *Challenging the Political Order: New social and political movements in Western democracies* (Cambridge: Polity Press), pp. 232–50.

Olson, M., 1968 *The Logic of Collective Action* (Cambridge, MA: Harvard University Press).

Parsons, T., 1964 *Social Structure and Personality* (New York: Simon & Schuster).

Perrow, C., ' The Sixties Observed', in Zald, M.N. and McCarthy, J.D. (eds), *The Dynamics of Social Movements: Resource mobilisation, social control, and tactics* (Cambridge, MA: Winthrop).

Pinard, M.,1971 *The Rise of a Third Party: A study in crisis politics* (Englewood Cliffs, NJ: Prentice-Hall).

Piven, F. Fox and Cloward, R.A., 1995 'Collective Protest: a critique of resource mobilisation theory', in Lyman, S. (ed.), *Social Movements: Critiques, concepts, case-studies*.

Piven, F. Fox and Cloward, R.A., 1977 *Poor People's Movements* (New York: Pantheon).

Piven, F. Fox and Cloward, R.A., 1992 'Normalizing collective protest', in Morris and McClurg Mueller (eds), *Frontiers in Social Movement Theory*, pp. 301–25.

Raschke, J., 1985 *Soziale Bewegungen Ein historisch–systematischer Grundfib* (Frankfurt: Campus).

Riesman, D., 1961 *The Lonely Crowd* (New Haven, CT: Yale University Press).

Roth, R., 1989 'Fordismus und neue soziale Bewegungen', in Wasmuht, U. (ed.), *Alternativen zur alten Politik? Neue soziale Bewegungen in der Diskussion* (Darmstadt: Wissenschaftliche Buchgesellschaft), pp. 13–37.

Rucht, D., 1988 'Themes, logics and arenas of social movements: a structural approach', in Klandermans (ed.), *From Structure to Action: Comparing social movement research across cultures*, pp. 305–28.

Rucht, D., 1991 'Sociological Theory as a Theory of Social Movements? A critique of Alain Touraine', in Rucht (ed.), *Research on Social Movements: The state of the art in Western Europe and the USA*, pp. 348–53.

Rupp, L. and Taylor, V., 1987 *Survival in the Doldrums: The American women's rights movement 1945–1960* (New York: Oxford University Press).

Ryan, B., 1992 *Feminism and the Women's Movement: Dynamics of change in social movement ideology and activism* (New York and London: Routledge).

Scott, A., 1990 *Ideology and the New Social Movements* (London: Unwin Hyman).

Shefner, J., 1995 'Moving in the Wrong Direction in Social Movement Theory', *Theory and Society*, 24, 595–612.

Smelser, N.J., 1962 *Theory of Collective Behaviour* (New York: Free Press).

Snow, D.A. and Benford, R.D., 1988 'Ideology, Frame Resonance and Participant Mobilisation', in Klandermans, Kriesi and Tarrow (eds), *From Structure to Action: Social movement participation across cultures*, pp. 197–217.

Snow, D.A. and Benford, R.D., 1992 'Master Frames and Cycles of Protest', in Morris and McClurg Mueller (eds), *Frontiers in Social Movement Theory*, pp. 133–55.

Snyder, D. and Kelly, W.R., 1979 'Strategies for Investigating Violence and Social Change: illustrations from analyses of racial disorders and implications for mobilisation research', in Zald, M.N. and McCarthy, J.D. (eds), *The Dynamics of Social Movements: Resource mobilisation, social control and tactics* (Cambridge, MA: Winthrop), pp. 212–34.

Tarrow, S., 1983 *Struggling to Reform: Social movements and policy change during cycles of protest* (Ithaca, NY: Centre for International Studies, Cornell University).

Tarrow, S., 1988 'National Politics and Collective Action: recent theory and research in Western Europe and the United States', *Annual Review of Sociology*, 14, 421–40.

Tarrow, S., 1989 *Democracy and Disorder: Protest and politics in Italy 1965–1975* (Oxford: Oxford University Press).

Tarrow, S., 1990 *Challenging the Political Order: New social and political movements in Western democracies* (Oxford: Oxford University Press).

Tarrow, S., 1991 'Comparing Social Movement Participation in Western Europe and the United States: problems, uses and a proposal for synthesis', in Rucht (ed.), *Research on Social Movements: The state of the art in Western Europe and the USA*, pp. 392–420.

Tarrow, S., 1991 'Struggle, Politics and Reform: collective action, social movements and cycles of protest', *Western Societies*, 21.

Taylor, V., 1989 'Social Movement Continuity: the women's movement in abeyance', *American Sociological Review*, 54, 761–74.

Taylor, V. and Whittier, N., 1992 'Collective Identity in Social Movement Communities: lesbian feminist mobilisation', in Morris and McClurg Mueller (eds), *Frontiers in Social Movement Theory*, pp. 104–30.

Tilly, C., 1976 'Major Forms of Collective Action in Western Europe 1500–1975', *Theory and Society*, 3, 365–75.

Tilly, C., 1978 *From Mobilisation to Revolution* (Reading, MA: Addison-Wesley).

Tilly, C., 1979 'Repertoires of Contention in America and Britain', in Zald, M.N. and McCarthy, J.D. (eds), *The Dynamics of Social Movements: Resource mobilisation, social control, and tactics* (Cambridge, MA: Winthrop), pp. 126–55.

Tilly, C., 1984 'Social Movements and National Politics', in Bright, C. and Harding, S. (eds), *Statemaking and Social Movements: Essays in history and theory* (Ann Arbor: University of Michigan Press), pp. 297–317.

Tilly, C., 1993 *European Revolutions 1492–1992* (Oxford and Cambridge: Blackwell).

Tilly, C., Tilly, L. and Tilly, R., 1975 *The Rebellious Century, 1830–1930* (Cambridge, MA: Harvard University Press)

Touraine, A., 1971 *The May Movement: Revolt and reform* (New York: Random House).

Touraine, A., 1981 *The Voice and the Eye: An analysis of social movements* (Cambridge: Cambridge University Press).

Touraine, A., 1984 *Solidarity: The analysis of a social movement in Poland 1980–1981* (Cambridge: Cambridge University Press and Paris: Editions de la Maison des Sciences de l'Homme).

Turner, R. and Killian, L., 1957 *Collective Behaviour* (Englewood Cliffs, NJ: Prentice-Hall).

Turner, R., 1983 'Figure and Ground in the Analysis of Social Movements', *Symbolic Interaction*, 6:2, 175–81.

Zald, M.N., 1987 'The Future of Social Movements', in Zald, M.N. and McCarthy, J.D. (eds), *Social Movements in an Organizational Society: Collected essays* (New Brunswick, NJ: Transaction Books), pp. 319–36.

Zald, M.N., 1991 'The Continuing Vitality of Resource Mobilisation Theory: a response to Herbert Kitschelt's critique', in Rucht (ed.), *Research on Social Movements: The state of the art in Western Europe and the USA*, pp. 355–83.

Zald, M.N., 1992 'Looking Backward to Look Forward: reflections on the past and future of the resource mobilisation research program', in Morris and McClurg Mueller (eds), *Frontiers in Social Movement Theory*, pp. 326–48.

Zald, M.N. and McCarthy, J.D., 1977 'Resource Mobilisation and Social Movements: a partial theory', *American Journal of Sociology*, 82:6, 1212–22.

Zald, M.N. and McCarthy, J.D. (eds), 1979 *The Dynamics of Social Movements: Resource mobilisation, social control, and tactics* (Cambridge, MA: Winthrop).

Zald, M.N. and McCarthy, J.D. (eds), 1987 *Social Movements in an Organizational Society: Collected essays* (New Brunswick, NJ: Transaction Books).

Zurcher, L.A. and Snow, D.A., 1981 'Collective Behaviour: social movements', in Rosenberg, M. and Turner, R. (eds), *Social Psychology: Sociological perspectives* (New York: Basic Books), pp. 447–82.

2 • Louise Ryan

An analysis of the Irish suffrage movement using new social movement theory

DURING my PhD research at University College Cork in the early 1990s my choice of subject matter was frequently the cause of raised eyebrows. I was told that the Irish suffrage movement was the appropriate domain of historians not sociologists. I countered this criticism by explaining that I was analysing the suffragists using the identity-oriented school of social movement theory. However, I was then told that it was anachronistic to apply theories derived for 'new social movements' to a historical movement. Nonetheless, with the encouragement of my supervisor Piet Strydom, I persisted with my research. My effort to overcome the scepticism of others was probably valuable practice for my viva, in which I had to convince my external examiner, leading social movements theorist Klaus Eder, that analysing the suffragist campaign using a framework of NSM was not only possible but also fruitful.

Over the last ten years working as an academic in Britain, my research has taken me in different directions, but I have retained an interest in social movements (Ryan 2001). During those years much work has been done on social movement theory, but debates about the relationship between, and relevance of, NSM theories and historical movements continue unabated. In this chapter I revisit and update my PhD research, drawing upon a range of theorists including Verta Taylor (1999) and Della Porta and Diani (1999). My aims here are twofold: on the one hand, in choosing the Irish suffrage movement I seek to challenge the assertion that such a movement was entirely distinct from NSMs; on the other hand, I argue that the NSM theoretical framework may prove very useful in facilitating a deeper and more wide-ranging understanding of the suffrage movement. I aim to show that rather than having been a simple 'votes for women' lobby group, the suffrage movement can be understood as complex and multifaceted; illustrating several of the characteristics usually associated only with *new* or contemporary movements.

NSM theories

Della Porta and Diani define social movements as 'informal networks, based on shared beliefs and solidarity, which mobilise about conflictual issues, through the frequent use of various forms of protest' (1999:16). Movements may be fairly fluid and loosely structured, but they do involve a sense of belonging and shared beliefs. Social movements often generate ideas and beliefs that are widely considered new, challenging and even shocking, and thus represent a challenge to what is taken for granted and *the norm* in society at large. Therefore, social movements are engaged in an oppositional–conflictual relationship. This opposition is made manifest in different forms of protest. Throughout their 1999 book Della Porta and Diani focus on NSMs, while acknowledging many of the concerns that have been expressed about their so-called *newness*. In this section I explore the concept of the NSM in some detail.

The school of NSM theories emerged in the 1970s–1980s and continues to inform many studies of protest groups and social mobilisation (see, for example, Hourigan 2003; Todd and Taylor 2004). The work of Alain Touraine (1981, 1985) and Alberto Melucci (1980, 1985) has been instrumental in theorising NSMs. According to Touraine, in modern times there have always been two main movements – the elite and the social movement – vying against each other. From the middle of the 1800s to the 1960s the main social movement was the labour movement that vied against the capitalist State.[1] However, Touraine claims that there has recently been a shift away from this type of conflict to a new scenario. In post-industrial Western societies groups like those of the anti-nuclear movement emerge to oppose the technocratic elites who control information and decision-making in society' (Touraine 1981, 1985: 781–2; North 1998). My aim here is not to rehearse Touraine's arguments in detail. I am concerned primarily with his construction of NSMs as *new* based on the assumption that they share characteristics that are unique to the present period and are distinct from the characteristics associated with *old* social movements (OSMs).

Prior to the 1960s there was a tendency to treat social movements as potentially dangerous, irrational, chaotic, violent and threatening (Zirakzadeh 1997). The new approach to social movements that emerged in the 1970s–1980s developed in response to the types of movement that were perceived as *new*, e.g. the peace movement, the anti-nuclear movement, the student movement and the environmental movement. However, I would argue that these new theorists, because of their focus on contemporary movements, were rather too uncritical of the ways in which older social movements had been theorised. There was a tendency to accept the somewhat simplistic and one-dimensional notions of pre-1960s' social movements.

Those theorists assume that NSMs differ markedly from earlier movements.

Of course, the main movement to which these newer movements are compared is the labour movement. The distinction between new and old movements is intended as far more than merely temporal: it symbolises a significant shift in the interests of social movements (Eyerman and Jamison 1991: 23). Drawing on the work of Habermas, many theorists assume that NSMs are responding to increasing administrative intervention in the social and symbolic processes, the so-called colonisation of the life world. NSMs accept the State and the economy but wish to create more space in civil society for social autonomy, plurality, right to difference, etc., based on the universal principles of the formal democratic State (Cohen and Arato 1984: 269–70). However, while theorists like Alberto Melucci (1995, 1996) continue to emphasise that NSMs represent new forms of mobilisation and action, others are critical of the dichotomy between new and OSMs (Eyerman and Jamison 1991; Bagguley 1992; Ray 1993; Calhoun 1995; Martin 2004).

Any simplistic, polarised construction of old and new movements omits the continuities and similarities that persist over time across various movements. This weakens the explanatory power of NSM theory in two key ways:

1 Narrow constructions of *old* social movements have led to the simplification of these diverse and complex movements. I believe that before we embark on an appraisal of NSMs it is necessary to first understand what OSMs really stood for. OSMs have been described as campaigns for material and instrumental needs, centred on issues like citizenship. However, if OSMs are defined simply in terms of the labour movement then this is not representative of all the many smaller social movements that existed in the late 1800s and early 1900s. Indeed, as Larry Ray (1993) argues, movements like the women's suffrage movement were not only concerned with citizenship but also raised issues around identity. The difference between the *old* women's movement and the *new* women's movement may not be as marked as some theorists have implied (*ibid*: 61–2). Ray strongly disputes the old–new dichotomy: 'claims to novelty are exaggerated and ahistorical since contemporary demands have long histories, and movements like environmentalism, pacifism, feminism were significant around 1890–1900 or before' (*ibid*: 61). In addition, because older social movements were thought to have a dominant and centralised leadership structure, it has been assumed that these movements can be understood simply by studying the decisions of the leaders. As I have argued at length elsewhere (Ryan 2001), this assumption about leadership underestimates and misrepresents the loose nature of leadership and the diffuse nature of decision-making within some OSMs.

2 The second way in which the old–new dichotomy weakens the explanatory power of NSM theory relates to the narrow definition of *new* movements. Several critics have argued that the conceptualisation of NSMs needs to be

reassessed (see, for example, Martin 2004). Theorists like Offe and Melucci have constructed NSMs as lifestyle- and identity-oriented. These movements are perceived as being concerned with *post-material* issues such as alternative health care, etc., and seek to defend civil society against colonisation by the State. Melucci (1995) argues that his original analysis of NSMs has been much misunderstood and simplified by both those who use the concept and those who have criticised it. He says that it was only ever intended as a temporary critical tool to help understand the types of movement that were emerging in the late 1970s and early 1980s, i.e. in the post-industrial information society. However, regardless of how Melucci himself may have intended the concept to be used, there is no doubt that the term NSM has been taken on by a wide range of theorists and has influenced the way a generation of social protest has been analysed and understood. While Melucci continues to defend the newness of NSMs, one of problems with his work that leaves it open to so much criticism is its 'high level of abstraction' (Martin 2004: 42). It is rarely applied to detailed case studies of particular movements. Recent empirical research suggests that many NSM theorists have been highly selective in their examples of *new* movements and fail to consider the wide array of contemporary movements that continue to be concerned with *old* issues. For example, Martin (2004) shows that many new movements, such as the peace and environmental movements, continue to campaign around material issues like global poverty and Third World debt.

Nonetheless, many of the concepts developed by NSM theorists are extremely valuable and the analysis of collective identity formation, self-reflexivity and submerged networks as cultural laboratories is very useful in understanding the internal dynamics of social movements. However, the extent to which this analysis is relevant only to new movements remains a contentious issue. Unlike Melucci, one theorist who has applied his theory to a specific social movement is Klaus Eder, and I contend in the next section that his work helps to challenge the simplistic old–new binary.

Challenging linearity

In his attempt to assess the emergence of NSMs within a historical context Eder (1993) argues that it is important to look beyond the labour movement as a typical example of an OSM. He points out that the labour movement does not represent the diversity of social movements in the past. Thus, unlike Touraine, Eder acknowledges the plurality of movements that have existed throughout the modern era; he also sees the similarities and connections between these movements across time periods.

Eder's work represents an important corrective to the linearity of the old–new dichotomy and provides an example of how continuities may be traced across social movements over time. He does not see NSMs as entirely *new* in a historical sense: 'Counterculture movements have existed since the beginning of modernity. The social movements that created civil society have always been accompanied by sectarian groups looking for a more spiritual form of life in civil society' (1993: 136). While Eder argues that there is a significant difference between old and new movements, he still believes that a relationship, and a historical link, exists between them. In applying his theories to social movements of the past and the present, Eder looks at one movement – environmentalism – in particular and traces its development over the last two centuries. By examining one movement over time, he illustrates the historical links between an old and new movement and clearly demonstrates that the labour movement was not the only social movement of the late nineteenth century.

Craig Calhoun has similarly challenged the 'historical misrepresentation' present in NSM theories (1995: 178). He argues that the transition from OSMs to NSMs located within the transition from industrial to post-industrial society is a linear developmentalism that simplifies the changes and continuities of social protest over time. He suggests that a re-examination of movements from the eighteenth and nineteenth centuries will reveal many characteristics similar to those attributed to NSMs. Under the intriguing title *New Social Movements of the Nineteenth Century*, Calhoun argues that theorists like Melucci have exaggerated the extent to which the labour movement 'ever was a unified historical actor with a single narrative and disciplining institutional structure' (*ibid*: 178). He goes on to argue: 'Throughout the early nineteenth century, communitarianism, temperance, and various dietary and lifestyle movements attracted hundreds of thousands of adherents in both Europe and America' (*ibid*: 180).

In challenging the assumed uniqueness of NSMs, Calhoun then applies their key characteristics to movements from the nineteenth century. Drawing on a very wide sweep of groups, from abolitionists to utopian socialists, he demonstrates the presence of direct action strategies, identity politics, non-hierarchical structures, loose membership networks and experimental lifestyles. These qualities are usually assumed to be uniquely associated with NSMs. I agree with Calhoun when he goes on to argue that despite its misrepresentation of history, NSM theory is valuable in providing a framework that may enhance the study of all social movements across historical and geographical contexts. Indeed, recent empirical research shows that the analysis of identity issues can be applied to a much wider array of movements than NSM theorists have recognised (Hourigan 2003: 64). However, while Calhoun's arguments and his framework are very useful, one could criticise him for drawing on so many diverse examples. In attempting to demonstrate the range of 'NSMs' in the nineteenth century he offers a plethora of brief descriptions but no detailed analysis. He chooses different examples to illustrate each point and so does not relate all the characteristics to any one particular group or movement. Drawing on Calhoun's framework of NSM characteristics, I focus on just one example and assess the extent to which this movement demonstrates a range of qualities and can thus be described as approximating an NSM.

Calhoun (1995) cites the women's movement as an example of an early social movement that illustrates continuities over time. The feminist movement has been in existence for over 150 years, although for much of that time it has been latent. Apart from the mass mobilisations of the 1960s and 1970s, women previously mobilised in many countries worldwide (including developing countries like India) at the beginning of the twentieth century in pursuit of legislative reform and cultural–attitudinal change. However, as Verta Taylor (1999) argues, the invisibility of gender issues within social movement theory may explain why the women's movement has not been fully researched as an example of a social movement.

Gendering social movement theory

Until recently political sociologists and sociologists of social movements rarely evoked gender as a force in the emergence and development of social movements. This is not surprising, since the field of social movements, especially compared with other areas of study, has been remarkably untouched by the gender scholarship produced in the social sciences over the last decade (Taylor 1999: 8).

Nickie Charles (2004) argues that, with very few exceptions, the leading social movement theorists are men. This is all the more remarkable given the fact that women are so active in the NSMs so beloved by theorists – the peace, the environmental, the animal rights and the anti-nuclear movements. Despite their interest in identity, these male theorists largely ignore gender identity. As Charles says 'it is almost as if social movement theory exists in a parallel gender-neutral universe' (*ibid*: 262). Charles echoes Verta Taylor's argument that a theory addressing the intersections of gender and social movements is not only useful but necessary. Attention to gender is essential for a thorough and accurate explanation of collective action because the gender-neutral language that characterises much social movement theory obscures the role of gender within the mobilisation, organisation and stratification of movements. In addition, Taylor (1999) argues that gender as a set of cultural beliefs and ways of interacting with others figures heavily in many identity-oriented movements. She adds that a gender analysis of social movements is important because movements have often played a crucial role in processes of resistance and change around gender issues.

Taylor's approach seeks to merge the insights derived from classical collective behaviour theory, resource mobilisation and the NSM school of thought. She is interested both in how gender is constructed, debated and challenged within the movements, and also in the gender regime of the institutional context within which a movement is embedded. The wider gender regime provides an important backdrop to the mobilisation, strategies, claims and collective identities of the actors. She goes on to argue that 'treating gender as an analytic category in the construction of collective identity illuminates the role that gender symbolism plays in socially constructed solidarities that mobilize collective action' (*ibid*: 23). Taylor concludes that the exclusion of women's movements and a gendered analysis of social movements has led to fundamental inadequacies in the theorisation of social movements. A social movement analysis informed by a gender analysis would benefit social movement theory but would also benefit our understanding of women's movements.

While Charles (2004) applies her analyses to contemporary women's movements, Taylor (1989) went further and developed an analysis of women's groups in the US during the 1940s–1960s, the period between the so-called first-wave and second-wave movements, and this has led to the concept of 'movements in abeyance'. Taylor argued that the apparent chasm between first-wave and second-wave feminism reinforces the image of a nadir period during which no feminist activity occurred. Her research shows that feminist activity of the 1940s–1960s provided a crucial seedbed for the growth of the women's movement in the late 1960s and early 1970s. Thus the so-called second-wave feminist movement did not emerge out of a vacuum but had roots that stretch back to the nineteenth century.[2] Taylor argued that because social movement theorists have ignored a wide range of women's collective action, they have become preoccupied with other types of movement that may not accurately represent the true range and depth of social protest in society at any given time.

Similarly, Karen Offen argues that the tendency towards a dichotomy of old and new women's movements leads to the unhelpful split between so-called first-wave and second-wave feminism, and that this grossly misrepresents the complexity of the early women's movement (1992: 74–5). It also underestimates the continuity of concerns among feminists across the generations.

Thus Taylor's view of movements in abeyance is helpful in challenging the apparent *newness* of the modern women's movement. However, it is necessary to go further and also challenge the apparent *oldness* of the earlier women's movement. In my view, Taylor does not take this argument far enough to explore the extent to which a gendered analysis of the women's movement across time may add true range and depth to an understanding of social protest in the past. I believe that applying a gender analysis to past social movements will help to develop a more thorough understanding of the ways in which movements engaged with the gender regime, as well as with the mobilisation, strategies, claims and collective identities developed by these movements.

Because the importance of gender and gender issues has been neglected by so many social movement theorists, early women's movements such as the suffragists have either been ignored completely or else misrepresented by social movement theories as single-issue political lobby groups.

Analysing the Irish suffrage movement through NSM theory

Research on suffrage activism has tended to focus largely on the pursuit of the vote. Thus the movement may be misunderstood not only as a single-issue pressure group but also as reformist campaign demanding inclusion in formal democratic institutions. However, a new historiography of the early women's movement has been emerging over the last decade (Holton 1992; Offen 1992). This work reassesses the complexity and multifaceted nature of feminism in the nineteenth and early twentieth centuries. My research seeks to go beyond the narrow focus on enfranchisement to uncover the complexity of identities, actions and motivations behind the suffrage movement. Drawing on Eder's work (1993), it is possible to argue that this movement represented an alternative or, in his words, countercultural movement which engaged with and frequently criticised the dominant discourse and agenda of the Government and the main social movement of that period, the Irish nationalist movement.

Calhoun (1995) questions whether or not the following criteria are unique to NSMs:

- issues of identity;
- defending the lifeworld;
- politicisation of everyday life;
- non-class-based mobilisation;
- non-hierarchical/non-instrumental;
- direct action;
- overlapping commitment.

I ask similar questions of the Irish suffrage movement.

The term 'Irish suffrage movement' may be applied to a loose amalgam of scattered groups of varying sizes, which began in the 1870s reaching its peak of activity between 1908 and 1914.[3] In 1908, the Irish Women's Franchise League was set up by Hanna Sheehy Skeffington and Margaret Cousins (Murphy 1989; Ward 1997). Influenced by British militants, the IWFL described itself as a militant group but never engaged in the level of militancy associated with the British Women's Social and Political Union. The majority of Irish suffrage groups which sprung up around the country were constitutional and opposed militant tactics. Thus it would be simplistic and inappropriate to apply the British dichotomy of militant suffragettes versus constitutional suffragists to the Irish context (Cullen Owens 1984). In Ireland, the suffrage movement was split in other, potentially more divisive, ways. For example, the Munster Women's Franchise League was a constitutional group made up of unionists such as the authors Somerville and Ross and the ardent nationalist Mary MacSwiney. The alliance between suffragists who wanted Irish independence and those who supported the Union with Britain was uneasy and, in the case of the Munster Women's Franchise League, short lived (Ryan 1995). The Irish suffrage movement can be defined as a loose, segmented network of diverse groups with a multiplicity of leaders (Ryan 2001). The diverse and scattered nature of the movement is reflected in the establishment of the Irish Women's Suffrage Federation by Louie Bennett in 1911. This umbrella group had over twenty affiliated societies (Cullen Owens 1984). Membership of the movement as a whole was fluid and fluctuating, making it difficult to accurately assess but, at its height the movement claimed to have approximately 3,000 members (*Irish Citizen*, June 1912).

In studying any social movement of the distant past, it is not possible to interview actual members, so that some other means of uncovering their views has to be sought. While most activists remain anonymous and lost to history, some women and men wrote books, pamphlets and articles, and these are helpful in constructing images of how they visualised the movement and its aims. Such writings, however, are limited in that they offer the views of individuals who may not have been representative of the movement as a whole. For that reason, I have chosen to concentrate on the organ of the movement, the *Irish Citizen* newspaper published between 1912 and 1920. With several editors over its eight-year life span and hundreds of different contributors, this newspaper is invaluable in capturing the various concerns, interests and debates that occupied activists. As the only forum providing a space for all movement members to express their views, the *Irish Citizen* is a lively source in which topics were often discussed at length over weeks or months, drawing on a range of diverse voices. Through this source the researcher gains some insight not only into a range of interests but also into the active process of debate and collective learning in which the contributors were engaged. This is not to suggest that the *Irish Citizen* is completely inclusive and represents the views of all suffragists. Nevertheless, for the purposes of this analysis, I maintain that the paper provides a valuable opportunity to test the applicability of NSM theory to this *old* movement.

Issues of identity were clearly important to all suffragists, and terms like 'suffragist' and the more militant 'suffragette' were powerful signifiers both of strategy and of belief in and commitment to a controversial cause. However, issues of identity ran deeper than that, and the notion of being a *feminist* as opposed to simply a suffragist illustrated the concern with a wider array of interests than just enfranchisement. Most of the contributors to the *Irish Citizen* described themselves as feminists and analysed the relationship between suffragism and feminism:

> What is called the Votes for Women movement is but a side-issue of a much greater and more far-reaching problem. It is true that the Votes for Women movement is the chief manifestation of Feminism in these countries; but though public attention has been particularly focused on this one phase of Feminism, the girl who first defied conventions by riding a bicycle ... the poorest and meanest woman anywhere who is revolting against the conditions of her life and longing for a chance to relieve its monotony – all these are part and parcel of the great uprising amongst women (Margaret Connery, *Irish Citizen*, 28 December 1912).

Although Connery's article offers a broad definition of feminism in an international context, Irish feminists also debated issues of national identity. The growing tensions between Irish nationalists, unionists and the British authorities informed relations between Irish and British feminists (Ward 1995) and Irish and American feminists (Murphy 1989). Irish feminist action in international pacifism also raised questions about identity across national boundaries (Ryan 1997). In addition, on a more philosophical level, Irish feminists continued the tradition of early feminist writers in analysing the meaning of female identity, social constructions of femininity and the influence of biological instincts (Hazelkorn 1989; Ryan 1996). Such topics were discussed with particular reference to the First World War:

> In the manhood and womanhood of the future no tinsel of trumpets or flags will seduce into the insanity of recklessly destroying life ... Not because women lack courage, not because we admit physical incapacity, not because we assume higher virtues than men, will women declare against war, but solely and simply because women alone appreciate at its highest the value of human life. (Margaret McCoubrey, *Irish Citizen*, 27 February 1915)

The extent of differences between the sexes was hotly debated and, as the latter extract illustrates, such analyses were often complex and indeed contradictory. Feminists frequently argued that men and women were simultaneously different and equal. The qualities of female identity were seen as both equal and in some cases superior to traditional masculine qualities (Ryan 1996, 1997).

Pacifist campaigns against the First World War offer just one example of the many global links between feminist groups in the early twentieth century. Gatherings like the Hague Peace Congress and the Zurich Peace Congress, and organisations like the Women's International League for Peace and Freedom, gave feminists a transnational platform. Irish feminists maintained regular contact with women's groups in America, Europe and further afield, including for example India.[4] Despite tensions around nationalism, Irish women travelled frequently to Britain, and British women like Emmaline Pethick Lawrence and

Sylvia Pankhurst were well-known supporters of Irish suffragism. The *Irish Citizen* carried regular reports on campaigns around the world, firmly locating Irish feminism within a global movement. While it is important to acknowledge the cultural specificities of the Irish movement (Ryan 1997), it is equally important to recognise the extent to which movements forged links across national boundaries. Melucci (1995) argues that there is a planetary or transnational dimension to NSMs. But clearly movements such as the suffragists had begun to develop a transnational focus long before the age of global communications.

Calhoun (1995) argues that NSMs are assumed to be particularly involved in 'politicising everyday life'. However, as he points out, feminist groups have long been associated with the slogan 'The personal is political'. While this may be considered unique to post-1960s' NSMs, there is evidence to suggest that so-called 'first-wave' women's movements were also concerned with the complex relationship between the private and the public sphere (Holton 1992; Offen 1992). In discussing the activities of early twentieth-century Irish feminists it is important not to focus exclusively on their campaigns for access to the formal political sphere and extending the roles of women in the public sphere generally. Several feminists went further and called into question the public–private split. By calling public attention to private abuses of women and children in the home, they offered a critique of social structures rather than merely demanding inclusion in them. These women attempted to reveal the widespread extent of domestic violence in Irish society and pointed to economic dependence as a key factor in forcing women to keep their abuse silent and hidden. 'An age-old tradition prevails that in matrimonial affairs what transpires in the home must be carefully concealed from the world without' (Mrs Priestley-McCracken, *Irish Citizen*, September 1919). Mrs Priestley-McCracken added that such privacy 'gives a sense of security to the stronger, fiercer and more dominant partner'. She argued that women are forced to stay in violent relationships and to keep them secret because of their economic dependence on men. She claimed that the legal profession were completely on the side of men and offered no help to women who complained of brutality. The legal profession contributed to the view that it is a man's prerogative to beat his wife. This analysis went beyond a mere critique of private patriarchy: the article calls into question the relationship between the private world of the home and the very public world of the courtroom. In this way, links are drawn between power, privilege and exploitation across the spheres, from domesticity to public institutions. The male domination of the legal institutions was a point repeatedly made in the *Irish Citizen* (Ryan 1996).

I challenge Cohen's claim (1983) that the suffrage movement was concerned merely with the inclusion of women in formal political institutions. Eyerman and Jamison have also described OSMs as being concerned with access to 'bourgeois culture' (1991: 153). However, this emphasis on access and inclusion underestimates the degree of feminist critique. These women certainly sought inclusion on juries and all public bodies and committees. However, there was also a critique that went further and challenged male-defined morality, laws and rules, and male-controlled work practices. In other words, early twentieth-century feminists challenged the dominant codes of knowledge, authority and morality in society. They wanted to change society rather than merely be included in it: 'society as at present constituted must go' (Hanna Sheehy Skeffington, *Irish Citizen*, 4 January 1913).

It may appear, on the surface, that feminists wished to enhance the regulation of all aspects of life in order to protect women and girls against violence and abuse. However, I argue that, in common with many social movements, the feminists' agenda blended together both a defence of the integrity of the life-world and demands for its regulation. On the one hand, many contributors to the *Irish Citizen* demanded legislation to outlaw the exploitation of women in the workplace and in the home. However, on the other hand, several also demanded an end to the regulation and control being exerted on women by male-dominated institutions like the Church: 'In all ages men have been great sticklers for the observance of a code of conventional morality – on the part of women' (M.K.C., *Irish Citizen*, November 1917).

According to M.K.C., the standard-bearers of this modesty cult were the priests. From the privileged position of the pulpit, where no woman could challenge them, priests lectured women on their dress, lifestyle and behaviour. The article is forthright in its criticism of such traditional and discriminatory practices: 'Women have now outgrown their swaddling clothes, and they decline to be scolded and put to stand in the corner like naughty children.' I am not suggesting that all suffragists were openly critical of the Church; however, there were several women who were prepared to verbalise their disapproval of its practices and the attitudes of the clergy. For many feminists, freedom of self-expression, freedom of movement and assembly, as well as freedom to dress and behave in unconventional ways, were important aspects of being a feminist. In my view, this represents something approximating a *defence of the lifeworld*.

Calhoun (1995) indicates the range of strategies and tactics employed by social movements in the nineteenth century, and he points to the suffrage movement as a good example of direct action tactics. In the Irish context militancy was not as widely used as in Britain: most Irish suffragists were constitutional rather than militant activists (Ryan 1994). Nevertheless, women did employ a range of inventive strategies aimed at achieving publicity for their various campaigns. Within the conventions of early twentieth-century norms and values, women continued to be denied space within civil society; therefore, every march and public gathering addressed by women was a defiance of tradition. Throughout its eight-year history, the *Irish Citizen* testifies to the inventiveness of women and their methods of 'direct action' in gaining publicity. Soon after her release from prison Hanna Sheehy Skeffington wrote a letter to the paper:

> It is gratifying to realise that Sergeant Thomas, by his assault on me, and the police who illegally attempted to break up the protest meetings, have unwittingly rendered us a great service, and giving a fine impetus to our movement by rousing public indignation against police methods and the ways of police magistrates. (13 December 1913).

As Eder (1993) has argued, in each historical period smaller, alternative, social movements have frequently been ignored or even marginalised because of the presence of larger, more dominant, social movements. The Irish suffrage movement has been neglected or at best simplified in Irish history. This is a reflection in part of the ways in which nationalism, nationalist movements and militancy have dominated all accounts of the late nineteenth and early twentieth centuries. The relationship between the suffrage and nationalist movements was fraught with tensions and bears many of the hallmarks of feminist and nationalist clashes elsewhere in the world (Yuval-Davis 1997). The nationalist men, especially the militant wing of the nationalist movement, believed that the suffragists should postpone their campaign for enfranchisement until after Irish independence. This was also the line taken by Ireland's representatives at Westminster (Ward 1989). Although many suffragists did support the idea of Irish self-determination from Britain they were dubious about postponing female enfranchisement until after Home Rule had been won (Ward 1995). In fact the Irish suffrage movement was made up of nationalist women, unionist women and those who were suspicious of both positions (Hazelkorn 1989). The movement attempted to overcome party loyalties in negotiating a tricky path between their needs as women and the needs of their nation – be that Irish independence or the Union with Britain.

Some Irish suffragists offered a critique of the ways in which nationalist discourse constructed women in limited and traditional roles (Ryan 1995). This feminist critique of nationalism is extremely important in highlighting the extent to which a hegemonic national identity was being challenged and resisted by the women's movement many decades ago. Some suffragists believed that nationalism dominated the Irish political agenda to the exclusion of crucial issues such as education, employment and sexual violence. Louie Bennett, founder of the Irish Women's Suffrage Federation, wrote: 'Probably no country has suffered more severely than Ireland as the victim of purely masculine political ideals' (*Irish Citizen*, 18 April 1914)

As mentioned earlier, it is difficult to know how many activists were involved in the movement or to categorise activists into specific socio-economic groupings. However, based on the written accounts that do exist, it seems that the movement was not simply a class-based formation. It is probable that, like NSM activists today, many members were middle class, but it is obvious that women from working-class and upper-class backgrounds were also involved. Attempts were made to forge alliances with trade unions like the Irish Women Workers' Union, and several reports on factory working conditions were published in the *Irish Citizen* (see for example 2 and 9 August 1913). However, some women felt that the suffrage movement was dominated by a middle-class agenda (see Duggan, *Irish Citizen*, 20 February 1915). Nevertheless, despite the suggestion of class bias, it is probably fair to say that the movement was not a class-based formation. Moreover, in attempting to bring together women from across a range of socio-economic groups, the suffrage movement perhaps encountered similar tensions to those faced by some NSMs (Todd and Taylor 2004).

The membership of the suffrage movement was fluid and flexible and, although each group had its own elected committees, presidents and secretaries, the movement as a whole was fairly non-hierarchical. As I have argued at length elsewhere (Ryan 2001), there was no one leader, and though clearly some suffragists were more famous than others, several different women exerted influence over the movement. As editor of the *Irish Citizen* for many years, Hanna Sheehy Skeffington might be seen as particularly important,[5] though as the founder of the umbrella group the Irish Women's Suffrage Federation, Louie Bennett was certainly influential; and one of the oldest campaigners, Anna Haslam, was revered by many.[6] The diversity and fluidity of membership reflected the range of different but overlapping campaigns within the movement. Pacifism, nationalism, trade unionism, child welfare, education campaigns and temperance were all important aspects of feminism, and members were often involved in several of these either simultaneously or serially.

Conclusion

So, what can we conclude about the relevance of NSM theory to the study of the Irish suffrage movement? The suffragists existed in a different historical context: they were not actors in a post-industrial society. But, it is misleading to configure collective action through a duality of industrial versus post-industrial, as that simplifies all OSMs as protests over the production and distribution of goods. The Irish suffragists were active in a society that was partly industrial but also largely agricultural; in any case, they were not engaged in a conflict about the means of production.

Melucci (1995) insists that NSMs are analysed in a complex, thorough and probing way; however, there remains a tendency to present OSMs in a rather simplistic and one-dimensional way. If the complex, probing and theoretically sophisticated analysis is also applied to OSMs such as the suffragists then a much more interesting picture begins to emerge. Calhoun (1995) argues that the application of identity-formation theory, or the identity-oriented paradigm, to OSMs can be fruitful. For example, the analysis of contemporary social movements as cultural laboratories, or hothouses, within which new ideas are propagated and nurtured is useful for understanding the radicalness of some OSMs. The suffrage movement was a coalition of numerous small networks, many of which had been in existence for years as latent, submerged, laboratories of cultural innovation. Melucci (1995) says that public spaces, rather than the narrow and official political arena, are the primary location of NSMs. However, because the suffragists were denied any access to political spaces they had to make maximum use of public spaces, and they came up with some very inventive ways of occupying and utilising the spaces that were available to them.

Existing sources, such as the *Irish Citizen*, suggest a high level of self-reflexivity[7] on the part of suffragists who engaged in debates about the meaning of feminism and the ways in which a feminist identity could be realised and shared within the suffrage movement. While suffragists forged transnational links in Europe, North America and Asia, issues of ethnicity, class, religion and nationality were complex and often uncomfortable for suffragists as they tried to develop a collective identity. But these issues remain complex and contentious for many of the much-lauded NSMs today. Suffragists were engaged in producing new codes and challenging the dominant logic of patriarchal society. Much of the vicious opposition to the suffrage movements was a reaction to the challenges posed by a feminist analysis of male-dominated society.

According to NSM analyses, social movements provide participants with a safe space to develop and express new ideas that are essentially challenging to the status quo. These ideas, lifestyles and aspirations may well be viewed by the wider society as outrageous, dangerous, immoral, or even simply dismissed as ridiculous. Once these ideas have been developed and new identities invented the movements then play a key role in communicating them to a wider network through alternative newspapers, bookshops, workshops, magazines, radio, internet, websites, etc. Through these media, movements can succeed in circulating quite radical and even subversive ideas.

I suggest that the suffragists were engaged in a similar process of creating radical ideas and aspirations, challenging the male-dominated status quo, and developing new feminist identities, initially in small, safe spaces but then later circulating these through their alternative press, public meetings, and by chalking pavements, making public speeches, etc., but also through more disruptive means such as heckling politicians, noisily and forcefully occupying public spaces and, on occasion, damaging public property. Clearly, in the early twentieth century, the suffragists did not have access to the range of mass media available to movements today, but that should not lead us to underestimate their inventive efforts at circulating radical feminist ideas to a reluctant and even hostile society.

As Eder (1993) has indicated, it is important to consider the cyclical nature of social movements. Movements evolve and go through different stages during their life cycle; e.g. movements that were once active and eruptive like a volcano of new ideas can later settle down into routine activity. Overtime, movements become part of the social complex and no longer appear quite so radical. However, that does not mean we should underestimate just how radical and earth-shattering these movements appeared when they first emerged. Suffragists were considered quite shocking in the early twentieth century. To use Verta Taylor's argument (1999), women's movements were challenging patriarchal authority and critically engaging with the existing gender regime. The radical-ness of their ideas, aspirations and methods must indeed have seemed like a volcanic eruption in the early twentieth century.

Notes

1 The idea of the labour movement as the primary social movement of the nineteenth and early twentieth centuries owes much to Marxist analysis. The labour movement is usually associated with organised labour such as the trade union movement.

2 For a discussion of women's movements in Ireland during the 1940s–1960s and an application of Taylor's theory of movements in abeyance see Linda Connolly (2003).

3 There is insufficient space in this chapter to offer a descriptive history of the Irish suffrage movement. Three books have been written about the movement see Cullen Owens (1984), Murphy (1989) and Ryan (1996). In addition, there have been numerous articles including Ward (1995), Ryan (1992, 1994, 1995 and 1997).

4 Links between the Irish and Indian suffrage movements were forged by the work of Margaret and James Cousins. The Cousins were co-founders of the Irish Women's Franchise League and also regular contributors to the Irish Citizen. They went to live and work in India in 1913 where Margaret Cousins became actively involved in the Indian suffrage movement. For more information about the Cousins's involvement in Indian politics see Candy (1994).

5 For more information about Hanna Sheehy Skeffington and her role in the Irish feminism see Ward (1997).

6 A discussion of Anna Haslam's contribution to feminism in Ireland can be found in Cullen Owens (1984).

7 Self-reflexivity is a critical awareness and engagement with identity and the role of the self in social action. Melucci (1995) sees this as a crucial element of new social movements, but I believe that early feminists also demonstrate self-reflexivity.

Bibliography

Arato, A. and Cohen, J., 1984 'Social Movements, Civil Society, and the Problem of Sovereignty', *Praxis International*, 4:3, 266–83.

Bagguley, P., 2004 'Unemployment, Protest and Democracy', in Todd, M. and Taylor, G. (eds), *Democracy and Participation: Popular protest and new social movements* (Lanham, MD: Rowman & Littlefield).

Bagguley, P., 1992 'Social Change, the Middle Class and the Emergence of New Social Movements: a critical analysis', *Sociological Review*, 40, 26–48.

Calhoun, C., 1995 'New Social Movements of the Nineteenth Century', in Traugott, M.

(ed.), *Repertoires and Cycles of Collective Action* (London: Duke University Press).

Candy, C., 1994 'Relating Feminisms, Nationalisms and Imperialisms: Ireland, India and Margaret Cousins's sexual politics', *Women's History Review*, 3, 581–94.

Charles, N., 2004 'Feminism, Social Movements and Political Order', in Todd, M. and Taylor, G. (eds), *Democracy and Participation: Popular protest and new social movements* (Lanham, MD: Rowman & Littlefield).

Cohen, J., 1983 'Rethinking Social Movements', *Berkeley Journal of Sociology*, 27, 99–113.

Cohen, J., 1985 'Strategy or Identity? New theoretical paradigms and contemporary social movements', *Social Research*, 52, 663–716.

Connolly, L., 2002 *The Irish Women's Movement: From revolution to devolution* (Basingstoke, Palgrave).

Cullen Owens, R., 1984 *Smashing Times: A history of the Irish suffrage movement 1889–1922* (Dublin: Attic Press).

Della Porta, D. and Diani, M., 1999 *Social Movements: An introduction* (London: Blackwells).

Eder, K., 1993 *The New Politics of Class: Social movements and cultural dynamics* (London: Sage).

Eyerman, R. and Jamison, A., 1991 *Social Movements: A cognitive approach* (Cambridge: Polity Press).

Hazelkorn, E., 1989 'The Social and Political Views of Louie Bennett', *Saothar*, 13, 32–44.

Holton, S., 1992 'The Suffragist and the Average Woman', *Women's History Review*, 1:1, 9–26.

Hourigan, N., 2003 *Escaping the Global Village: Media, language, and protest* (Lanham, MD: Lexington Books).

Martin, G., 2004 'New Social Movements and Democracy', in Todd, M. and Taylor, G. (eds), *Democracy and Participation: Popular protest and new social movements* (Lanham, MD: Rowman & Littlefield).

Melucci, A., 1980 'The New Social Movements: a theoretical approach', *Social Science Information*, 19, 199–226.

Melucci, A., 1985 'The Symbolic Challenge of Contemporary Movements', *Social Research*, 52, 789–816.

Melucci, A., 1995 'The New Social Movements Revisited', in Maheu, L. (ed.), *Social Movements and Social Classes* (London: Sage).

Melucci, A., 1996 *Challenging Codes: Collective action in the information age* (Cambridge: Cambridge University Press).

Murphy, C., 1989 *The Women's Suffrage Movement and Irish Society in the Early 20th Century* (New York: Harvester Wheatsheaf).

North, P., 1998 'Exploring the Politics of Social Movements through "Sociological Intervention": a case study of local exchange trading schemes', *Sociological Review*, 46:3, 564–82.

Offe, C., 1985 'New Social Movements: challenging the boundaries of institutional politics', *Social Research*, 52, 817–68.

Offen, K., 1992 'Defining Feminism: a comparative historical approach', in Bock, G. and James, S. (ed.), *Beyond Equality and Difference* (New York: Routledge).

Todd, M. and Taylor, G. (eds), 2004 *Democracy and Participation: Popular protest and new social movements* (Lanham, MD: Rowman & Littlefield).

Ray, L., 1993 *Rethinking Critical Theory: Emancipation in the age of global social movements* (London: Sage).

Ryan, L., 1992 'The *Irish Citizen* Newspaper 1912–1920: a document study', *Saothar*, 17, 105–11.

Ryan, L., 1994 'Women Without Votes: the political strategies of the Irish suffrage movement', *Irish Political Studies*, 9, 119–39.

Ryan, L., 1995 'Traditions and Double Moral Standards: the Irish suffragists' critique of nationalism', *Women's History Review*, 4:4, 487–503.

Ryan, L., 1996 *Irish Feminism and the Vote* (Dublin: Folens Publishers).

Ryan, L., 1997 'A Question of Loyalty: war, nation and feminism in early twentieth-century Ireland', *Women's Studies International Forum*, 20:1, 21–32.

Ryan, L., 2001 'The Cult of Personality: reassessing leadership and suffrage movements in Britain and Ireland', in Barker, C., Johnson, A. and Lavalette, M. (eds), *Leadership and Social Movements* (Manchester: Manchester University Press).

Taylor, V., 1989 'Social Movement Continuity: the women's movement in abeyance', *American Sociological Review*, 54, 761–74.

Taylor, V., 1999 'Gender and Social Movements', *Gender and Society*, 13:1, 8–33.

Touraine, A., 1977 *The Self Production of Society* (Chicago, IL: Chicago Press).

Touraine, A., 1981 *The Voice and the Eye* (Cambridge: Cambridge University Press).

Touraine, A., 1985 'An Introduction to the Study of Social Movements', *Social Research*, 52, 749–88.

Ward, M., 1989 *Unmanageable Revolutionaries* (London: Pluto Press).

Ward, M., 1995 'Conflicting Interests: the British and Irish suffrage movements', *Feminist Review*, 50, 127–47.

Ward, M., 1997 *Hanna Sheehy Skeffington: A life* (Cork: Cork University Press).

Yuval-Davis, N., 1997 *Gender and Nation* (London: Sage).

Zirakzadeh, C., 1997 *Social Movements in Politics: A comparative study* (London: Longman).

3 · Linda Connolly[1]

The consequences and outcomes of second-wave feminism in Ireland

FEMINISM emerged as both a form of transnational politics and an intellectual current over two centuries ago. The women's movement is one of the most globalised forms of protest that continues to operate in contemporary societies. Its importance, therefore, as a global social, political, cultural and intellectual project cannot be underestimated in the field of social movements analysis or, indeed, general social theory.

Giugni (1999: xi) writes that researchers have generally given more attention to the origins and trajectories of social movements than to their *impact* on routine politics, their social environment, other social movements and the participants in movements. This chapter explores the question of how we can think about and study the political and cultural impact of second-wave feminism in the context of Ireland. Recent debates in the field of social movements theory concerning the consequences and outcomes of social movements are illuminated and developed (Della Porta and Diani 1999; Giugni, McAdam and Tilly 1999; Schussman 2002). Following more than three decades of second-wave activism, it is now possible to look back and reflect on the wider impact this phase of feminism has had both in the private and in the public sphere in Irish society. The extent to which the goals of various second-wave feminist campaigns and groups have advanced change in key areas is discussed in some depth below. However, in essence, the women's movement in Ireland has persistently mobilised a plurality of actors, groups and strategies both within submerged networks and in more hierarchical groups and organisations over time and place. Any analysis of movement *outcomes* must therefore be able to work through the diffuse nature and actions of social movements.

In view of all this, the question of outcomes is essentially problematised in this chapter. The example of the women's movement in Ireland is developed to illustrate both the potential and the limitations of theories and research on the outcomes produced by social movements. The analysis will also attempt to move existing studies of feminism in Ireland beyond their focus on national institution-based policy outcomes to address the cultural outcomes of feminism

[58]

and the women's movement in Ireland as well as the development of feminism as a cultural project *in itself.*

Developing a research agenda

The analysis provided in this chapter is based on over twelve years' research and fieldwork. An extensive research agenda has incorporated innovative methods (including intensive interviews with activists, archival research/documentary analysis of sources produced by movements, analysis of media accounts of feminist activism and cultural analysis) – and also theoretical analysis of the emergence of the first and second waves of feminism in Ireland, as well as the activism of the women's movement in the intervening decades between these two peak waves, a period of 'movement abeyance' (Taylor 1989; Connolly 1996). The research has produced different studies, including a monograph based on over fifty intensive interviews with activists conducted in the 1990s (see Connolly 2002) and a government-funded archival research project entitled 'The Irish Women's Movement: documenting Irish feminisms' (see Connolly and O'Toole 2005). Comparative research in the arena of women's social movements has also been developed (Connolly 2005).[2] This research programme has therefore reached a stage where an in-depth theoretical appraisal of movement outcomes is possible in the case of Irish feminism.

Throughout the duration of this research several theoretical and substantive questions in the social movements paradigm have been addressed. For example, elsewhere I have provided an analysis of the Irish women's movement at the meso level of movement theorising (Connolly 1996, 2002). Initially in this research programme, analysis at the meso- or process-oriented level of theorising social movements was in large part due to the state of movement analysis in Irish studies: when I began working on feminism in a social movements framework in 1992, very little was known about how (never mind why) the women's movement in Ireland, North and/or South, had persistently mobilised *as a social movement* in the period from the mid-nineteenth century to the present. In fact, I was unable to access many of the sources on social movements theory in Irish libraries – I had to import the literature on RMT and NSMs through interlibrary loan. Feminism was not treated as a social movement with a long and continuous history in Ireland; rather, it was generally referred to in mainstream analysis as a sporadic form of protest that seemed to emerge from time to time out of nowhere. As a consequence of all this, the impact of this *movement* in Ireland has not been studied or theorised – a situation compounded by the fact that social movements, in general, have been neglected in the dominant interpretation of the *modernisation*/socio-cultural development of modern Ireland, which was viewed primarily through the lens of the State and formal political structures and institutions.

The research conducted raised several challenges in the comparative analysis of women's social movements which tended to either ignore the Irish case or treat it as weaker and/or later than feminism *elsewhere* (see Connolly 2005 for a discussion). The notion that Irish women were 'late-developers', or less progressive, in comparison to women in other European countries, when second-wave feminism emerged was questioned (Connolly 2002). My research produced extensive evidence to show that second-wave feminism in Ireland did not emerge much later than elsewhere in Europe and the Anglo-American sphere. Nor was feminism in Ireland stimulated *directly* or simply caused by events and developments in other countries (such as the European Union and Anglo-American feminist activism). In short, Irish women are and were not that impressionable. Besides, as Irish women's historians have widely demonstrated, there was already a long-standing history of feminist activism in Ireland when a vibrant second wave resurged internationally (Beaumount 1999). In short, the alleged *lateness* of second-wave feminism in Ireland derives from associating women in predominantly Catholic and post-colonial societies with an innate and essential traditionalism. The distinct and continuous development of feminism both up to and after the 1960s is obscured in this kind of analysis/essentialism.

One of the key findings of the first stage of this research was that the second-wave women's movement did not suddenly emerge from nowhere in Ireland in the late 1960s. More accurately, the women's movement in Ireland was characterised by a high degree of organisational continuity *throughout* the last century: the first and second waves of feminism were *directly linked* by a network of activists who mobilised a network of organisations in the 1940s that amalgamated new activists as well as long-standing activists from the first wave (Connolly 1996). Activists in this network (such as Hilda Tweedy, who was founding member of the Irish Housewives' Association in the 1940s) later went on to mobilise prominent liberal feminist organisations during the second wave of feminism in Ireland. The ad hoc group that called for a National Commission on the Status of Women in 1968, for example, was composed of members of this network. An innovative approach was developed, using a snowball sampling technique, in order to trace and reveal the networks of feminist campaigns and groups in Ireland throughout the twentieth century, as well as their extensive links with international feminist groups and campaigns (for a discussion of networks see Della Porta and Diani 1999: 110–35). In the case of second-wave feminism in Ireland, therefore, the so-called break between the *new* and the *old* social movements, central to the development of the NSM paradigm in continental Europe, was challenged (see also chapter 2 in this volume) and a theory of movement abeyance was developed in some depth (Connolly 2002).

As these examples show, in-depth empirical research was necessary in order to tackle unsupported speculation about the Irish women's movement (a widespread problem in mainstream Irish studies and in the comparative analysis of feminism, which I have criticised elsewhere – see Connolly 2004) and to estab-lish the true complexity and longevity of this transnational movement in the context of Irish culture and society. Furthermore, it prevented the formulation of a simplistic connection between structural conditions, modernisation and the emergence of second-wave feminism. Although changing structural conditions and international developments buttressed and combined with feminist politi-cal goals in Ireland (including the mobilisation of feminism in the US, the relaxation of sexual norms in the 1960s, the growth of international television as a medium for secular ideas, the entry of Ireland into the EEC, the expansion of female education, the demands of the labour market and the economic modernisation project of the state), an existing network of activists was critical in harnessing the mobilisation potential of the women's movement in the 1970s, when political opportunities arose and the cultural climate began to change.

Having developed a painstaking research agenda involving intensive inter-views with activists, later research involved in-depth analysis of archives that originated *from within* feminist groups and organisations. The Attic Press–Róisín Conroy Collection, at the Boole Library, University College Cork (catalogue code: BL/F/AP), was generated and collected by Róisín Conroy as co-founder and publisher at Attic Press and as an activist in the Irish women's movement. The materials were deposited in the Boole Library at University College Cork by Conroy in 1997. The archive covers the years 1963–91 and contains 133 boxes plus ephemera. 'The Irish Women's Movement: document-ing Irish feminisms' is a collaborative research project, which was established in the Sociology Department at University College Cork in 1999. The project formed one major strand of an integrated research initiative at the university that was funded by the Government of Ireland's first Programme for Research in Third Level Institutions (PRTLI 1) and represents the first time any Irish government has funded a university-led study and analysis of the legacy of femi-nism and the women's movement in recent Irish history. The project studied the changes that have occurred in Irish women's lives since the late 1960s, focusing in particular on the role of feminist politics and the women's movement in these developments. Documentary analysis and evidence gathered suggested that second-wave feminism is a multifaceted intellectual, political, social and cultural movement that did not just affect (some) women's lives from the 1970s onwards – rather, it is a transnational movement that has consistently exerted pressure through various means on the social, cultural and political order that has transformed modern Irish history and society, more generally, in recent decades.[3] An attempt to analyse and theorise the diverse and uneven outcomes of second-wave feminism is timely, therefore, in the case of Ireland.

That a growing corpus of documents has become increasingly available in recent years to Irish women's movement researchers, both in official library collections and on a more informal basis, has created exciting possibilities in the movement paradigm. Archives produced by movements themselves have not been used extensively in the field. An extensive range of primary materials that have not been available in the public domain since their initial use in political activism (both in the Róisín Conroy–Attic Press Archive, in other collections and in activist sources provided and consulted informally) were researched and uncovered in 'The Irish Women's Movement: documenting Irish feminisms' project. The end result is an examination of the development of second-wave feminism in Ireland through the prism of a range of documentary sources that originated *from within* the women's movement itself (including the minutes of meetings, position papers, flyers, press releases, photographs, artifacts, political art, posters, magazines and other publications, as well as banners and other movement objects).

The extensive movement documents and archives studied provided an intimate portrayal of feminist activism, in all its diversity, in the period from the late 1960s to the 1990s. The minutes of meetings and position papers produced by groups, for example, demonstrate in great detail the multifarious strategies, politics and goals of the women's movement. Much of the project concentrated on using these documents to reveal the political nature of second-wave feminism as a social movement – how feminists collectively organised, networked, strategised and effectively mobilised a unique and forceful movement in several arenas. However, the archival material also revealed the symbolic and cultural dimensions of activism, and these are discussed below. In other words, social movements have a range of potential effects in the social, political and *cultural* realms. The project sought to move forward existing analyses of the women's movement in Ireland by focusing on feminism as a multifaceted social movement; moreover, it also attempted to connect (or reconnect) feminism more explicitly to the profound social and cultural transformation that has characterised *modern* Ireland since the 1960s.

Theorising outcomes

One of the underlying rationales for studying social movements is that they are important social phenomena that often lead to significant change at the level of individuals, organisations, communities, and societies ... First, what can be said about the range of potential outcomes or consequences of social movements? Second, what are some of the problems associated with identifying social movement consequences or outcomes and how would you, as a researcher, solve some of these problems? (Schussman 2002: 1)

The study of movement outcomes is extremely complex. In agreement with Schussman (*ibid*: 3): 'The tasks in a developing research agenda on movement outcomes are ambitious and weighty, both empirically and theoretically.'

Nevertheless, the research programme described above has established a strong basis for exploring recent approaches to the consequences and outcomes of social movements. What follows in this chapter therefore is an attempt to apply some recent theoretical insights concerning the outcomes of movements to a particular field – Irish feminism.

Theorists in the movement field have, in general, been more interested in theorising the factors that lead to cycles of growth or decline of NSMs than in consequences/outcomes. At the same time, a presumption that movements by definition create *change* is widespread. The RMT framework elucidates the kinds of political opportunities that are important to the growth of social movements and how the position of a social movement in a cycle of protest affects opportunities for mobilisation and collective action. In addition, the circumstances in which movement organisations cooperate and compete with one another, how victories and defeats affect subsequent mobilisation and the impact of counter movement activity are considered. RMT provides a useful emphasis on the actual processes of mobilisation and movement dynamics. As we have seen in chapter 1, however, it has been criticised for its inability to accommodate less formal and widespread cultural dimensions of social movements.

The emphasis on policy outcomes in the social movement literature is largely a result of the dominant role played by resource mobilisation and political process theories during the last few decades (see chapter 1 for a discussion). Yet, at the same time, SMOs are expressive forms of action that aim to spawn a changing *consciousness* across society and produce cultural and cognitive change. In agreement with Giugni (1999), while the cultural effects of movements are more problematical to study empirically than their political effects, insofar as it is more difficult to measure them, it is nevertheless possible to attempt empirical research on cultural outcomes of movements, as we will see later in this chapter: 'Collective action ... is not limited to political aspects. Social movements also have a cultural dimension, and scholars are increasingly acknowledging the need to study this aspect of movements more deeply (e.g. Morris and McClurg Mueller 1992; Johnston and Klandermans 1995)' (Guigni 1999: xxiii).

The NSMs perspective has focused more explicitly on the relationship between movements and socio-cultural change. However, problems also arise in this paradigm in the assessment of outcomes. In agreement with Foweraker (1995: 3):

> New social movement theory often assumes large processes of historical or societal transformation, which remain unproven. Resource mobilisation theory makes bold methodological assumptions that can offend a sense of cultural context. Both kinds of theory can too easily assume a consensual view of 'normal politics' which provides a benchmark for subsequent definitions;

and both kinds of theory are prone to increasing introspection that removes them from the sources and lived experience of social struggle. Where this occurs, the theory is often marred by wishful thinking, and begins to make icons of its object of study.

The complex issue of whether feminism in Ireland has had a presence sufficient to affect women's lives in a variety of contexts, outside of visible or elite organisations, is a key question in this chapter. Feminism has had a generally transformative and sometimes revolutionary goal in Irish society over an extensive period. However, to what extent has this been realised in the most recent wave of activism? And how can we study and theorise the outcomes of second-wave feminism in Ireland? A central problem in connecting social movements to outcomes is that of causality: 'Even when social change occurs in the most dramatic fashion possible, as in revolution, the connection between change-seekers and the revolution is difficult to conclusively draw' (Schussman 2002: 1). For some theorists, the experience of 'acting collectively'/collective action is considered to have a transformative impact primarily on individual participants (the biographical impact of activism). Feminism, for instance, has been charged with merely representing the interests of a particular class of women (primarily in the arena of employment) and of having achieved little transformative impact on society as a whole. For others, a more direct causal relationship between collective action and general social change is envisaged. Yet, in reality, it is extremely difficult to diametrically connect social movements and SMOs to the actual changes they seek.

Schussman (*ibid*) demonstrates how numerous scholarly efforts have been undertaken to both specify what is meant by outcomes and develop theoretical perspectives that lend themselves to understanding outcomes. As suggested earlier, these efforts range from outcomes at the level of individuals and organisations to the level of policy and regime change. An early conceptualisation is found in Gamson (1990) who classifies outcomes at the level of organisation; Gamson suggests that two important consequences of insurgency for organisations are: first, acceptance as a legitimate contestant for power, implying some level of access to the polity; and, second, the receipt of new advantages, that is the gaining of some material objective or desired benefit. For Gamson, these items roughly constitute movement 'success', and he argues that insurgency and bureaucratic organisation are correlated with such achievement.

Scholars have since attempted to move beyond organisational outcomes and resources to the level of policy, which is also difficult to evaluate (see Giugni et al. 1999). Schussman (2002: 2) reviews how Soule et al. (1999) considered the extent to which specific legislative activity (roll-call votes and hearings on women's issues) correlates with protest. The authors found that such legislative change is to some extent dependent on the mobilisation of women's SMOs, but to a greater extent is based on trends in women's labour-force participation (*ibid*: 251). In short, they suggest that outcomes attributed to movements can in fact be a consequence of *other* social forces – such as broad structural change and the demands of the economy. Alternatively, seeking some middle ground Diani (1997) treats network ties and social capital as outcomes in their own right, exploring the extent to which movement activity creates social capital for its participant members and organisations (see Schussman 2002: 2 and Niamh Hourigan's chapter for a more extensive analysis). In this framework, the grandiose outcomes typically attributed to movements are not prioritised. Rather, network formation is in itself a critical outcome. Diani, using the example of the gay and lesbian community, demonstrates how movement-developed social capital is a critical outcome (see Paul Ryan's chapter in this volume for a similar argument and Niamh Hourigan's chapter).

Giugni et al. (1999) have developed a comprehensive programme for analysing the consequences of movements. Since institutions change more slowly than policies, the need to study how movements can alter social as well as political institutions is emphasised. For instance, we know that specific campaigns have in some way or other successfully contributed to the generation of *change* in the arena of family law in Ireland (e.g. in relation to domestic violence and divorce legislation). However, how can we develop a theoretical understanding of the relationship between an instance of change and activism? Moreover, in the long term, to what extent if any have feminist ideas in this arena progressively changed how we construct family and intimate relationships in everyday life? As already stated in the introduction to this text, in addition to affecting policy and the law, SMOs are expressive forms of action that aim to spawn a *changing consciousness* across society and produce cultural and cognitive change. Much of the action of the women's movement in Ireland has also been in the sphere of culture and cultural production (such as consciousness raising, community education, personal development, art, film, music and writing). As a consequence of all this, a model that can accommodate the political–institutional, the socio–cultural, the ideological and the countercultural consequences and outcomes of Irish feminist activism is developed in this chapter

The development of second-wave feminism in Ireland

The task of assessing the outcomes of second-wave feminism in Ireland has been greatly facilitated by the development of substantive research and writing in this field over the last decade (for example, Smyth 1993; Connolly 1996; 2003; Galligan 1998; Connolly and O'Toole 2005). We now know a lot more about the *hidden* history and dynamics of second-wave feminism in Ireland. Most commentators date second-wave Irish feminism from 1968, when the Irish

Housewives' Association and the Association of Business and Professional Women established an ad hoc committee to call on the Government to establish a National Commission on the Status of Women. The resurgence of a distinctive new wave of feminist activism was especially evident in Irish society by 1970, when the *Report of the First National Commission on the Status of Women* was published and the defiant and pioneering radical group, the IWLM, emerged in the public arena. Although recent research points out that ongoing feminist work sustained in the aftermath of the Civil War in the 1920s until the end of the 1960s directly links second-wave feminism organisationally with activism originating in earlier decades of the century, in comparison with previous decades the women's movement transformed and grew significantly in impact and size throughout the 1970s. The second wave is clearly a distinct period of activism that merits in-depth analysis. A period of movement advancement, incorporating the growth of both larger national women's organisations (notably the Council for the Status of Women) and networks and a parallel expansion of grassroots radical activism on a national scale (including, the IWLM, Irish Women United (IWU), Women's Aid and the Rape Crisis Centre) occurred in this decade. Primary mobilising issues included contraception, rape, domestic violence, social welfare provisions, family law and equality in employment.

By the 1980s, although the direct action of the women's movement scaled down significantly in comparison with the previous decade, many existing feminist groups were beginning to mainstream more intensively. Several organisations acquired limited government funding and premises, for example, in this period. At the same time, new movement centres and campaigns were emerging. Pro-choice campaigns were particularly prominent in the aftermath of a national referendum and pro-life amendment to the Constitution in 1983. By the end of the 1980s, women's groups had also begun to form in local communities in very significant numbers. And in the field of education, women's studies was developing, while in Irish cultural life the work of feminist artists, intellectuals and writers flourished.

In the 1990s, the professionalism of a now *established* women's movement was evident and longstanding feminist activists focused much of their energies in mainstream contexts and in institutions. The election of Mary Robinson, a prominent feminist activist and lawyer since the 1970s, as President of Ireland in 1992 seemed to epitomise this trend. For many commentators, however, the 1990s signalled the onset of a post-feminist era or, at best, a third wave of feminism characterised more by political fragmentation and identity politics than by feminist solidarity. Young women are considered to have rejected feminism and the women's movement in this period. And yet empirical research suggests that new campaigns and concerns did emerge with vigour in the 1990s – for example, the reaction of the public to the *X* case[4] and the associated campaign for abortion information and women's right to travel was notable (see Connolly and O'Toole 2005).

Although major studies of the development of the second-wave women's movement have recently appeared in Irish studies (Galligan 1998; Connolly 2002; Connolly and O'Toole 2005), orthodox interpretations of social change in Ireland continue either to ignore or else to diminish feminism as a minor political player. The possible impact of this important movement has been either written out or underplayed in distinguished accounts of social change and modernity. At the same time, Irish feminist studies have focused more on the dynamics and mobilisation of the women's movement than on its *impact*. Yet, as new sources (such as, the Attic Press–Róisín Conroy Collection) reveal, second-wave feminists launched and formulated a highly organised agenda which targeted and instigated fundamental change in a wide range of arenas. Lack of attention to the question of outcomes in the field has therefore compounded the underplaying of feminism in mainstream analysis of social change and modernity in the Irish context.

In agreement with Crossley (2002: 8), 'movements are important because they are key agents for bringing about change in societies'. In this light, it is shortsighted to ignore social movements or consider them less important than the family, the economy or the state, for example. The women's movement is undoubtedly a major consideration in the allegedly rapid transformation Irish society has undergone in recent decades. However, as I have demonstrated above, analysing *change* in relation to social movements is a very complex matter. Sophisticated methodologies and theories of movement outcomes are especially required. Second-wave feminism has not had any kind of simplistic or straightforward *impact* in terms of social and cultural change in Ireland. First, individual movements are never the only direct cause or source of change in any given arena – often campaigns and activism will have unintended consequences. Second, the campaigns and agendas of second-wave feminists have not *always* been successful in Ireland, even in periods of widespread mobilisation such as the 1970s (see Connolly 2002). On the other hand, small-scale mobilisation and action have sometimes resulted in considerable success. Third, looking at social and cultural resistance to feminism is as important as feminism itself in any critical account of the outcomes of social movements. For example, the involvement of the women's movement in decriminalising contraception in the 1970s provoked a backlash in the form of an influential counter-right pro-life campaign that was to have a powerful impact on the women's movement, Irish politics and Irish society in general throughout the 1980s. One of the main outcomes of a social movement is often to stimulate counter-movements (e.g. the pro-life movement in Ireland) and related movements (e.g. both the gay and lesbian movement and the men's movement in Ireland were strongly motivated by the prior activism of the women's movement). And, fourth, movements can be considered mere symptoms of broader social forces rather than as overt agents or carriers of *change* in themselves.

Recent theories of movement outcomes can be drawn upon to explore, in a complex manner, the influence that diverse strands of feminist activism and thought have had, and continue to have, in a number of key arenas. Drawing on the research agenda outlined above, the rest of this chapter will proceed to examine a range of diverse *outcomes*.

Problematising the political–institutional consequences of activism

Much research in the field has focused on the political–legal outcomes of movements. Specifically in the arena of institutional change, a range of evidence documenting tangible outcomes compliant, in some way or other, with feminist goals and objectives can be identified. These outcomes were identified in the research described above, both in the meticulous analysis of newspapers in the period covering the second wave and in the archives of the second-wave Irish women's movement. The emergence of visible feminist organisations, networks and concerted campaigns can also be postulated as an *outcome*. A sample of those outcomes, in chronological order, includes the following:

1968   An ad hoc committee representative of several long-standing women's groups presented a memorandum to the Taoiseach calling for the establishment of a National Commission on the Status of Women.

1970   Government set up First Commission on the Status of Women.
        First meeting of the radical Irishwomen's Liberation Movement (IWLM).

1971   *Chains – or Change?*, the manifesto of the IWLM, was published and the group appeared on the *Late, Late Show*, broadcast nationally, and gained national publicity.
        Women's Progressive Association formed (later re-named the Women's Political Association).
        Commission on the Status of Women published *Interim Report on Equal Pay*.

1972   The organisations Action, Information, Motivation (AIM) and Cherish established.
        Report of the Commission on the Status of Women published.

1973   Council for the Status of Women established.
        Civil Service (Employment and Married Women) Act 1973: removal of the marriage bar in the Civil Service, local authorities and health boards.
        Social Welfare Act provides for Deserted Wives and Unmarried

Mothers' Allowance.

Mary Robinson introduces Private Members Bill to the Seanad (Senate) to amend the 1945 Criminal Law (Amendment) Act and the Censorship of Publication Acts 1929 and 1945.

1974   Women's Representative Committee set up by Minister for Labour to implement the recommendations of the *Report of the Commission on the Status of Women.*

Supreme Court ruling in favour of Mary McGee, finds the ban on the importation of contraceptives for private use unconstitutional. Supreme court recognises the existence of a constitutional right to marital privacy.

Máirín de Burca and Mary Andersen take a case to the Supreme Court, claiming the 1927 Juries Act, which effectively barred women from sitting on juries, was unconstitutional.

Anti-Discrimination (Pay) Act passed.

Social Welfare Act grants payment of Children's Allowance to mothers. Provision for payment of an allowance to single women over 58 years and to the wives of prisoners.

Maintenance Orders Act provided for a reciprocal enforcement of maintenance orders between Ireland and the UK.

Women's Aid opens its first refuge.

IWU, a radical feminist organisation, formed.

1975   International Women's Year.

IWU holds its first public meeting at Liberty Hall and adopts ICTU Working Women's Charter.

UN Decade for Women inaugurated in Mexico.

1976   Contraceptive Action Programme launched by IWU.

European Commission rejects Irish Government's application for derogation from Commission's Directive on Equal Pay.

Juries Act passed following de Burca–Andersen case, which deemed conditional exclusion of women from jury lists to be unconstitutional.

IWU invades the 'male only' 40–foot bathing area at Sandycove.

Family Law (Maintenance of Spouses and Children) Act passed.

Family Home Protection Act passed to prevent family home being sold unknown to the family or without the prior consent of both spouses.

1977   First Rape Crisis Centre opened in Dublin.

Six women elected to the Dáil; first-preference votes for women increase from 42,268 to 81,967.

Six women elected to the Senate.

Employment Equality Act resulted in establishment of the Employment Equality Agency.

Unfair Dismissals Act passed.

1978   'Women Against Violence Against Women' march to protest against rape and sexual assault.

1979   Two women elected to the European Parliament.
        Máire Geoghan Quinn appointed to the Cabinet, the first woman since Constance Markievicz in 1919.
        Health (Family Planning) Act passed restricting sale of contraceptives to bona fide couples only.
        Women's Right to Choose Group formed.
        Campaign for an Irish Women's Centre launched.

1980   First Irish Pregnancy Counselling Centre established.
        Opening of Dublin Women's Centre.

1983   Open Door Counselling established in Dublin following Irish Pregnancy Counselling Centre's financial collapse.
        Abortion referendum results in Article 40.3.3 of the Constitution of the Irish Republic, guaranteeing the 'right to life of the unborn'.
        Irish Feminist Information established.
        KLEAR established.

1984   Anti-Reagan demonstration by Woman Against Disarmament.
        Attic Press, feminist publisher, established.
        University College Dublin (UCD) Women's Studies Forum established.

1985   UN Global Women's Conference at Copenhagen.
        Róisín Conroy's High Court Case and the Repeal the Social Welfare Code Campaign.

1986   Nuala Fennell appointed Minister of State for Women's Affairs.
        Divorce rejected by the electorate in a national referendum.

1987   Interdisciplinary Congress held in Dublin.

1990   Mary Robinson elected President of Ireland.
        WERRC established at UCD.

1992   Abortion Information and Right to Travel referenda passed.
        20 women elected to Dáil Éireann.
        Decriminalisation of homosexuality

1993   Report of the Second Commission on the Status of Women published.

1995   Divorce referendum accepted.
        Regulation of Information Act introduced.
        Green Paper on Abortion published.

Collective action is not, however, limited to these visible or well-known outcomes. Nor can all these outcomes be attributed to feminism *alone*. Tangible outcomes were often co-generated by other factors (EEC directives and sympathetic elites, for example). Furthermore, the successes of the movement and the extent to which movements (in this case the Irish women's movement) fail to achieve their goals merits equal attention. The varying short- and long-term impact of outcomes is also a consideration. For instance, the campaign that resulted in the removal of the marriage bar in Irish law did not automatically result in a massive entry of married women into the Civil Service in the 1970s. The significant entry of married women into the labour force in Ireland happened later in the context of the changing demands of the economy. In other examples, legislative change was in fact *preceded* by social change – artificial contraception was being used and provided illegally for some time before it was legalised in 1979, and thousands of Irish women have abortions in the UK each year despite the fact that abortion is still outlawed in Ireland. Although outcomes that coincide with specific campaigns and instances of feminist activism can be identified in the political-legal arena, further analysis of the multiplicity of factors that *combined with feminism* to produce these outcomes is essential.

Socio-cultural change

Increasingly, movement analysis is a field that can apparently address the cultural as well as the more obvious political impact and outcomes of feminism.[5] Giugni (1999: xxiii) suggests that 'collective efforts for social change occur in the realms of culture, identity, and everyday life as well as in direct engagement with the State'. Movements do not operate exclusively at the level of revolution, mass mobilisation and major legislative change – they also problematise the ways in which we live our everyday lives and calls for changes in the private as well as the public sphere. But, how can we study socio-cultural change vis à vis social movements?

Socio-economic data and biographical accounts, which were integral to the research programme described above, demonstrate that Irish women's lives, roles and self-image have changed considerably since the 1970s (see Byrne and Leonard 1997). The transformation in public discourse about women and gender as well as the transformation of gender relations in everyday life in Ireland are also palpable. For example, it is not unusual for a woman living in Ireland today to openly have her child or children (typically 1.6 of them) in more than one type of family or relationship in her life course.[6] And increasingly she will choose to work outside as well as inside the home. The workplace is no longer a predominantly male space. The average number of children an Irish woman will have has significantly decreased in the period since contraception was provided illegally by the women's movement in the 1970s and partially legalised (for married couples only) in 1979. However, as stated above, cultural change preceded legislative change: women were deciding to control their fertility and have fewer children *before* the law changed. The law was subverted by thousands of women – for example, the pill could be prescribed to regulate or alleviate menstruation but not for fertility control. Irish women used this loop-hole to access the pill for *other* purposes.

To what extent was feminism implicated in these developments? Was feminism not rejected by a large number of women/the public generally in Ireland – who regarded radical feminists, in particular, as extreme? Although the Irish public has not always readily supported the demands of feminists and the women's movement since the 1970s, the range of questions and debates that were propelled into the public arena by this movement over time have had a wider political and cultural effect. The women's movement progressively gained a level of attention (especially negative attention) through its more controversial actions, as well as its institutional–political strategies, which injected a new culture of questioning in the public and private spheres (concerning, for example, intimate relationships, sexuality, family life, marriage, parenting, work, technology and health). As Paul Ryan demonstrates in chapter 4, the dominant religious, medical and legal discourses, through which men and women had understood and 'framed' their roles and sexuality for over a century, were challenged by feminism and other movements. A new discourse of individual sexual fulfilment gradually filtered through the emergence of a range of NSMs in Ireland, including the gay and lesbian movements. It was feminist activism, in particular, which brought many issues that were previously out of bounds and stigmatised in the Irish public sphere into the open for the first time (such as rape, sexuality, abortion, contraception, single motherhood and domestic violence). Irish society and public debate were, by the late 1960s, still influenced by Catholic social teaching (see Inglis 1998). For example, when the IWLM organised a public meeting in the Mansion House, Dublin, in 1971 it was completely unheard of for a woman to stand up and publicly declare herself to be an 'unmarried mother' – as one woman did (she received a standing ovation). Single motherhood was considered shameful in Ireland at that time and children born outside of wedlock were discriminated against in the law and put up for adoption in large numbers. Moreover, unmarried mothers were commonly hidden and institutionalised until their babies had been put up for adoption. Likewise, domestic violence was generally considered a private issue to be dealt with primarily within *the family*. And the priest in Ireland was one of the main sources of advice on family planning through the confessional.

A fundamental challenge to the striking cultural conservatism that characterised Irish society for much of the twentieth century emerged from within a whole range of reformist movements that mobilised from the 1960s on, the women's movement being one of the most significant. The fact that several of the founding members of the IWLM and its organisational offshoots were journalists facilitated the entry of feminist issues into the public arena and discourse. An entire page of most of the national newspapers was devoted to women's issues and provided a forum for publicising the demands of the women's movement – since the editors of those pages were members of the IWLM. Second-wave feminist thought and interventions opened up and provoked a wide-ranging questioning of long-established attitudes to Irish women and values that had permeated public institutions and private life through the media, in particular. The actions of an organised and active women's movement over the last three decades can therefore be said to have contributed in no small way to the generation of a new language, discourse and cultural space in modern Ireland – as well as the substantive changes in policy and the law, traced above.

Direct action v. mainstreaming; disruption v. moderation

Any analysis of short- to long-term movement outcomes must also take the plurality of strategies and tactics that were mobilised by the women's movement into account. The benefits of mainstream/political action over direct/radical action was a subject of much debate in the women's movement itself and in the analysis of social movement outcomes (see Giugni 1999 and Gamson 1990). Bouchier (cited in Randall 1987) suggests that *both* an autonomous, informal, non-hierarchical *and* a formal mode of organisation ensure movement survival. In the case of the women's movement, an autonomous radical movement sector was necessary to develop a collective consciousness and to recruit activists who would not participate in more hierarchical liberal organisations (which have tended to be led by white, middle-class and professional women) and formal politics. The grassroots radical group structure of the 1970s in Ireland and elsewhere was a necessary means to provide the intersection between personal and social change – the essence of the 'personal is political' (Dahlerup 1986: 14). At the same time, a significant number of women in Ireland chose to work within the established political institutions and political parties to advance feminism. According to Galligan (1998), these women have succeeded, to a considerable extent, in reconstituting formal political discourses to be more inclusive of women and women's concerns.

Radical direct action and mainstream activism produce very different outcomes. In terms of outcomes, the loose, small-group-based structure evident in the 1970s was dramatically successful in uniting energies and developing new radical perspectives in Irish public debate. However, this form of activism often resulted in a large turnover of activists and a range of unsuccessful or short-lived initiatives. The more formal, hierarchical aspect of the Irish women's movement (the Council for the Status of Women, now called the National Women's Council, for instance) has been more enduring in organisational terms – but has it been stronger in impact? Ryan suggests:

> Because contemporary theoretical analyses of feminist ideology were originally formulated within either a Marxist or radical feminist perspective, liberal feminism was generally viewed negatively in terms of both ideology

and activist method. Yet, it is this segment of the movement which constitutes the majority of participants in the United States, and it is largely liberal feminists who can be found in rape crisis centres, abortion clinics, monthly strategy meetings, pickets, marches, state legislative sessions, and congressional hearings. Liberals, it appears, are short on theory but long on activism. (Ryan 1992: 2)

However, mobilising inside *the system* had both advantages and disadvantages in securing movement objectives in the second wave. While for some commentators it is a sign of success for a social movement if it has an impact on the established institutions and ideologies, in the process the movement itself will change and perhaps diminish. One of the key outcomes of the second wave, mapped in the research outlined above, was the professionalisation and mainstreaming of the women's movement, from the 1980s on especially. The implications of the recent professionalisation of Irish feminist organisations (the Rape Crisis Centres, for example) and the perceived decline of radical feminist grassroots mobilising was reflected upon by a number of interviewees in my research. They expressed concern about the long-term impact of mainstreaming, the coopting of activists by political parties and established institutions, and the demobilising effect of professionalising movement organisations.

Participation in autonomous feminist organisations, on the other hand, raised women's consciousness about radical feminism and contributed to their politicisation as they came to see the connections between a range of issues and the larger system of gender inequality. Through personal experience, activism and the wider diffusion of radical feminist ideas in the media and in feminist texts, magazines, publications, an increasing number of women have become aware of the political rather than the personal nature of their problems – their consciousness has been raised. Radical feminist ideas were not confined to what were considered the 'radical' organisations (like the IWLM and IWU) over time, however. Organisations such as the National Women's Council (NWC, formerly the Council for the Status of Women), which have been pursuing equality within the legislature since the early 1970s, have progressively adopted explanations for women's oppression in a number of areas that are more consistent with original radical theorising – including the right to travel for an abortion, the causes of rape, the complexity of reproductive choice and gay rights/sexuality.

During the 1990s the women's movement continued to professionalise and mainstream. While it may have less visibility as a radical protest movement, its political power as a set of professional lobbying organisations is increasingly recognised. Moreover, the women's movement has been extremely effective at establishing durable and autonomous women-centred institutions that mobilise both within and outside of the State and its institutions. For example, the provision of services like women's aid refuges, legal advice centres and reproductive health services have been crucial in thousands of ordinary women's lives in Ireland across all social classes. Thousands of Irish women would not have accessed the pill if a family planning clinic had not provided it, nor would they have escaped a violent situation without economic and practical assistance and refuge; thousands wanted to have an abortion in the UK but did not know how, and many felt they could never, in their lifetime, reveal that they were raped or abused. In all these situations, the women's movement *began* the process of cultural and discursive change through practical everyday assistance/services in a range of arenas. However, long-standing services have also been extremely effective as lobbyists and in campaigns. Apart from these issues being a target of political change and mobilisation, they exhibit Eyerman and Jamison's understanding (1991) of how social movements attempt to bring about cognitive change in society: through the creation of a distinctive worldview; the articulation of an alternative set of technological principles; and new ways of disseminating knowledge, especially the rejection of conventional distinctions between 'experts' and others (see Tovey 1999: 35).

These examples show that the achievements of the women's movement have impinged more widely on Irish women's lives than a narrow focus on liberal rights/policy change suggests. At the same time, equality measures in the liberal approach have had both quantitative and qualitative consequences. The strategy of getting more women into the Civil Service, the legal profession, academia, etc., has to *some* extent challenged the patriarchal values and image of public institutions and the workplace. The very presence and visibility of even a minority of women in the professions and in positions of power is a symbolic challenge to the predominant work culture, even if working women are not predominantly feminists. Ironically, part of the cultural effect of feminism is that women who chose not to participate in the women's movement or define themselves as 'feminist' have benefited greatly from the efforts and successes of the women's movement in the workplace – while avoiding the negative labelling often ascribed to 'feminists' in the public sphere.

For Ryan (1992: 89), there are two central contributing factors to current orientations in feminist practice and activism:

1 There are more similarities than differences in philosophy among establishment feminists today, indicating a less concerted social movement. In recent years, feminist thought has evolved into a comprehensive ideology and discourse that addresses a whole spectrum of social and political questions, from human rights to nationalism to environmentalism

2 There is a new way of understanding feminism and social change in cultural terms. For instance, long-term activists now often describe feminism as a process. Feminism is important therefore not just because it has mainstreamed and diffused into the institutions of the State, but because it

intertwines with the biography and personal development and growth of many women who have lived through the second wave.

Outcomes and ideologies

Any consideration of the impact and outcomes of feminist activism in Ireland must also conceptualise the cultural as well as political–institutional dimensions of activism. The fluid relationship between theoretical stances, ideologies and strategies evident in the women's movement further problematises the question of outcomes. In the history of the Irish women's movement, there is no simple or direct causal relationship between liberal feminist actions and policy change, for example, despite the widely held assumption that liberal feminism unproblematically and directly impacts public policy. The women's movement in Ireland has frequently been stereotyped as a unified entity in debates about its outcomes and impact. However, various second-wave feminist groups constantly worked to confront, debate and overcome real *differences* among themselves or between Irish women (see Connolly 2002 for an in-depth analysis). In the process, a multifaceted movement with a variety of outcomes was created.

Recent feminist theoretical approaches that emphasise difference, as well as new studies of the history of the movement itself, have established the complexity of the Irish women's movement. On the other hand, where differences have been acknowledged there has been a tendency to perceive these only in terms of strife and conflict, or through the stereotype of 'women fighting with each other'. However, the very diversity of the women's movement is in many ways its lifeblood, and reflects the movement's engagement with a range of social, cultural and political perspectives, as well its own ability to change and continue as societal and historical circumstances demand. In 'The Irish Women's Movement: documenting Irish feminisms' project (Connolly and O'Toole 2005), we outlined the main groupings, or kinds of feminist stances, within feminist politics in order to address how these were expressed within the Irish context. Liberal feminists tend to lobby for equal rights for women within the existing structures of society. In general, liberals consider the status quo to be established. Although this position tends to be criticised by other feminist activists, this kind of feminist work is crucial to the mainstreaming of feminist values and rights within the wider structures of society, especially the political and legal systems, and has accomplished many important rights for women in Ireland since the 1970s.

This investment in the status quo differentiates liberals from socialist feminists. Unlike Marxist feminists who worked for women's rights within wider leftist groupings, socialist feminists formed groups within the women's movement and campaigned against class inequality alongside gender inequality – and established a sense of solidarity with women workers and trade unionists in the international arena. Initially (particularly in North America) radical feminism was associated with those who prioritised sexual oppression. As a consequence, early radical feminists and lesbian feminists tended to be grouped together. However, over time, radicalism became associated with feminists who were more involved in grassroots activism and for whom social and cultural revolution was intrinsic to their politics.

In the Irish context, groups such as the IWLM and the IWU , among others, could be characterised as radical feminist groups. Direct action is more associated with radical than with liberal feminism – and events such as the Contraception Train can be read very clearly as radical feminist actions. Separatist feminists in North America, for instance, attempted to create self-sustaining female communities and to withdraw as much as possible from patriarchal society. Separatism was not really a dominant feature of feminism in Ireland, although there were elements of separatist values in the establishment of women-only spaces during the period. Activists involved in mainstream Irish politics, socialist politics, republicanism, civil rights and housing rights at times cooperated in campaigns, and solidarity between dissimilar groups and theoretical perspectives was not uncommon. Furthermore, activists who concentrated their activism primarily within feminist groups often held different and, at times, oppositional political stances – such as those within the core group of the IWLM who differed over the stated aims of the group and whether or not direct action tactics (such as the Contraception Train) would alienate the public with regard to the demands of the women's movement. In terms of a history of ideas within Irish feminist activism, there is therefore room for much further investigation. Innovative theoretical approaches were conceptualised by Irish activists throughout the period covered in this study. Although the distinct project of mapping in detail the development of feminist theories in the documents of the Irish women's movement was beyond the scope of 'The Irish Women's Movement: documenting Irish feminisms' project, several perspectives were revealed.

Organisations with either an axial reformist (women's rights) or radical (women's liberation) public identity undoubtedly *overlapped* in the second-wave period in Ireland. Furthermore, *both* styles of activism were combined and informed distinctive organisations, to varying degrees, as the 1970s progressed. In the case of the Irish women's movement, there was significant coalition and interaction between organisations aligned to styles of activism labelled women's rights and women's liberation groups, as the movement progressively advanced. Consequently, the observable movement style of these two sectors is not based on the direct translation of hegemonic feminist ideologies into specific, rigid types of activism and outcomes.

Essentially, feminist theory is something that changed and evolved throughout the second wave, and terms referring to different feminist ideologies – radical feminism, liberal feminism, etc., changed over time and were not as fixed as we tend to view them today. A sense of clarity or of distinct lines drawn between particular groups and theoretical perspectives is not really evident in the documents relating to Irish feminist activism, for example, which were the product of extensive debate and engagement in various groups. It may have been possible in the larger urban centres of North America to form groups espousing a particular theoretical stance; but, given the scale of the Irish movement, there tended to be a lot of fluidity between groups, individuals and particular political stances. For instance, the same names often crop up both in feminist campaigns considered 'liberal' or 'radical' (see Connolly 2002 for an extensive discussion). Any consideration of movement consequences and outcomes must therefore be able to accommodate the often fluid and amorphous relationship of social movement activism and ideologies. Fundamentally, ideas were formulated at the level of discourses that were produced through negotiation and debate across the women's movement and in the wider society.

The consequences of feminism as a countercultural project

I have explored above how the women's movement worked to create legal–political as well as socio-cultural change in both the private and public spheres in Ireland. However, following Melucci (see chapter 1), feminism can also be understood as a kind of cultural project *in itself*. Melucci (1996) draws our attention to the new forms of cultural politics in contemporary society in which social movements are engaged, arguing that social movements are concerned principally with solidarity and conflict in the cultural realm. For Melucci, the most important political function of movements is as signs, or messages, which highlight hidden conflicts and problems.

Feminist activists and the women's movement engaged widely in countercultural activities (such as consciousness raising and self-education projects) and in cultural production in Ireland. Second-wave feminism was in itself an educational project. When feminist activists in the early 1970s questioned the status quo in newly formed women's groups, they began to unpick their own socialisation, read against the grain, challenge hegemonies and reconstruct the world from women's own perspectives. Early initiatives in Irish feminist studies tended to be based in voluntarily run women's centres, or located within small networks of friends who set up reading groups and consciousness-raising groups (or as they were called in the US 'rap groups') where a group of women would come together to discuss a particular issue. From the 1960s on, feminist ideas also diffused more widely and transnationally through texts and publications. Feminist thought was therefore never confined to the women's movement of any given country. The wider availability of feminist texts coincided with the beginning of a relaxation of censorship laws in Ireland in this period. During the second wave, feminist theories and books were hotly contested both within the Irish women's movement and in the wider society, especially in the media. Theoretical perspectives evolving within Anglo-American feminist activist groups were published and became core reading for feminists in Ireland as in other countries from the 1960s on. The work of prominent theorists such as Betty Friedan and Germaine Greer, to name just two, were read and discussed openly in reading groups, consciousness-raising sessions, political meetings, classrooms, public debates and conferences in Ireland. More recently, the writings of Naomi Wolf and others have been widely debated and read.

The kinds of cultural productions that emerged during the second wave remain largely under-researched and under-represented in movement studies. The issues of artistic representation, and the ways in which second-wave feminist activism constructed a counterculture that critiqued and subverted mainstream values were widely addressed in the research project reported on by Connolly and O'Toole (2005). The research revealed that there was quite a distinct 'feminist culture' during the period encompassing the second wave, ranging from iconic songs to literature, from street theatre to film and video groups, and from visual arts to specific styles in food and clothes. However, as Tina O'Toole has written (see *ibid*), arriving at definitions of just what that feminist culture consisted of is a difficult task – do we focus on what tends to be seen as 'high culture' (theatre, visual arts, literature) or concentrate on elements of street or 'popular culture' (feminist newspapers, slogans on t-shirts, protest chants)? The division of culture into 'high' and 'popular' proves impossible during a period when a poem written by an activist is chanted by a crowd at a protest march, is later published in a feminist newspaper and goes on to form part of the collection of an emerging writer, for example.

Furthermore, it is not possible to describe the kinds of cultural production associated with the Irish feminist movement as a singular *culture*, which can be categorized as one whole aspect of the feminist activisms of the period. Neither is it possible to reflect on this 'culture' as a specific space, cut off from other aspects of politics, culture and society. Elements of other alternative movements and cultural forces on the national and international stages – such as folk music, co-operative living, vegetarianism, left-wing ideologies and protest marches – as well as the demands and influences working within the various cultural arenas themselves, intersected with the spaces being opened up to feminist scrutiny in Ireland.

Given that this is a vast area, 'The Irish Women's Movement: documenting Irish feminisms' project provided a survey of the general arena of cultural production, focusing on some of the cultural work specific to the women's movement. Clearly, much work has already been done on some aspects of late twentieth-century Irish feminist cultural production, particularly in the realms of literature, film and the visual arts. For example, in the visual arts in Ireland it is possible to see distinct trends and changes that came about in this field as a direct result of second-wave feminism. Many women artists were activists who belonged to feminist groups, and some established groups and initiatives specifically to promote and collectivise the work of feminist artists during this period. An ad in the first issue of *Wicca* magazine[7] (1977) states:

> Women artists will exhibit their work in the gallery of the Project Arts Centre, 15 May to 9 June. Approx. 20 women – non-professionals, professionals and students working in a variety of mediums – have been selected by a panel to have their work shown. Male-run institutions frequently reject work by women and galleries because they work in 'unacceptable' mediums such as ceramics and fabrics and they are not always neutral, intellectual and formal, say the organisers of the exhibition. (BL/F/AP/1498, Attic Press Archive)

The Women Artists' Action Group was formed by Pauline Cummins in 1987. The main aim of the group was to provide a forum for women artists, who had up until this point 'reacted [to the feminist movement] alone, in their studios' but without any space for collective action ('Art Beyond Barriers', WAAG, National Library of Ireland, Ir. 700: 106). Other artists worked within community-based programmes to bring about change. Just as the feminist movement influenced the work of these artists, their work informed and commented upon the changes in Irish society brought about in part by the feminist movement. Installations such as 'Sounding the Depths' (Walsh and Cummins, Irish Museum of Modern Art, 1992) challenged and interrogated representations of the female body, and the way in which women had been positioned in Irish culture and society.

Areas such as women's writing and art tend to be neglected in mainstream social movements theory. Yet, this kind of work reached the wider culture and society, not only in Ireland but internationally. This is reflected in other areas of cultural production that emerged from or in tandem with the Irish women's movement, such as the National Writers' Workshop, which Eavan Boland facilitated in 1984, and which was aimed at encouraging women's literary work. In addition, in the academy, women's studies and feminist theory flourished from the 1980s on and resulted in an active research agenda and high level of publications in Ireland. Feminist texts also reached and raised the consciousness of a wider constituency of women who did not live near centres of activism or may not have had the confidence, freedom or time to participate in the women's movement.

Archives and documentary sources proved, in the research programme described above, to be a particularly innovative way of theorising movement outcomes at the cultural, political and biographical levels. The kinds of material held by feminist archives are somewhat different from those found in more traditional archives, which tend to focus on conventional documents. The 'documents' in feminist archives can sometimes run to three-dimensional objects such as badges, signs and whistles, as well as banners and t-shirts – a reminder of the kinds of objects which narrate the cultural life and histories of social movements. According to O'Toole, a key element of this archival material is what could be described as 'graphic feminism' – the posters, flyers, newspapers, cartoons, magazines, graffiti and banners, as well as slogans on t-shirts and badges which played a central role in the activism of this period (see Connolly and O'Toole 2005 to view a range of these sources). Graphic material was a focal point of feminist activism during the second wave, and is situated at the point where visual culture, activist symbols and political strategies meet. Images on posters were direct, vivid and memorable: for example, the image on the cover of the IWLM manifesto *Chains – or Change?* Visually attractive posters, made and designed by activists, that are held in the Róisín Conroy–Attic Press Archive, advertised key events such as the first public meeting of the IWLM at the Mansion House in 1971, meetings of the Society for Sexual Liberation in the late 1970s and a range of other meetings, demos and conferences. Flyers and pamphlets in the archive advertised meetings, but also disseminated booklists of further feminist reading and provided information relating to contraception, abortion and equal pay issues. Further analysis of these sources will undoubtedly demonstrate the wider cultural diffusion of feminism beyond the political–legal arena – and indeed beyond its own nexus.

Conclusion

In a complex society, the social construction of gender relations is responsive to an array of social processes – and not just to the women's movement. Feminism is clearly not the sole ingredient in the profound transformation that has occurred in gender relations in Ireland in recent decades. Therefore I have made no attempt in this chapter to crudely aggregate, or totalise, the impact/outcomes of second-wave feminism. Having said that, a basic premis of this chapter is that the women's movement (and indeed social movements in general) is a major but neglected consideration in the rapid transformation Irish culture and society has undergone in recent decades. Furthermore, its significance as a social and political (albeit predominantly mainstream) movement is as evident as ever in contemporary Irish society, despite a so-called decline in activism. However, this chapter concludes that although outcomes can and should be studied in depth in the movement paradigm, in effect, the outcomes of the women's movement can never be *conclusive*. Feminism throughout it's history has constantly been transmogrified by the multifarious dynamics, strategies and ideologies that have mobilised the women's movement, over time and place, as well as by multiple mediating processes and macro social forces in the wider society.

Moreover, the outcomes desired by feminism are not nearly *concluded*.

The durability and continuity of the women's movement in Ireland is now well established. However, how can we arrive at a general assessment of its outcomes in light of its legacy? Some of this chapter has drawn on in-depth empirical research to correlate second-wave feminism with some considerable institutional gains in the arena of women's rights. However, several questions about the assumed polit-ical–legal outcomes of second-wave feminism were raised. More in-depth analysis of other plausible contributing factors in particular instances of legislative and policy related changes must also be conducted in order to arrive at a more accurate view. Ireland's entry into the EC, for example, in the early 1970s was significant and needs to be studied in more depth.

Furthermore, it has demonstrated how the women's movement has been equally concerned with self-transformation (women's liberation) and with creating a counter culture – aspects of social movements that require more research and theoretical analysis in the field. The memoirs of feminist activists in Ireland (Nell McCafferty and June Levine have published autobiographies, for instance) as well as intensive interviews can be used to further develop and theorise the biographical outcomes of activism. This kind of research can also be used to develop Diani's conceptualisation of networks and social capital. The life-long relationships developed through feminist networks and the develop-ment of feminist communities were significant issues in the research outlined above. Moreover, the extent to which the language and framework of second-wave feminism can be said to influence individual's lives in Ireland today, especially women's lives, can be studied further by conducting qualitative research in the arena of family life, personal relationships and sexuality, for example. The transformation of intimacy that has been conceptualised by soci-ologists of the family can, for instance, be associated with the wider diffusion of the language and politics of women's liberation in the media as well as in popular discourse.

Despite the complexity of theorising the outcomes and consequences of social movements at the individual, organisational, structural and cultural levels, undoubtedly the women's movement has been a significant force in Ireland. By its very presence feminism has symbolically challenged the domi-nant masculinist code of Irish society. The survival of the women's movement in Ireland over the last three decades has, however, been in large part due to the way in which second-wave feminism often managed to create an impres-sion of being a larger movement than it was, as well as through generating the notion of 'a common cause' among Irish women – a collective identity. As a consequence, the original goals and priorities of second-wave feminism in Ireland have recently been subject to a profound revision and critique by women who feel they were excluded from the main agenda or 'left behind' by the mainstream women's movement in the 1970s and 1980s. New collective voices are beginning to transform the women's movement, as we have recently known it – the *outcome* of which remains to be seen. Questions such as the role of rural and working-class women in Irish feminism and the influx in recent years of female migrants into Ireland – many of whom are working in domestic service in order to facilitate the entry of middle-class women into the workforce (an occupation dominated by Irish female emigrants in times past) – pose new challenges in Irish feminist activism and debate. In the process, new movement centres have flourished, such as locally based women's groups (Byrne 1997). Fundamentally, these developments suggest that the *outcomes* of the second-wave women's movement in Ireland are, consequently, incomplete and therefore *still unfolding.*

Notes

1 Some material in this chapter is adopted from *Documenting Irish Feminisms* (Connolly and O'Toole 2005). Tina O'Toole must be given full credit for researching and writing the material on feminism and culture.

2 I conducted comparative research on feminism in Ireland and Quebec in 1999, using the archive of the Canadian women's movement at the University of Ottawa.

3 In addition to producing a book, the Irish women's movement project incorporated several other activities: a detailed bibliography of Irish feminist studies and research was produced and is published on the internet (see the project website www.ucc.ie/wisp/iwm); conferences, workshops, a series of public seminars as well as a public exhibition were held; an integrated project website was developed; the contents of feminist archives and collections in Ireland were collated and documented; movement photographs, artefacts, symbols and images were recorded and reproduced; an international network of experts/researchers in the field was established; and comparative research was advanced. This work will continue in University College Cork in cooperation with research partnerships established with colleagues in other institutions, nationally and internationally.

4 In February 1992, Judge Costello granted an injunction in the High Court preventing a pregnant 14–year-old rape victim from leaving Ireland to have an abortion in England. Amid public outcry, the Supreme Court overturned his decision two weeks later to allow her to go, ruling that 'if it is established ... that there is a real and substantial risk to the life, as distinct from the health, of the mother, which can only be avoided by the termination of her pregnancy, such termination is permissible'. Here, the Court held that there was a real and substantial risk of suicide if the pregnancy continued; thus the termination was permissible, even in Ireland. However, where no such risk existed, both information and possibly travel could be prevented in the interest of safeguarding the right to life of the 'unborn'. The Government then entered a Declaration to the Protocol, saying that it would not be used to restrict travel or information.

5 According to Della Porta and Diani (1999: 228), a number of scholars have attempted to indicate in classifications and typologies the components of social movement success. In one of the first major accounts of movement outcomes, Gamson (1990) made a distinction between new gains (tangible changes in public policy on issues raised by protest) and levels of acceptance (changes movements bring about in

systems of representation).

6 Recent census data suggests that one in three births is now outside marriage in Ireland compared to just over one in five in 1995. In Dublin City the proportion of births outside marriage in the first quarter of 2004 was 48.8 per cent (source: CSO).

7 *Wicca* is an Irish feminist magazine that is in the Attic Press Archive at UCC – these magazines were informally published and did not have proper dates, citation, etc.

Bibliography

Beaumont, C., 1999 'Gender, Citizenship and the State in Ireland, 1922–1990', in Brewster, S., Crossman, V., Becket, F. and Alderson, D. (eds), 1999 *Ireland in Proximity: History, gender, space* (London and New York: Routledge), pp. 94–108.

Bouchier, D., 1983 *The Feminist Challenge: The movement for women's liberation in Britain and the USA* (London: Macmillan).

Byrne, A. and Leonard, M. (eds), 1997 *Women and Irish Society: A sociological reader* (Belfast: Beyond the Pale).

Byrne, N., 1996 'The Uneasy Relationship between Feminism and Community', in Smyth, A. (ed.), *Feminism, Politics, Community*, WERRC Annual Conference Papers (Dublin: UCD), pp. 24–7.

Byrne, P., 1997 *Social Movements in Britain* (London: Routledge).

Connolly, L., 1996 'The Women's Movement in Ireland: a social movements analysis 1970–1995', *Irish Journal of Feminist Studies*, 1:1, 43–77.

Connolly, L., 2002 *The Irish Women's Movement: From revolution to devolution* (Basingstoke: Palgrave).

Connolly, L., 2003 *From Revolution to Devolution: The Irish women's movement* (Dublin: Lilliput Press).

Connolly, L., 2004 'The Limits of Irish Studies: historicism, culturalism, paternalism', *Irish Studies Review*, 12:2, 139–62.

Connolly, L., 2005 'Comparing the Women's Movements of Ireland and Quebec', *Canadian Journal of Irish Studies* (forthcoming).

Connolly, L. and O'Toole, T., 2005 *Documenting Irish Feminisms: The second wave* (Dublin: Woodfield Press).

Crossley, N., 2002 *Making Sense of Social Movements* (Buckingham: Open University Press).

Dahlerup, D., 1986 'Is the New Women's Movement Dead? Decline or change of the Danish movement', in Dahlerup, D. (ed.), *The New Women's Movement: Feminism and political power in Europe and the US* (London: Sage), pp. 217–44.

Della Porta, D. and Diani, M., 1999 *Social Movements: An introduction* (London: Blackwell).

Diani, M., 1992 'The Concept of Social Movement', *Sociological Review*, 40:1, 1–25.

Diani, M., 1997 'Social Movements and Social Capital: a network perspective on movement outcomes', *Mobilisation*, 2:2, 129–47.

Evason, E., 1991 *Against the Grain: The contemporary women's movement in Northern Ireland* (Dublin: Attic Press).

Eyerman, R. and Jamison, A., 1991 *Social Movements: A cognitive approach* (Cambridge: Polity Press).

Foweraker, J., 1995 *Theorizing Social Movements* (London: Pluto).

Galligan, Y., 1998 *Women and Contemporary Politics in Ireland: From the margins to the mainstream* (London: Pinter).

Gamson, W.A., 1990 *The Strategy of Social Protest* (Belmont, CA: Wadsworth [1975]).

Giugni, M., 1999 'Introduction: social movements and change', in Giugni, M., McAdam, D. and Tilly, C. (eds), *From Contention to Democracy* (Lanham, MD: Rowman & Littlefield).

Giugni, M., McAdam, D. and Tilly, C. (eds), 1999 *From Contention to Democracy* (Lanham, MD: Rowman & Littlefield).

Inglis, T., 1998 *Moral Monopoly: The rise and fall of the Catholic Church* (Dublin: University College Dublin Press).

Johnston, H. and Klandermans, B., 1995 *Social Movements and Culture* (Minneapolis: University of Minnesota Press).

Levine, J., 1982 *Sisters: The Personal Story of an Irish Feminist* (Dublin: Ward River Press).

Melucci, A., 1996 *Challenging Codes: collective action in the information age* (Cambridge: Cambridge University Press).

Morris, A.D. and McClurg Mueller, C. (eds), 1992 *Frontiers in Social Movement Theory* (New Haven, CT: Yale University Press).

O'Connor, P., 1998 *Emerging Voices: Women in contemporary Irish society* (Dublin: IPA).

Randall, V., 1987 *Women and Politics: An international perspective* (London: Macmillan).

Ryan, B., 1992 *Feminism and the Women's Movement: Dynamics of change in social movement ideology and activism* (New York and London: Routledge).

Schussman, A., 2002 'Movement Outcomes: a review and agenda', CBSM Prelim., question no. 4, Conference of the American Sociological Association, October 11.

Smyth, A., 1993 'The Women's Movement in the Republic of Ireland 1970–1990', in Smyth, A. (ed.), *Irish Women's Studies Reader* (Dublin: Attic Press), pp. 245–69.

Soule, S., McAdam, D., McCarthy, J. and Su, Y., 1999 'Do Movements Matter? The impact of women's movement activity on congressional action', paper presented at the Annual Meeting of the American Sociological Association, Chicago, August.

Taylor, V., 1989 'Social Movement Continuity: the women's movement in abeyance', *American Sociological Review*, 54, 761–74.

Tovey, H., 1999 '"Messers, Visionaries and Organobureaucrats": dilemmas of institutionalisation in the Irish organic farming movement', *Irish Journal of Sociology*, 9, 31–59.

Coming out of the dark: a decade of gay mobilisation in Ireland, 1970–80

THE IRISH Gay Rights Movement (IGRM) was founded in 1974 and further contributed to the ongoing transformation taking place within the field of Irish sexuality throughout the decade. The dominant religious, medical and legal discourses, through which men and women had understood their sexuality for over a century, were now increasingly challenged by a new discourse of individual sexual fulfilment that had gradually filtered through the emergence of NSMs. The IGRM was at the forefront of this challenge. It provided a crucial link between individual and collective actors who entered the public sphere armed with a new language to speak of gay sexuality, freed from the sinfulness and criminality with which it had been associated. My focus in this chapter is at the level of local structure (Buechler 2000) where individual biographies intersect with local, national and global structures. Local structures are important because movements require them to propel individuals into collective actors. Furthermore, these local structures often become sites of grievance and resistance. Buechler (*ibid*: 149) suggests we consider such movements that privilege the local structure in this way, for example the women's movement, as a subset of other social movements. My discussion extends this recognition of the local to the study of the Irish gay movement. In doing so, I recognise the limitations of Rose's exclusively political and legalistic account (1994), which remains the only substantive treatment of the emergence of the movement in Ireland.

My telling of the story of the Irish gay movement is different. I chart the personal journey of David Norris, Edmund Lynch and Bernard Keogh[1] as they reflect on founding the IGRM and on the personal and financial risks their involvement brought to their lives. Biographical approaches to the study of social movements allow us to see how individual activists shape and are shaped by the organisations in which they campaign (Roth 2000: 303). On this national stage, while these men were inspired by the climate of social unrest throughout Europe at the time, their parents and families, the jobs they held and the existing sexual world they had created prior to the movement mediated their participation.[2] My understanding of the gay movement is dependent on an appreciation of this personal story, which helps us understand the social and political development of the movement's aspirations and the internal power struggle to control its agenda. It sheds new light on the strategies employed as the movement engaged its political and judicial adversaries and the importance of the media as the new medium in which NSMs would communicate their message.

Previous studies of gay movements abroad do not provide a good precedent in privileging the role of the local structure. In the US Dufour's analysis (1998) of the mobilisation of gay activists examines three pieces of legislative change – decriminalisation of homosexual activity; statutory anti-discrimination measures; and hate crime laws – to chart the movement's effectiveness. Using the example of Chicago, Dufour (*ibid*: 62–71) suggests that the mobilisation of gay business people and the concentration of urban residents in districts like Lakeview were crucial in infiltrating city politics and forging alliances with other minority groups to institute change. Licata's overview (1985) of the movement takes a similar perspective: it is a sweeping historical review of processes of social change, locating the development of gay rights in eight stages from 1908 to 1979, highlighting urbanisation, civil rights unrest and subsequent institutional change. Across the border, Kinsman's detailed account (1987) of the Canadian movement, while essentially structural and legalistic, does give a brief insight into the people behind the mobilisation. Key reform figures in the political, religious and civil arenas are identified and go some way in bridging the gap between structural change and the local, everyday, lived experience. In her account of the Australian lesbian and gay movement Burgmann (1993) too prefaces her discussion by acknowledging the individual stories of lesbian and gay men growing up during the twentieth century, although in keeping with other accounts she concentrates on challenges to the state, the Church and medical power over homosexuality. There are other accounts of social movement mobilisation that place the individual and the motivation of activists centre stage. McAdam's study (1988) of the Summer Project in Mississippi in 1964 which saw 1,000 white northern university students head south to help the registration of black voters is a good example. McAdam's work is motivated by an interest in personal biography and how it shaped and is shaped by history (*ibid*: 4). The lives of the volunteers and the New Left movement as a whole were transformed by these months of collective action and are revealed through his interviews with them. Roth's study (2000) of working-class feminisms takes a similar approach. She conducted sixteen life-history interviews with activists in the Coalition of Labour Union Women in the United States, analysing the data around concepts of identity, injustice and biographical continuity. Her study again demonstrates the interface between personal and social change, with life histories capturing the formation of collective identity at both personal and organisational levels (*ibid*: 317).

There are difficulties in studying social movements (Altman 1971: 113). Movements are often loosely structured, with a cross-cutting membership often without clear leadership, which make their attempts to reconstitute civil society difficult to assess. Their emergence can be traced to the structural changes in European and American society in the latter half of the twentieth century that brought about the conditions suitable for a new form of protest to emerge. There were new actors, new lines of confrontation, new adversaries to be fought in a social and political climate that saw a decline in traditional class antagonism. As trade union movements moved increasingly within the parameters of government toward social and economic partnership, class conflict declined as a focus of mobilisation, with workers channelling their grievances through movements organised around ethnicity, sex and sexual orientation (Touraine 1981: 13). The reasons for these mobilisations are complex. For Weeks (1985: 191) the mobilisation of sexual identities is dependent on complex social and political conditions where people in urban meritocratic societies become aware of their oppressed condition and find the intellectual leadership to voice their discontent. Certainly it can be argued that much of Weeks's conditions were present in Ireland during the period under study. The abandonment of protectionism in favour of free-market economics contributed to unprecedented levels of industrialisation and urban growth, freeing people from the agrarian economy and the sexual repression associated with it. Similarly, the shift from the inheritance of property to educational credentials was crucial in achieving an economic independence of family and community.

Making everyday gay life visible in Irish society

The four years of second-wave feminist agitation prior to the founding of the IGRM was an influential legacy for the movement.[3] The tactics employed by the women's movement provided a blueprint to subsequent groups in the art of promoting their message through the media, while persuading decision-makers of the merits of their arguments through different forms of social protest. Intellectually, it was believed that the feminist movement could also provide the theoretical context in which to theorise gay and lesbian oppression within a patriarchal society.[4] Ultimately, the women's movement was central in challenging the connection between sex and reproduction. The removal of sex from the realm of married reproduction would be central to the gay movement's initial claims for legitimacy, resting on the belief that contraception would bring a decrease in the policing of all premarital sex, including gay sex.

One of the organisations established in the wake of second-wave feminism agitation was the Union for Sexual Freedoms in Ireland. This umbrella organisation oversaw the creation of local branches throughout Irish universities. Lecturer in English David Norris attended a meeting at Trinity College called the Sexual Liberation Movement (SLM).[5] He was not the only gay man to do so. Men like Norris were convinced that their lives could only be improved by fighting for their rights under the broader banner of sexual liberation. The reality was that the SLM was not fighting for *their* sexual rights. Although the majority of those who attended that first meeting were gay, the SLM's primary focus was campaigning for the availability of contraception. While homophile organisations like the Mattachine Society had existed in the US for some twenty years before the Stonewall riots, no such tradition had existed in Ireland.[6] Norris already had a keen interest in civil rights issues in Northern Ireland and the US, and while *his* personal life had yet to become political, this was something that would soon change. The reluctance of some in the women's movement and the broader campaign for sexual liberation to pursue the legitimate issue of gay rights when many gays and lesbians were actively involved in the campaign for reproductive rights, made the argument for the formation of a movement all the more convincing (Connolly 2002: 122). Norris certainly believed this to be the case.

> *David Norris:* The first couple of meetings were very altruistic indeed because we spent our time discussing how to obtain contraceptives for heterosexuals, and we wrote a letter to the *Irish Times.* And eventually some of us got fed up with that and said: 'Look! Wait a minute, there are eight of us here, seven fairies and a question mark, and why are we doing this? These bloody heterosexuals rule the world they ought to be able to look after themselves.'

> *Edmund Lynch:* We all loved the big debates in the SLM, we could wax lyrical about patriarchy and contraception and Northern Ireland, but the reality of our own lives was so much more pressing, so much more urgent. The reality was we were still facing a possible prison sentence at that stage but there was this surreal reluctance to deal with our lives, preferring instead to talk about women, blacks in Alabama or Catholics on the Falls Road.

Norris and Lynch advocated an organisation that would specifically agitate for gay rights and campaign for social outlets for gay people throughout the country while lobbying to achieve its political ends. Arguments ensued, but Norris and his supporters left the SLM to found the IGRM in 1974. Calling the organisation the Irish Gay Rights Movement was significant in itself. It was a direct challenge to the construction of nationalist sexuality as exclusively heterosexual and the relegation of homosexuality to a marginal *other* in Irish society. It would also assert the constitutional right of all men to equality under the law.

For Norris, Lynch and others it would bring their everyday gay lives into the public gaze where they would be examined, contested and defended. Della Porta and Diani (1999: 93) argue that when stigmatisation exists from outside, the construction of an autonomous identity is difficult to achieve, reducing the chances of effective collective action. The decision was not an easy one.

> *Edmund Lynch*: We knew not everybody would go with us, we knew that it was a personal decision for each person to make. A lot of it was hidden behind what was the best strategy for us to take, but in reality it was stepping outside Trinity on a Monday evening and identifying yourself as a gay man, and you can't begin to imagine how hard and what a leap into the unknown that was! A lot of people didn't want a gay movement to happen because they thought it would disturb their lifestyles, their parties. I was still living at home. I had told my parents and my brothers and sisters that I was gay because I could not go out and found a movement without letting them know. (*Laughs*)

While politics of the local structure may start at the level of the self, it moves beyond these issues of self-actualisation to a broader national and then a global stage. For Norris and Lynch the political path taken to construct meaningful sexual lives in the SLM would end not on the national stage but in the European Court of Human Rights.

The coming-out of the gay movement in Ireland

The local structure now became a site of grievance and resistance for the men who founded the IGRM. They would set about explaining and defending their everyday lives primarily through the media. The first stop in this defence was the courts. During 1973 and 1974 alone, forty-three men were sentenced in the District Court for acts of gross indecency under the Labouchere Amendment to the Criminal Law Amendment Act 1885. Gross indecency remained undefined and could be interpreted broadly as any intimate contact between men. Journalist Nell McCafferty, writing in the *Irish Times* (9 December 1975), reported from Dublin District Court Four where two men were bound to the peace for one year following charges arising from their arrest after having been found having sex in a public toilet. The presiding judge, Justice Ua Donnchadha, remarked that it was a most 'unnatural performance'. Between 1962 and 1972 there were 455 convictions under the legislation (Hug 1999: 207), undermining the view that the legislation was largely dormant in this period.

Sex in public places remained a feature of many gay men's lives during this period. Lynch acknowledges the social side of public sex in Ireland.

> *Edmund Lynch*: Even the toilets were [social]! There was this wonderful toilet down in – well, I thought it was wonderful – down on Capel Street Bridge. It was Victorian, and you could see all the feet underneath so you knew who was there. It was one of those … well, I was nervous going into the toilets, but we all did them, sometimes successful, sometimes not, but it was the only place for people to go.

Men were, however, humiliated by the State and the judiciary if they were caught engaging in public sex. The IGRM's task was not just to defend the men accused, but also to refute the legislation itself and the State that supported it. Following the lead of US organisations, the IGRM did organise sympathetic solicitors to support its members in gross indecency cases, motivated by the belief that it was the stigma associated with the court appearance that led most to plead guilty to the charges, allowing the legislation to remain uncontested.

> *David Norris:* There was a daylight aspect to being gay, as well, which was political and it was looking for your human rights. And we were educated by the fact that a number of people contacted us because they had gotten into trouble with the police, and as a result we developed a kind of embryo legal service, with people like Gareth Sheehan – who's not gay– who represented people for us in court. And we had a 100 per cent success rate … Because of the submissive attitudes of gays they [the police and the judiciary] had coming in, all [gay men] in a state of humiliated collapse … It's not our position to stand with our heads bowed in the dock and be sentenced and subject to abuse and scorn from the bench as the unfortunate Oscar Wilde was.

Norris believed that breaking the cycle of shame around homosexuality would be crucial in creating the conditions necessary for people to come together in some form of collective action. He also identified the Catholic Church as key in preventing those conditions coming about by maintaining a sense of shame around sexuality.

> *David Norris:* The Roman Catholic Church for hundreds of years invaded human sexuality simply because they knew how to capture hearts and minds: you grab them by the balls and their hearts and minds will follow. Because once you've got somebody prepared to accept your rulings in the most intimate and personal [areas], and cultivate a climate of shame about these things, then you are in a very powerful position.

The shame surrounding homosexuality was of course part of a broader process of embarrassment and guilt in Irish society related to the body and sexuality. Inglis (1998: 138–9) tracks this strategy to the nineteenth century when the Catholic Church sought to instil a sense of shame and guilt about sexuality to produce 'internally controlled bodies', which were essential to its control of public morality. This shame and guilt was transmitted in the privacy and isolation of the confessional. To overcome this, gay men had to feel that they were not alone in Ireland. A similar situation existed in the US. Katz (1976: 43) suggests that invisibility was the greatest obstacle to improving the everyday lives of gay men, overcome only by a collective identification. The IGRM tried to capitalise on this budding sense of community and the real desire of gay men to meet others like themselves by taking the movement to the people. Norris explains:

> The other thing we did was go all over the countryside and we would take [out] advertisements in local papers and just give a phone number to ring and then we'd hire a room in a hotel in Cork or Dundalk, and we'd agree to meet people in the foyer over a cup of coffee. And, I mean, the tremendous relief expressed in people's faces just simply from seeing another gay person in the flesh and knowing you could talk directly, that you weren't alone.

This strategy was also beneficial to the IGRM. By establishing contacts throughout the country the movement was able to draw on the wide range of skills and talents that people possessed, putting them to use in organisational work, magazine design and financial and legal advice.

Mobilising resources and devising strategy

Each member of the IGRM brought unique resources that were utilised in the pursuit of the movement's aims. Norris and Lynch were public-sector workers and possessed a degree of security in their employment that others did not share. The birth of the IGRM in Trinity College is significant. While most of those who attended the SLM meetings had no association with Trinity, it offered a symbolic refuge from a State still perceived to be under the influence of Catholicism. More directly, Trinity, free from church and state control, with a long history of political dissent since the foundation of the State helped create the intellectuals necessary for the emergence of NSMs in Ireland.

> *David Norris*: Trinity was a liberal place with a general disposition towards permitting and tolerating debate. Noel Browne, Eoin Sheedy Skeffington, Mary Robinson – all these people were in that tradition, and the freedom and the room to manoeuvre was granted to people with whom the authorities disagreed. Outside, people assumed that everything alien – and homosexuality was alien – came out of Trinity.

The expansion of third-level education had brought forward new actors that challenged the authority of traditional intellectuals of Irish society.[7] The gap between the leaders and the led had narrowed considerably. Here, I am referring specifically to the role of Roman Catholic priests and the power they assumed in the field of Irish sexuality. The resistance to this power, spawned in NSMs and universities, challenged the effects of power that were located in the knowledge and competence of others, designated 'experts' in a specific field. New experts on homosexuality were about to emerge in Ireland at this time. Grounded in the politics of identity, they would represent an individualised resistance to those acknowledged 'experts'.

NSMs have been characterised by their middle-class composition. Specifically, it has been the 'new' middle classes like those working in public sector occupations like education, health, media or students waiting to join these professions that have been most visible in NSMs. Melucci (1996: 298–9) argues that among these occupations the most likely to be involved in NSMs are those that have had previous experience in collective action and possess certain organisational or leadership abilities. This certainly seems to be the case in the Irish context.

Norris had been involved in the CRM in Northern Ireland and certainly would have possessed the intellectual capital to articulate the movement's aims. More significantly, I believe Norris possessed the necessary cultural capital, in both its objectified and embodied forms, to not merely launch the movement but to 'put the establishment and legislation on trial', by defending men brought before the courts on charges of gross indecency.[8] Norris, born into a Protestant family, possessed little beyond his family's heirlooms – furniture, paintings – and a long association with Trinity College passed down from generations. His appearances in court, alongside solicitor Gareth Sheehan, represented a considerable challenge to both the judiciary and the Gardaí (Hug 1999: 210).

> *David Norris*: I would be wearing a three-piece suit, a Trinity tie, [carrying] a briefcase, looking terribly respectable, and give character evidence. The Gardaí were used to people coming in a state of collapse, saying 'I'm guilty, I'm terribly sorry, please don't … '. When we started defending – and we had a string of successes – they realised it wasn't worth their while. And it went down to zero. They stopped prosecuting.

His dress, accent and confidence contrasted sharply with the shame with which Irish gay men had previously stood, head bowed, before the judiciary. The IGRM also possessed less tangible assets. Britt and Heise (2000: 264) argue that a key resource which a social movement possesses is an 'emotional capital', an anger, a feeling of injustice that mobilises individuals into collective action. The IGRM's founders possessed this form of capital in abundance.

For Gramsci (1971: 10), each emerging group needs to recruit intellectuals to whom they became organically linked, challenging the dominant ideological position of the established intellectuals. Similarly, Eyerman and Jamison (1991: 99) suggest that in NSMs it is the movements themselves that create the intellectuals they need. In her analysis of the women's movement in the US, Freeman (1979: 173) makes a related argument that people cannot all make the same contribution to a movement that requires only a limited amount of *specialised* resources due to the point of diminishing returns. The crude harnessing of these resources in the IGRM caused some disquiet among its members.

The ability of movement intellectuals to communicate their message to the public through the mass media is critical to a movement's survival, often turning leadership into celebrity over night (Giltin 1980: 3). Others certainly did not always appreciate Norris's position as movement spokesperson in the IGRM.

> *David Norris*: I had a fairly wide margin of freedom because of my background, [and] because my parents were dead; I had a job that was reasonably secure ... So I could speak out and became a spokesman, and some of the other people who were politically talented, and talented in an organisational way, because of the nature of their employment felt they couldn't, and that led to a kind of irritant between us because people went 'There he is pushing himself out again.'

Norris drew attention to the movement on many levels. He was perceived by many as exotic in Irish society. He had assumed a position as a leading scholar of James Joyce. Joyce, who had left Ireland in 1904, remained an outsider to Irish society and a constant critic of the nationalist literary revival, preferring to live in exile in Europe until his death in 1941. Norris's elevation to the position of spokesman goes beyond the Weberian concept of a charismatic leadership to include the possibility of carrying the professional and financial risks associated with collective action. This dimension is argued by McCarthy and Zald (1977: 1212–41), though it goes against earlier theorising (e.g. Olson 1965) that claimed that, since movements produced collective rewards, few individuals would bear any personal costs in achieving them. This was not the case with Norris.

McCarthy and Zald's analysis of social movements is a largely structural explanation for collective behaviour, concentrating on the material resources like money and labour, but has also evolved to appreciate the organisational skills and expertise individual activists bring to a struggle. Through this appreciation of individual resources we can connect the biographies of the founding members of the IGRM within the political climate in which they operated. Lynch identifies these pragmatic considerations when considering the leadership.

> *Edmund Lynch*: I said: 'David [Norris], point one, you're more articulate than I am; point two, you come from a minority religion; and point three, and the most important point of all, [is] that both your mother and father are dead.' Mine are still alive and they were the practicalities of being gay in Ireland at the time.

The IGRM needed more than a public face to succeed; it needed to develop strategies to maintain a high media profile for its activities. Founding member of the IGRM, Edmund Lynch had joined Radio Telifís Éireann[9] (RTÉ) in 1969 and developed a key role in alerting journalists as to the newsworthiness of an emerging gay movement story.

> *Edmund Lynch*: I didn't do newspaper interviews. I knew that was David's thing not mine. My job was, I wouldn't say manipulate the media, but to inform the media whether it was a good story, whether there was a good spin on things. Knowing the content and format of what constitutes a good news story was really helpful in getting our message across.

[*94*]

This relationship with and knowledge of the media would provide a tactical advantage throughout the decade. Four years later, as the political campaign for decriminalisation entered a crucial stage, the relationships developed with gate-keepers of media organisations would bear fruit. Lynch's knowledge of news organisations enabled the subsequent Campaign for Homosexual Law Reform (CHLR) to shape their press releases to meet the demands of news routines and newsworthiness. However, Lynch was not the only link the CHLR had to journalists.

> *Edmund Lynch*: Our access to journalists was really based on our individual relationships with them, but it did help that a lot of journalists who were writing about us had been students of English and David Norris had taught a lot of them, and certainly that had a great effect. But one phone call could have a huge public impact. Like the time I remember being sent down to a USI meeting in Wexford to speak about gay rights, and being refused the first night and talking to a journalist friend of mine who ran an article the following day: 'GAY ACTIVIST REFUSED' (*laughs*) Not surprisingly, they let me speak the next night.

RTÉ also took up the gay movement as a news story. Cathal O'Shannon's documentary on homosexuality, shown in July 1977, beamed footage from an IGRM disco in Parnell Square, showing happy, dancing (albeit almost in the dark) homosexuals, into the nation's living rooms. An *Insights* documentary by Ruth Dudley Edwards, shown in November 1979, concluded that patriot Patrick Pearse was a latent homosexual. This was challenging material, undermining a vision of Irishness that had been carefully crafted long before the birth of the nation in 1922. It also represented the further erosion of the Catholic Church's control over Irish civil society and the nature of the debate now conducted in the public sphere. This domination of the public sphere by the Church had been centred on the control of the discourse and language with which it operated but also the manner in which it was mediated to the audience by intellectuals and public figures who supported the Church's view of social life (Inglis 2000: 55). The IGRM would be one of many movements and interest groups that challenged the Church and put forward an alternative language and framework to understand both the self and society. The media facilitated this by encouraging debate and discussion on non-traditional alternatives to Catholic family life and, crucially for Inglis (2000: 57), in the 'expression and fulfilment of the self'. For Giddens (1994: 124) the power of the social movement rests in the ability to alter this discursive domain by facilitating discussion that questions traditional practices. He singles out both the women's movement and the ecological movement as being the most effective in revisiting these key assumptions about the nature of modern social life. I argue that the IGRM played a similar role. Through the media Norris introduced a new language and an alternative understanding of Irish men's sexual lives. This posed a direct challenge to public figures like bishops and priests who now had to defend *their* account of sexuality as *the truth*. As Lynch's interview illustrates, social movements like the IGRM proved considerably more adept at mastering the new realities of debate in the public sphere than did its competitors.

The structure and the tactics that the IGRM employed did not evolve in a vacuum; they were influenced by the development of gay movements in Britain and the US. The IGRM adopted little of the radicalism of organisations born in the wake of the Stonewall riots when the international gay movement adopted a brief experiment with revolutionary sexual politics. Licata (1985: 180) shows how in the US the GLF's broad-based campaign to remove all forms of sexual, racial and economic exploitation through a non-hierarchical, loosely structured, organisation was challenged by the formation of the Gay Activist Alliance. The Alliance, while still based on the principle of direct action, was located within the realm of established politics, where issues of tax, employment, housing and the full participation of gays and lesbians in the political process were stressed (Altman 1971: 110). There was a return to leadership, to membership and to constitutions. By the time of the emergence of the IGRM in 1974, the trend towards negotiation over confrontation had been established, and Norris would seek out political allies and the respectability they could bring to the movement's objectives. Given the country's geographical and cultural proximity to Britain, it would be expected that the evolution of the gay movement there would have had a far greater effect on developments in Ireland.

There were, however, specific dynamics that made this evolution a very different experience on both sides of the Irish Sea. In Britain the foundation of the GLF had embraced the same ideological framework as its sister movement had in the US and had interwoven gay liberation within a radical, broad based, rejection of oppression. Watney (1980: 65) argues that gay liberation was allied to those suffering from racial oppression and a rejection of bourgeois models of mental health. Crucially, for Watney, liberation was impossible within the alienation present in capitalist modes of production. The parallel development, in 1971, of the Campaign for Homosexual Equality (Marshall 1980: 78) provided a model closer to the IGRM's, one with a similar concern with legislative reform, the extension of social facilities and a willingness to woo the political establishment to achieve its aims.

Questions remain whether the conditions were present in Ireland that existed in other affluent liberal democracies of Western Europe, North America and Australasia in facilitating the expansion of a contemporary gay movement in the 1970s. Altman (1980: 54) suggested that for homosexual identity to develop a society must be urban, secular and affluent. He draws a distinction between countries of Southern Europe like Italy, Spain and Greece where homosexual practice was widespread but who had yet to reach the economic conditions of their northern neighbours. Several factors militated against the development of a widespread identity in Ireland. The affluence that Ireland experienced in the late 1960s and early 1970s was short lived as worldwide recession fuelled by the 1973 oil crisis and poor political financial management of the economy plunged Ireland into an economic freefall from which it was slow to recover. These economic conditions were not conducive to the extension of the commercial gay scene, so vital for the increased visibility that would foster the development of a gay identity. The inclusion of the gay commercial world into mainstream consumerist society that Altman suggests occurred in North America and Western Europe in the 1970s and would take another twenty years before it became a reality in Ireland.

The blossoming of a commercial gay ghetto that could provide the necessary refuge for an emerging homosexual identity had to be supported by a high level of urbanisation. Even within urban areas, traditional communities and practices coexisted with more modern ones. There had been only a marginal decline in attendance of Mass by Irish Catholics in the 1970s, while the Catholic Church continued to hold considerable control in education (Inglis 1998: 224). Using the 1960s as a benchmark between traditional and modern Ireland is limiting. The erosion of traditional values is for Altman (1980: 59) part of a broader social and cultural shift that occurred in post-industrial societies during the 1970s and is central to answering the question of why gay social movements increased their visibility so much in this period. Such a cultural shift was slower to come about in Ireland. Consider the position of women in society. The 1970s brought key pieces of employment legislation that promised equal pay (1976) and lifted the marriage bar (1973) that prevented women entering the Civil Service, but, as O'Connor (1998: 36) argues, the proportion of women actually entering the labour force during the decade was small. Similarly, while no marriage bar existed in other areas of employment like banks, a cultural expectation that women would leave work on marrying existed, institutionalised by a marriage gratuity made payable to the women (O'Connor, 1998: 38). Cultural acceptance of the movement and its visibility within society was slower to develop in Ireland because the movement and the individuals within operated under criminalisation and a threat of prosecution.

Improving the quality of everyday life for gay men

The aims of the IGRM were two-fold: to provide a safe outlet for men and women to establish friendships and relationships, while using the income generated by these ventures to fund counselling facilities; and to lobby for political activities that would bring about decriminalisation. After renting venues in three separate locations throughout the city, the IGRM finally combined its offices and social venue in one building, on Parnell Square in Dublin. It attracted a wide clientele. Openly gay activists dismayed by the conservative nature of the movement mingled with those still deep in the closet.

> *Edmund Lynch:* People came to the discos on motorbikes, some choosing different names, some people were married, and a lot of people came from the country. I remember one who used to come all the way down from Sligo and then back to Sligo to milk the cows that following morning.

> *Bernard Keogh:* The first few discos we organised were on a voluntary basis. We thought a few would come, but people came out of the woodwork, hundreds of them, so we started charging.

This diversity would, however, make consensus as to the movement's objectives almost impossible to realise. Norris too saw the difficulties in communicating with such a diverse membership.

> We tried to reach people through posters and leaflets, but it meant we had to access a very amorphous population group. They were not concentrated in any area, social group, they were spread right through the population at a level of approximately 10 per cent, and so getting information to them was very difficult.

The relationship between the social and political wings of the IGRM was at times uneasy. For many, the success of discos run by the IGRM marked not the beginning of the movement but the end, as one of its key objectives had been realised. Men could dance, socialise, have sex and fall in love all under the cover of darkness in the relative safety of the Parnell Square premises. For some like Norris, Lynch and Keogh, this marked only the beginning. No political activity could take place without the income generated by the discos, and some argued that this money should be reinvested in more social events and the establishment of contacts with people throughout the country. In reality, the provision of social events was draining the IGRM of resources and the energy of their members, leaving little time for political action.

> *Bernard Keogh:* The IGRM was all very 'general secretary this' and 'chairman that' but at the end of a disco in Parnell Square we'd all be scrubbing out the toilets.

> *Edmund Lynch:* It was exhausting! There were times when I was coming in from a hard day's work – I tended to work long hours, that's the way television works – and then I'd have to do work down in the centre, then the disco work, and probably cleaning out toilets at the end of the night.

The IGRM was not the first gay organisation to face this dilemma. Marshall (1980: 82) argues that Britain's Campaign for Homosexual Equality (CHE) had struggled with reconciling the social and political sides of the organisation, a balancing act between the creation of a community to befriend and counsel and a more politically aggressive campaign to realise the broader objectives of the movement. In the IGRM, those like Norris and Lynch who advocated a more political agenda became marginalised. Some saw their removal as a purge of the intellectual wing of the gay movement, motivated by a reluctance to engage with their major political and religious adversaries.

> *Bernard Keogh:* Some people wanted to leave the law alone. They thought that people had a very nice lifestyle: they can go the pub, they can go cruising the loos down the quays. And if you focus attention on this [the legislation], the Gardaì will be forced to pay more attention, and that would disturb that cosy little lifestyle.

> *David Norris:* I was pretty unassailable, but they targeted people like Bernard [Keogh], people like that, so although I topped the poll, I had nobody to work with and was replaced as chairman ... And I said I'm not going to work in these circumstances and resigned from the committee to concentrate exclusively on the political side. There were only three or four others, the ones the other side wouldn't touch with a barge pole.

There is evidence to support Keogh's analysis. In the UK, in the first four years after the 1967 Reform Bill was passed, convictions for gross indecency increased 160 per cent (Kinsman 1987: 143). There was no doubt that increased political agitation would bring Irish gay men under similar police surveillance. Such political agitation would also bring this side of the movement into direct conflict with powerful conservative forces in Ireland. The IGRM continued to hold its social events, but those advocating the legal agenda of the movement splintered with the founding of the CHLR in 1977.

The CHLR: high-profile allies, headed paper and a filing cabinet

The new organisation founded by David Norris and his supporters had little resources, income or facilities. However, the CHLR did manage to launch the most high-profile campaign for gay rights since the movement's inception, consistently engaging with its political opponents. I believe the key to this success was the single-issue focus of the organisation; the cultivation of alliances with individuals and similar rights-based organisations, and the effective use of the mass media. Gamson (1990: 44) in his study of fifty-four American organisations found that the single-issue groups were by far the most successful in realising their objectives, and did so by maximising the use of their scarce resources. We should understand the development of the CHLR as a distinct SMO (Kriesi 1996: 153), complete with an organisational and professional structure to achieve its aims. This marked the separation of the movement's functions, with the remnant of the IGRM becoming the exclusive service provider to its members while political mobilisation was now the exclusive pursuit of the CHLR.

The CHLR was dependent on the high-profile nature of its patrons. Figures from the business and political worlds, like Victor Bewley, Hugh Leonard and Dr Noel Browne, lent their names and support. Government ministers were canvassed for support, while plans for a High Court challenge to test the constitutionality of the legislation were already afoot. The support of the trade union movement, the political left and reform professionals like theology professor Enda McDonagh and lawyer Mary Robinson were crucial.

> *David Norris*: There was a tiny number of people involved and our facilities were half a filing cabinet in my office in Trinity and some headed note paper, and I got some distinguished people, like the Dean of St Patricks Victor Griffith, Hugh Leonard, Victor Bewley, these sorts of people, Noel Browne, to act as patrons. Well that was a wonderful coup because the newspapers took us seriously. They gave us wonderful creditability, and there was only four of us and a couple of pages of headed paper! And still we were seen as an international conspiracy that was going to corrupt the Western world.

Similarly, the mobilisation of the pro-life movement a decade later was based upon largely unfounded fears about the strength and influence of those who supported a woman's right to choose. Although there was little public support for abortion in Ireland, Hesketh (1990: 5–6) argues, the pro-life movement suspected that the majority of Irish journalists and trade unionists were sympathetic to its introduction. This illustrates how effective courtship of media organisations could be in generating debate in the public sphere, debate largely beneficial to interest groups like the CHLR. The CHLR's attempt to turn members of the elite public into sympathisers was not a new tactic. McCarthy and Zald (1977: 1217) identified this strategy as part of their emerging RMT that is set against the traditional strategies social movements have pursued. Utilising elite public support and forging alliances with similar rights-based organisations continued to be employed by the successors of the CHLR right up to the decriminalisation of homosexuality in 1993.

Kriesi (1996: 156) argues that SMOs become more moderate in their aims and conventional in their tactics. The establishment's reaction to the increased visibility and stated objectives of the CHLR, however, proved anything but moderate. The Censorship of Publications Board banned the distribution of the English magazine *Gay News* in April 1976, while Dublin Corporation[10] withdrew funding from the Project Arts Centre after it brought a gay London based theatre company to perform the following year. Councillor Frank Sherwin PC explained his position in a letter to the *Evening Press* in February 1977.

> If people want to indulge in homosexuality then they should keep quiet about it. In my opinion these people are not only weak but also sick and they should not be permitted to contaminate others, especially the young.

Others sought to silence homosexuals more directly. The *Irish Independent* (5

July 1977) reported on the second attempt to burn down 'a homosexual meeting house' in Dublin, while a new affiliated organisation, the National Gay Federation, had its new premises at the Hirschfeld Centre targeted the following year. These tactics were not new. The *Evening Herald* (5 May 1975) had reported that arson was suspected in the burning down of Petticoat Market, a venue for a gay disco in Dublin. Norris describes the harassment against the newly opened Hirschfeld centre.

> The building had been attacked on and off since its opening, bricks through windows, crude bombs, hoax devices. Of course we also had petty harassment from those old remnants of the IGRM and we had difficulty in Fownes Street because it was such an old building, and that was alright 'cause we started off pre-Stardust[11], but once Stardust happened we were in the shit. We had the fire brigade round, the fire officer, the health officer! It was all very petty. Ironically, as you well know, the building was burned down in 1988.

The increased publicity surrounding the gay movement culminated with the constitutional challenge in November 1977. Arguing that the existing legislation that criminalised homosexuality was in contravention of article 40.1[12] of the Constitution Norris embarked on a three-year legal battle. The Jeffery Dudgeon case in the European Court of Human Rights found that the exclusion of Northern Ireland from the United Kingdom's 1967 Sexual Offences Act had violated Dudgeon's human rights. Despite such a precedent, the High Court ruled against Norris in October 1980, as did the Supreme Court three years later.[13]

The social aspirations of the gay movement were far more successful in this period. Norris and a few other supporters in 1978 established the Hirschfeld Centre that would provide many of the social and support services of the IGRM. But the Hirschfeld Centre marked a significant change in direction for the gay movement. Although driven by the same aspirations as its predecessor, I believe it was characterised by an increased professionalism and a greater legalistic structure. The Hirschfeld Centre was the company and the subsequent National Gay Federation (NGF) was to be its tenant, thus increasing control and minimising the financial risk to its founders. The shift towards professionalisation was essential for Norris based on his experience with the IGRM:

> I put ten grand of my own money into it and then gave the banks a mortgage on my house in order to restore the building ... I don't think any rational person would hand it all over to a fairly volatile voluntary committee because I'd be handing over my own financial and personal future.

Kreisi (1996: 154) identifies these processes of formalisation and professionalisation as central to the development of an SMO: a movement enters a phase where formalised leadership and bureaucratic structures are seen as more effective in gaining access to similarly structured state agencies. The founding of the

NGF in 1978 was a success story, providing 'the largest and most successful gay organisation Ireland had ever seen' (Norris, 1979: 10), placing the movement in a key position to make further political gains throughout the next decade. The new challenges the NGF would face in the 1980s arising from the Fairview murder,[14] and the emergence of HIV and AIDS, would further politicise its membership and strengthen the movement's institutional links with state agencies.

Conclusions

This chapter has argued that the local, everyday-life, dimension in the study of gay social movements has been neglected. As a consequence the emergence of the gay movement in Ireland has to be understood as more than just a product of the modernising forces that transformed economic and social life. The focus on the lives of the founders has sought to contextualise the movement and to illustrate its emergence as a consequence of the personal resources and capital of its founders. This is not to suggest that these men worked in a vacuum. They operated within a political and cultural context largely hostile to homosexuality. This has been shown in relation to the restrictions imposed by the broadcasting code governing RTÉ and its responsibility to uphold certain social mores; and it has been shown in the judiciary's treatment of men charged with gross indecency. The movement did however utilise channels of power in this context, often based on existing individual relationships in the political and cultural sphere, to operate at a level far beyond those existing resources.

Rose (1994: 3) points to the existence of a homosexual subculture in Dublin at the turn of the twentieth century to suggest that the founding of the IGRM merely placed an organisational structure on existing informal networks. Keogh explained how many gay men saw the movement as disruptive to that sexual order and wished to have no part in it. The emergence of the movement can also be explained by the previous politicisation of its leaders and their ability to use the intellectual and cultural capital they possessed to forward its objectives. Central to this was recognising the importance of the mass media in communicating the movement's message and becoming adept in shaping that message into a newsworthy format suitable for media consumption. The shape of the movement itself was influenced more by the ebb and flow of international gay politics. I suggest that the IGRM was founded in a conciliatory era where the trend of confrontation had been replaced by one of facilitation. Here the emphasis would be on the formation of alliances and engagement with state agencies. The GLF in the US and Britain had rejected attempts by older homophile organisations to assimilate the gay population into mainstream society by advocating the respectable pursuits of monogamy and gay marriage, while emphasising the sameness of gay and straight communities. The absence of a similar history of homophile organisations in Ireland led gay men to develop networks in other civil rights organisations of the period, before coming together to launch the IGRM, a process similar to that identified in the women's movement. It is within those networks that the possibility of schisms arises. Like the GLF and the Campaign for Homosexual Equality in Britain, the movement could never meet the diverse needs of the men and women it represented. Conflict within the IGRM centred upon the extent to which its membership rejected toleration as a political objective. The personal risks involved in the political campaign saw only a few embark on the long journey to achieve the coveted goal of decriminalisation, while others used their organisational ability to provide continued social and support services to the gay community.

Notes

1 David Norris and Edmund Lynch were founding members of the Irish Gay Rights Movement while Bernard Keogh was general secretary 1975–77. This chapter does not focus on the lesbian movement. Unlike lesbians in Britain and the US, most Irish lesbians had chosen to work within the broader church of the women's movement rather than with gay men in the IGRM. The movement developed under very different circumstances, finally breaking away from the remnants of Irish Women United to form the Liberation of Irish Lesbians in 1978. See Crone (1998: 343–7).

2 There had been student and worker unrest in Paris and throughout Europe in 1968 (see Caute 1988; Harman 1998), Stonewall riots resisting police harassment of the gay community in New York City, while the American CRM had inspired the Catholic community to resist Stormont's abuse of power in Northern Ireland (see Dooley 1998).

3 For a detailed analysis of second-wave feminism, see Connolly (2002).

4 The Gay Liberation Front (GLF) in Britain had used similar tactics to the women's movement, holding consciousness-raising seminars for its members. Ideologically they saw the family as a source of oppression of gays and women in society, and tended to theorise their respective positions as if they were a homogeneous group. See Watney (1980: 66–7).

5 On the background and childhood of Norris see Freedman (1995: 17–56).

6 For a discussion of these homophile organisations, see D'Emilio (1983: 196–219).

7 I am using the term traditional intellectual as defined by Gramsci (1971: 7–8).

8 My discussion of cultural capital is influenced by Bourdieu (1986: 24–8).

9 The IGRM used RTÉ and the print media to convey its message. In 1976, an RTÉ interview with Norris caused public disquiet leading to a ruling by the Complaints Advisory Committee that the station had broken its broadcasting code in the production of a programme by violating its social mores.

10 Now Dublin City Council.

11 The Stardust nightclub in Dublin burned down on 15 February 1981 claiming the lives of forty-eight people. The Fire Services Act (1981) was introduced after the disaster, following evidence that locked exit doors and barred windows impeded people's escape.

12 Article 40.1 of the Irish Constitution guarantees the right of citizens to equality before the law. A provision on the right to privacy that was successfully used in the 1973

McGee case overturning the ban on contraception was also invoked (see Hug 1999: 96–9).

13 For an overview of this legal contest for gay rights see ICCL (1990: 13–23).

14 Declan Flynn was murdered in an area known to be frequented by gay men in Fairview Park, Dublin in 1982. The suspended sentences handed down to his killers led to widespread outrage and public protests (see Rose 1994: 20–1).

Bibliography

Altman, D., 1971 *Homosexual: Oppression and Liberation* (Sydney: Angus & Robertson).

Altman, D., 1980 'What Changed in the Seventies?', in Gay Left Collective (eds), *Homosexuality: Power and politics* (London: Allison & Busby).

Bourdieu, P., 1986 'Forms of Capital', in Richardson, J. (ed.), *Handbook of Theory and Research for the Sociology of Education* (New York: Greenwood Press).

Britt, L. and Heise, D., 2000 'From Shame to Pride in Identity Politics', in Stryker, S., Owens, T.J. and White, R.W. (eds), *Self, Identity and Social Movements* (Minneapolis: University of Minnesota Press).

Buechler, S.M., 2000 *Social Movements and Advanced Capitalism: The political economy and cultural construction of social activism* (Oxford: Oxford University Press).

Burgmann, V., 1993 *Power and Protest: Movements for change in Australian society* (St Leonards: Allen & Unwin).

Connolly, L., 2002 *The Irish Women's Movement: From revolution to devolution* (Basingstoke: Palgrave).

Crone, J., 1998 'Lesbian Feminism in Ireland', in Smyth, A. (ed.), *Feminism in Ireland*, special issue of *Women's International Forum*, 11:4, 343–7.

D'Emilio, J., 1983 Sexual Politics, Sexual Communities: The making of the homosexual minority in the United States 1940–1970 (Chicago, IL: University of Chicago Press).

Della Porta, D. and Diani, M., 1999 *Social Movements: An introduction* (Oxford: Blackwell).

Dooley, B., 1998 *Black and Green: The fight for civil rights in Northern Ireland and Black America* (London: Pluto).

Dufour, C., 1998 'Mobilising Gay Activists', in Costain, A. and McFarland, A. (eds), *Social Movements and American Political Institutions* (Lanham, MD: Rowman & Littlefield), pp. 59–72.

Eyerman, R., and Jamison, A., 1991 *Social Movements: A cognitive approach* (Cambridge: Polity Press).

Freeman, J., 1979 'Resource Mobilisation and Strategy', in Zald, M.N and McCarthy, J.D. (eds), *The Dynamics of Social Movements* (Cambridge: Winthrop).

Freedman, V., 1995 *The Cities of David: The life of David Norris* (Dublin: Basement Press).

Gamson, W.A., 1990 *The Strategy of Social Protest* (Belmont, CA: Wadsworth).

Giddens, A., 1994 'Living in a Post-Traditional Society', in Beck, U., Giddens, A. and Lash, S., *Reflexive Modernisation: Politics, tradition and aesthetics in the modern social order* (Cambridge: Polity Press).

Gitlin, T., 1980 *The Whole World Is Watching: Mass media and the making and unmaking of the new left* (Berkeley: University of California Press).

Gramsci, A., 1971 *Selections from Prison Notebooks* (London: International Publishers).

Hesketh, T., 1990 *The Second Partitioning of Ireland: The abortion referendum* (Dublin: Brandsma Books).

Hug, C., 1999 *The Politics of Sexual Morality in Ireland* (Basingstoke: Macmillan).

ICCL, *Equality Now for Lesbians and Gay Men* (Dublin: ICCL, 1990).

Inglis, T., 1998 *Moral Monopoly: The rise and fall of the Catholic Church* (Dublin: University College Dublin Press).

Inglis, T., 2000 'Irish Civil Society: from church to media domination', in Inglis, T., Mach, Z. and Mazanek, R. (eds), *Religion and Politics: East–West contrasts from contemporary Europe* (Dublin: University College Dublin Press).

Katz, J., 1976 *Gay American History* (New York: Thomas Y. Crowell).

Kinsman, G., 1987 *The Regulation of Desire: Sexuality in Canada* (Montreal: Black Rise Books).

Kriesi, H., 1996 'The Organizational Structure of New Social Movements in a Political Context', in McAdam, D., McCarthy, J.D. and Zald, M.N. (eds), *Comparative Perspectives on Social Movements* (Cambridge: Cambridge University Press).

Licata, S., 1985 'The Homosexual Rights Movement in the United States', in Licata, S. and Petersen, R. (eds), *The Gay Past: A collection of historical essays* (New York: Harrington Park Press).

Marshall, J., 1980 'The Politics of Tea and Sympathy', in Gay Left Collective (eds) *Homosexuality: Power and politics* (London: Allison & Busby).

McAdam, D., 1988 *Freedom Summer* (New York: Oxford University Press).

McCarthy, J.D. and Zald, Z.N., 1977 'Resource Mobilisation and Social Movements: a partial theory', *American Journal of Sociology*, 82, 1212–41.

Melucci, A., 1996 *Challenging Codes: Collective action in the information age* (Cambridge: Cambridge University Press).

Norris, D., 1979 '"Homosexuals are Revolting": A History of the Gay Movement in Ireland', *In Touch*, 2(7)L 8–11.

O'Connor, P., 1998 *Emerging Voices: Women in contemporary Irish society* (Dublin: Institute of Public Administration).

Olson, Jr., M., 1965 *The Logic of Collective Action* (Cambridge, MA: Harvard University Press).

Rose, K., 1994 *Diverse Communities: The evolution of lesbian and gay politics in Ireland* (Cork: University of Cork Press).

Roth, S., 2000 'Developing Working Class Feminism: a biographical approach to social movement participation', in Stryker, S., Owens, T.J. and White, R.W. (eds), *Self, Identity and Social Movements* (Minneapolis: University of Minnesota Press).

Touraine, A., 1981 *The Voice and the Eye: An analysis of social movements* (Cambridge: Cambridge University Press).

Watney, S., 1980 'The Ideology of the GLF', in Gay Left Collective (eds), *Homosexuality: Power and politics* (London: Allison & Busby).

Weeks, J., 1985 *Sexuality and its Discontents* (London: Routledge).

Moving the immovable: the civil rights movement in Northern Ireland

> When the Civil Rights march on 5 October passed through the city of Derry it was met with a police baton-charge. Jonathan Adams, along with other elder policemen, had been called up from various counties in the North for the day. Not only because of a shortfall in numbers but also because outsiders would not be recognized. The air was rank with bigotry and acrimonious shouts like 'In the name of God let us through'. The whole affair, the police thought, would be restricted to a small side street, and here it was proposed that law and order would make its stand on a genuine footing. The police had been told beforehand that the march had not been properly endorsed by the Civil Rights movement, that it was directly republican, directly IRA. This was the perfect chance to settle old grievances. (Dermot Healy, *A Goat's Song*)[1]

THE origins of almost thirty years of political violence in Northern Ireland are inextricably linked to the failure of civil rights agitation in the late 1960s and early 1970s to achieve the objective of internal reform and democratisation of the unionist-dominated local State. The emergence of the Northern Ireland Civil Rights Association (NICRA)[2] heralded the temporary demise of irredentist nationalism and the formation of a social movement with a reformist agenda.

Two important issues arise in connection with this process:

1 The issue of the factors that led to the mobilisation and collective action has not been adequately addressed. Mainstream social movement theory as well as historical and sociological approaches to the problem of mobilisation tend to adopt a utilitarian and instrumental framework excluding or marginalising any analysis of the importance of values, ideologies, culture and identity. This chapter attempts to explain the emergence and eventual demise of the CRM by distinguishing between redistribution and recognition,[3] and stressing that, for many nationalists, cultural injustice was more significant as a mobilising factor than economic exploitation.

2 The implosion of the CRM after the shooting dead of civilians in Derry by British paratroopers in January 1971, an event which convinced many that

there could be no peaceful resolution to the problems facing Northern Ireland, posed the question of the use of state-sanctioned violence to repress ,calls for reform. The use of the police and army to repress dissent brought the question of legitimacy to the fore and ensured that policing was to become, and remain, a central factor in the subsequent conflict and its resolution.

Social movement theory and the Hobbesian problem

Social movement theory and research have tended to focus upon middle-class and peaceable movements in advanced industrial societies. In general, movements with a nationalistic, ethnic or religious dimension have been ignored as have the more general problems arising from the presence of competing identities. A further lacuna in the mainstream literature has been the neglect, until relatively recently, of political violence and in particular state-sponsored violence.

The analysis of some of the most persistent, intractable and often violent movements has been left to mainstream political scientists, journalists and those interested in peace studies and the problem of terrorism. Solidarity in Poland, the Palestinian Intifada and various nationalist movements in Europe are examples of movements generally ignored by social movement research.[4] Despite the fact that theories of collective action have developed an impressive array of theoretical approaches over the last thirty years the thrust of research has focused upon the motivations of individuals to the exclusion of the analysis of why and under what circumstances collective action takes place (Tarrow 1994; Buechler 2000; Crossley 2002). Part of the problem may lie with the dominance of the resource mobilisation paradigm which, by locating the analysis of social movements within a utilitarian framework and applying a rational choice model, places the question of costs and benefits at the centre of analysis.[5] When deprivation and grievance are linked to questions of identity, as they generally are in conflicts of an ethnic, national or religious nature, the weakness of the rational choice model becomes manifest. The resource mobilisation approach, by uncritically accepting the utilitarian model borrowed from Bentham's economic theory, faces severe problems in dealing with action which has a clear collective base. Collective action implies some form of collective identity, which, while not clearly articulated by individuals, is a component part of their everyday lives (Laraña et al. 1994).

There is a deeper ideological and political problem here. The political motivation of Bentham's original utilitarian approach was to connect possessive individualism – a theory of human behaviour – with a theory of human nature diametrically opposed to the collectivist ideas of socialism. By postulating the free-standing, universal, human actor as the locus of social action all contrary activity could be branded as irrational and amoral. As Piven and Cloward have pointed out (1992: 323): 'Like many malintegration analysts before them, resource mobilisation analysts have also reduced lower-stratum protest politics to irrational and apolitical eruptions.'

NSM theory, which is in part a response to the deficiencies of the rational choice approach, offers both insights and conceptual dead-ends when applied to movements such as the CRM in Northern Ireland. While there is a tendency to locate the dynamic of NSMs in the new middle classes (Offe 1985; Kriesi 1989; Eder 1993) there has been an increasing focus upon other factors, such as ethnicity, identity and gender, as crucial in the process of mobilisation. Melucci (1996) stresses the importance of collective identity in the formation of social movements and the capacity of people to both define and redefine the parameters of identity. The work of Habermas, while not dealing with the empirical dimension of social movements, has fostered a theoretical realignment towards cultural and symbolic forms of resistance (Habermas 1984; see also Crossley 2002) while the more philosophical interventions of Honneth and Nancy Fraser stress the importance of non-economic elements of exploitation, such as non-recognition and cultural exclusion (Honneth 1995a, 1995b; Fraser 2000; and see Alexander and Lara 1996). The work of Honneth, in particular, attempts to explain the mobilisation of groups with reference to cultural, psychological and non-economic and subjective factors, grounded in forms of disrespect and the denial of recognition to one group by another.[6] Honneth, following Hegel, replaces the utilitarian model of mobilisation with a theory grounded in the notion that people have normative and moral expectations concerning the way in which society and community is organised. Recognition can be denied at three different levels:

- that of personality, which erodes and undermines self-confidence;
- that of social organisation, which involves self-respect; and
- that of culture, which involves self-esteem.

Honneth (1995b: 131) empirically grounds his stress upon recognition by referring to everyday language: 'In the self-descriptions of those who see themselves as having been wrongly treated by others the moral categories that play a dominant role are those – such as "insult" or "humiliation" – that refer to forms of disrespect, that is, to the denial of recognition.'

Nancy Fraser's approach (1997, 2000; see also Fraser and Honneth 2003) complements and extends that of Honneth by giving the concept of recognition a more empirical content. According to Fraser there are two complementary component parts to contemporary struggles – redistribution and recognition. Although complementary paradigms of justice, they constitute distinct spheres of exploitation. In the contemporary world, where the salience of class conflict is much reduced, conflicts over recognition have moved centre-stage. Fraser writes:

The 'struggle for recognition' is fast becoming the paradigmatic form of polit-ical conflict in the late twentieth century. Demands for 'recognition of difference' fuel struggles of groups mobilised under the banners of national-ity, ethnicity 'race', gender, and sexuality. In these 'postsocialist' conflicts, group identity supplants class interest as the chief medium of political mobil-isation. Cultural domination supplants exploitation as the fundamental injustice. (1997: 11)

The struggle for recognition goes beyond the legal and formal. The argument over formal rights – such as the 'one man, one vote' demand of the CRM – is only one side of the coin. Both Honneth and Fraser stress the moral dimension of a truly democratic society where others are regarded as equals, imbued with the human characteristics and requisites for equal participation in the polity.

This approach is particularly instructive when applied to situations where ethnicity or competing identities play a significant role in community struc-tures. It is in such situations that utilitarian theory breaks down on the question of the empirical link between interest and action. In the contemporary world, there is simply no direct link between levels of deprivation, or economic disem-powerment, and political action. Within Ireland and Britain – to take one example- there are numerous pockets of deprivation, both urban and rural; yet few coherent examples, apart from those of Northern Ireland, of a minority taking serious collective action to redress cultural and economic grievances.

This problem has engaged the interest of some social movement theorists: 'If the social movement research of the last two decades has shown anything, it is that grievances are not sufficient to trigger social action' (Tarrow 1994: 177). Or, put another way, why do people fail to act collectively to redress their shared grievances when the source of those grievances is obvious? In the Irish case the master-frame used to mobilise collective action in the twentieth century became increasingly dysfunctional after the partition of the country in 1922. Although the structure of oppositional meanings remained intact in the culture of nation-alists in Northern Ireland, the traditional form of political action, armed resistance, seemed to have lost its dynamic.

The collective identity of Irish nationalists has its roots in the historical legacy of resistance to British rule, a legacy that dominated collective action in the nineteenth century. This identity was a complex interweaving of religion, ethnicity, collective historical memory, local allegiances and deeply felt griev-ances. When filtered through the lens of the political, two broad strands of resistance emerged: constitutional nationalism and militant republicanism. Although both positions shared the same objectives – Catholic emancipation, land reform and some from of independence from Britain- as well as sharing a common desire for a cultural revival – they were divided on the means to achieve these objectives. Constitutional nationalists abhorred political violence (although many like Daniel O'Connell were loath to condemn it) while militant republicans shared the conviction that Britain would only response to physical force. Irish independence was eventually conceded by Britain in response to a bitter guerrilla war, lending credence to the latter position. But for the nationalists living in a unionist dominated Northern Ireland, the victory was a hollow one. The new political entity of Northern Ireland was specifically constructed to ensure a built-in unionist majority, a reality which weakened a central moral and political argument of nationalists: that they constituted a majority of the population. As Piven and Cloward (1977) have stressed, for a movement to emerge, a strong cultural identity is not enough, as subordinate groups are often infected by pessimism and the fatalistic weight of past failure. Not only must people define the structures of society as unjust (nationalists in Northern Ireland were in agreement on this point), but there must be a belief that change is possible. A crucial objective of the unionist-dominated State was to convince nationalists that resistance would be futile.

Neutralising resistance and the denial of recognition

After the partition of Ireland, the Unionist Party in the North moved swiftly to consolidate its position. Any attempt to conciliate the nationalist minority was swiftly rejected, and the structures and composition of the state were blatantly sectarian.[7] A senior civil servant recalled that the Minister of Home Affairs (in effect the minister directly responsible for internal security) had made it clear to his staff that 'he did not want the most juvenile clerk or typist, if a papist, assigned for duty in his ministry (Bardon 1992: 498). The Minister for Agriculture, speaking in 1934, was more forthright:

> I recommend those people that are loyalist not to employ Roman Catholics, 99 percent of whom are disloyal; I want you to remember one point in regard to the employment of people who are disloyal ... you are disfranchising yourself in that way ... You people who are employers have the ball at your feet. If you don't act properly now, before we know where we are we shall find ourselves in the minority instead of the majority. (Quoted in Farrell 1976: 90–1)

The logic underpinning the exclusion of the minority was that Catholics could not be granted full civil rights unless they totally and unconditionally accepted the status quo and the principle of the Union with Britain. Therefore the price of acceptance for individual Catholics was the rejection of their fellow-nationalists, the majority of whom were not willing to grant legitimacy to the new State. Yet unambiguous loyalty to the crown, in itself, was often not enough to gain access to even the lowliest position. A Catholic gardener employed at Parliament Buildings, with a distinguished war record and a recommendation from the Prince of Wales, suffered, according to one historian, 'vile persecution'

(Bardon 1992: 497). The blanket denial of recognition to nationalists implied that even those Catholics who did not consider themselves to be nationalists were suspect because of their ethnic origins, and any effort to integrate themselves and advance through the system was either rebuffed or deflected. As long as even a 'tiny minority' of the nationalist population was suspected of disloyalty, recognition could not be granted to the minority as a whole. As Jennifer Todd (1993:197) comments: 'The practical moral community, in whose interests and for whose benefit the Union was maintained and partition imposed, was a Protestant one. Northern Catholics were written out of unionist political theory.'

Nationalist attitudes were in some ways a mirror image of the unionist stance without the coercive power of the latter. Many nationalists denied the legitimacy of the State and offered only the minimum of cooperation. The Catholic middle class tended to service its own community and avoid involvement with the State. The education system was organised on religious lines, as was the rudimentary welfare system, which existed before the welfare state reforms after the Second World War. Given the coercive and exclusionary nature of the State, such attitudes were understandable, but had the effect of bolstering and reaffirming unionists' attitudes that saw their own exclusion of nationalists as thereby justified.

Although the narrative of unionism was exclusionary in that it established hierarchical valuations that justified the subordination of the minority, nationalism was also exclusionary. The prelocutionary[8] nature of both narratives set up a zero-sum game which gave unionists the justification to use their social, economic and political power to enforce their domination. The problem that faced the nationalist population was not that which confronts most social movements: that of creating a collective identity (Gamson 1992; Melucci 1996), since such an identity was already present. The symbolic resources of nationalism were deeply embedded in a shared culture which expressed itself through shared cultural forms such as religion, music, sport, oral tradition, commemorations and communal celebrations. What was problematical, until the emergence of the CRM, was the transformation of this collective identity into political action. Traditional forms of resistance, based upon armed insurrection and networks of secret societies,[9] were ineffectual in the face of the extensive and elaborate repressive apparatus, which could be mobilised by the State[10] (Farrell 1983; Ellison and Smyth 2000). The nature of minority–majority relationships within the North, combined with a suffocating apparatus of repression and exclusion, meant that new forms of collective action could only emerge if collective identity could be mediated through the assimilation of new cultural meanings, which could lead to mobilisation. Ironically, it was the setting up of the welfare state in Britain after 1948 that established a framework through which traditional grievances could be filtered. The universalistic principles of social democracy presented a new language of reform which coupled with structural reforms to the labour market, education and the health service.

Important structural changes included rising participation of the minority in second- and third-level education, the increasing segmentation and feminisation of the workforce, the decline of traditional heavy industry and the expansion of the service sector. These structural changes were taking place against ideational shifts as the universalistic principles of social democracy began to filter into political discourse. The newly emerging framework offered the possibility of articulating personal and collective feelings of being treated as inferior citizens.

Mediating collective action

The pressures that led to the introduction of Keynesian economic management and social-democratic welfare reform in post-war Europe were largely absent in Northern Ireland. The socio-economic forces, which led to the implementation of reforms in Europe, were rationalised through an ideology that stressed equality, democracy and a general harmony of interests. Reform was encapsulated in a new version of universalism: equality of opportunity, access to education and social mobility and the promise of a rising standard of living and a redistribution of wealth through fiscal measures. The State, assuming a corporatist mantle, took upon itself the task of recasting the labour process in a Fordist mould and acting as midwife to the birth of the consumer society.

In the North there was little appetite for such far-reaching changes. Industry was mainly small scale and family owned, and the larger industries – shipbuilding, linen manufacture and engineering – did not readily lend themselves to reorganisation on Fordist lines (Isles and Cutbert 1957; Smyth 1985; Rowthorn and Wayne 1988). There were sharp divisions between the Catholic and the Protestant working class in ideological, organisational, spatial and sectoral terms, which made united action around a reformist agenda difficult if not impossible. At the institutional level, there was little enthusiasm on the part of the Unionist Party for the welfare state, and the Catholic Church was downright hostile.[11] The fact that Northern Ireland was part of the United Kingdom, however, meant that legislation implemented by the Westminster Parliament could not be rejected by Stormont without provoking a constitutional and political crisis.[12] The consequent unexpected, and to some extent imposed, modernisation of sections of the state apparatus was to have unanticipated and far-reaching consequences. With the crucial exception of the police and security apparatus, which was highly centralised, state bureaucracy under Stormont was decentralised and localised. Central government practised a non-interventionist and *laissez-faire* attitude towards most areas of governance, allowing local government to control such areas as public housing, roads, planning and, to a lesser extent, education. Given the ethnic and religious nature of spatial division this non-interventionist policy had the effect of reproducing the *status quo*. Informal links between the Unionist Party, the Orange Order and the Protestant commercial and industrial classes ensured that established patterns of industrial location, public housing and labour force composition were controlled to the advantage of the majority population. It was a system based upon stagnation and particularism: in order to maintain its political power the Unionist Party was forced to uphold local power structures while at the same time avoiding direct central government interventions.

The introduction of Keynesian management of the economy, a component part of the post-war settlement, undermined this reality and presented the Unionist Government with challenges it could not meet. The policy, emanating from London, of central direction of economic and regional development exemplifies this problem. As in the rest of the UK, the traditional heavy industrial base of the north-east had been in decline since the turn of the twentieth century. The demand fuelled by two world wars disguised the full extent of the underlying structural problems besetting the economy as employment in the staple (and Protestant-dominated) shipbuilding, linen and engineering industries continued to fall. The rate of unemployment in the 1960s, at 8 per cent, was double the UK average and there were signs of rising discontent among the Protestant working class at the loss of traditional sources of employment. The nationalist population suffered disproportionately from the lack of jobs with an unemployment rate of 16 per cent and a much higher rate of emigration (Rowthorn and Wayne 1988: 110ff.). The informal mechanisms of the segregated economy were not capable of coping with the disintegration of traditional industry and the Government was forced to apply the tools of the interventionist State to maintain the support of the Protestant working class:

> To keep their support [the Protestant working class] the government was forced to act and took vigorous steps to foster the development of new industry. Lavish investment grants, tax concessions and other inducements were used to attract British, American and continental firms to the province ... new jobs were being created but even more jobs were lost in declining industries and through the rationalising of existing enterprises. (Rowthorn 1981: 4)

The effect of central state intervention into planning and industrial location was to reinforce already existing structures of division. New industry was located predominantly in Protestant areas in and around Belfast, while, for instance, the predominantly Catholic city of Derry experienced levels of unemployment never falling below 15 per cent between 1950 and 1970. Unionists have argued that there were sound business reasons for new industry favouring the Belfast region, such as the presence of a skilled workforce, a developed infrastructure and closeness to the centre of administration. Brian Faulkner, one-time

Minister of Commerce (with responsibility for industrial development), offers this justification in his autobiography:

> Allegations that the nationalist areas were deliberately neglected are totally without foundation in fact. There was actually a government bias towards these areas: more generous financial inducements were available to firms to go to predominantly border areas ... the case of the Michelin tyre factory illustrates both the truth of this claim and the limitation of what the government could actually do ... we specifically offered them one million pounds extra government assistance if they went to Londonderry ... in spite of this, Michelin decided that it was in their interest to site the factory elsewhere and built it in the predominantly Protestant town of Ballymena in County Antrim. The government was, of course, accused of not really trying to get the factory for Londonderry, a shallow political criticism which I deeply resented. (Faulkner 1978: 27)

Faulkner may well have resented the accusations, but he failed to see that the rules of the game had been drastically altered. By accepting the principles of state intervention inherent in the social-democratic paradigm Stormont had implicitly taken on board direct responsibility for policies that had previously been shrouded in a mantle of unaccountability. By accepting the principles of the post-war settlement, the State was committed to promoting universalistic principles of equality and democracy through bureaucratic-rational intervention. Perhaps, as Faulkner had suggested, the State had little control over the locational decisions of multinational corporations but the nationalist population saw the situation differently. It interpreted the paucity of industrial development in Catholic areas as another example of the sectarian and unequal nature of the State. By accepting, however reluctantly, the principle of state intervention and the universalistic principles of welfare reform the Unionist Party had given the minority a crucial political and ideological opening. The effects of the implementation of welfare legislation compounded the problems encountered by the State in regional and economic development. Reforms in education, health and social security had a profound effect on the social structure of the North, as well as exposing ideological contradictions between the practices of the Unionist Government and social-democratic ideals. Since the general standard of living, the social class position and economic status of the minority was considerably lower than that of the Protestant majority, the introduction of the welfare state had a disproportionate effect on the former. The pressure to emigrate lessened, access to secondary and tertiary education increased, as did the overall standard of housing, health and welfare. These material and structural changes were matched by the gradual spread and acceptance of the culture of social-democratic ideals. A new political discourse of rights, equality, democracy and reform was displacing the dominant ideologies of nationalism and Catholicism, two dominant worldviews which were, in the Irish context, often indistinguishable. The discourse of the minority was gradually shifting away from the coercive, instrumental and asymmetrical nature of nationalist politics towards one based upon moral categories such as the demand that ritual humiliation be replaced by recognition in the form of the realisation of rights. In an interesting comment on a speech by John Hume (later to become leader of the moderate nationalist party, the SDLP, and one of the architects of the peace process) in 1965, Purdie comments: 'At a mass rally in the Guildhall (in Derry) ... Hume roused the crowd with a speech which made no reference to partition or nationalist grievances, but emphasised the common heritage and common interests of all the citizens of Derry' (Purdie 1990: 165).

By the middle of the 1960s the changes set in train after the Second World War were beginning to coalesce around new political opportunities for the minority: new groups and individuals were emerging with the capability of taking advantage of the new situation; the social structure had significantly changed with the consolidation of a new Catholic middle class; and new cultural ideas had taken root. This transformation had taken place despite the Unionist Government, which was ill-prepared and unwilling to deal with the inevitable demands for reform (Rose 2000: 31ff.).

The evolution of the CRM

In 1962 the IRA campaign which had been in train since 1958 came to an end. The campaign was misconceived from the beginning, with little popular support and with an objective – the overthrow of the Northern Ireland state – that was clearly not achievable. The failure of this latest military adventure on the part of republicans brought about a rethink of strategy among individuals and groups in the trade union movement, socialist groups and elements of the republican movement. John Hume's speech in Derry in 1965, mentioned above, was typical of the new thinking: to move away from traditional republicanism and nationalism and the belief that the State must be overthrown as a prerequisite for the establishment of equality and democracy towards a reformist position stressing the importance of changing the State from within. The author of the semi-official history of NICRA wrote: 'NICRA evolved from a diverse set of political aims and ideas which slowly came together to forge a unity based upon a common frustration with Unionism, a broad rejection of crude nationalism and a growing awareness of the need for an effective vehicle for political and legislative reform' (NICRA 1978: 5) .

NICRA was not the first group to agitate for civil rights in Northern Ireland, but its foundation in November 1966, and the broad support it enjoyed from a number of organisations, marked the beginnings of the creation of a mass movement.[13] The aims of the organisation were initially restricted to a focus upon legal and constitutional rights (*ibid*: 8):

- to defend the basic freedoms of all citizens;
- to protect the rights of the individual;
- to highlight all possible abuses of power;
- to demand guarantees for freedom of speech, assembly and association; and
- to inform the public of their lawful rights

For the first eighteen months of its existence NICRA avoided engagement with concrete grievances in areas such as housing, electoral practice and employment, confining its activities to what amounted to a letter-writing campaign to ministers. This proved to be as lacking in success as had been previous attempts to pressure the British Government to actively intervene in the affairs of the North (Purdie 1990: chapter 3).

Effectively, the political system in the North, and by extension that of London, was blocked and both incapable and unwilling to undertake reforms. As in Italy in the 1960s, the monopoly of power by one party (since 1922 in Northern Ireland and 1945 in Italy) blocked the possibility of democratic electoral change as well as consolidating the identification of state with government.[14] The Unionist Party had never felt accountable for the exclusion of the minority and felt responsible only to its own supporters. Occasional glimpses of the seamless interaction between the bureaucracy, the Unionist Party and local power structures have come to light. In an article in the London *Times* (24 April 1967) the former head of the design team for the new town of Craigavon, outside Belfast, told the newspaper that he had been warned by a source close to the Government that 'the Ulster government would not countenance any scheme that would upset the voting balance between Protestants and Roman Catholics in the area'. When the head of the design team resigned in protest Stormont launched a concerted campaign to discredit him (Rose 2000: 72–3). It soon became clear that there was an absence of a political opportunity structure[15] through which the demands of the reformers could be mediated. The existing political opportunity structures were closed and incapable of mediating and resolving conflicts due to the absence of suitable channels and the refusal of the British State to use its position as the superior constitutional and political actor to intervene. The constitutional and peaceful phase of agitation by NICRA lasted eighteen months amid increasing frustration at the lack of progress. All the factors necessary for mass mobilisation were already in place – a cognitive framework for collective action;[16] the identification of an adversary; the definition of a purpose and the overall objectives of the struggle (Melucci 1996: 292) – and by the summer of 1968 the leadership of NICRA was, somewhat reluctantly, ready to support those intent on taking protest to the streets.

Mediating conflict: the role of the police

In institutional terms, the State in the North rested upon two contrasting pillars. The bulk of decision making, as it affected the life of ordinary citizens, was made at local level. Local government had control over housing, significant areas of employment, local planning and infrastructural development. A network of formal and informal organisations, from local councils to the Orange Order, had entrenched power at local level and the support of the Unionist Government. This structure of control and patronage was central to the hegemony of unionism but it also meant that central government, even if it wanted to, had little room to manoeuvre as far as meeting the demands of the CRM were concerned. The very cohesiveness of the unionist all-class alliance depended upon the continuation of the semi-autonomous local politics of exclusion.

In contrast, the security apparatus was centralised and under the control of the Minister of Home Affairs. From the foundation of the State the police was organised on military lines and backed up by a large reserve force drawn almost exclusively from the majority community. The Special Powers Act gave almost unlimited power to the police and the Government to repress political dissent, and those powers were supplemented by legislation which was aimed at the repression of the cultural identity of the minority, such as laws forbidding the public display of flags and emblems (apart from the Union flag) and making it an offence to use street names in the Irish language (Ellison and Smyth 2000: 32ff.). The organisation, culture and politics of most policemen made them deeply suspicious of the minority and even the most innocuous demands were interpreted as a direct threat to the State and their position within it, both as Protestants and as policemen. The refusal of the State to countenance the demands of the minority made it inevitable that, when street protests began in the summer of 1968, the first line of confrontation would be with the Royal Ulster Constabulary, as the police force was then known. It is instructive to note that the question of policing and direct state repression did not figure in the list of demands put by NICRA although the RUC was central to the continued survival of the State. But as soon as confrontation between marchers and the police began, the question of repression swiftly rose up the agenda of grievances. Della Porta argues (1995: 189) that in Germany and Italy, during roughly the same period, 'political violence developed directly from the interactions between social movements and the police' – and the same was true of Northern Ireland. The role of the RUC was not simply one of surveillance and repression but also of controlling space. The practice of marching and commemoration is central to Protestant culture and can be seen as assuaging the insecurity of unionists and asserting their perceived right to the territory of Northern Ireland. The very fact that the minority was asserting its right to march was a challenge to the very basis of Protestant culture and perhaps explains why the middle-class leadership of NICRA was reluctant to embark on this type of protest.

As has been pointed out above, the CRM did not face a regime that was secure and stable in terms of support and legitimacy. The dependence of the State on repression was an index of the precarious nature of its existence, even though this was not immediately obvious to the minority, or indeed to the Unionist establishment itself. The Unionist regime resembled little more than an empty shell when faced with concerted and determined opposition. Without the political will or the structural means to grant concessions unionism responded in the way it knew best: with increased repression. It was this response to marches that fostered a sense of solidarity among the minority and pushed NICRA down the road of collective action and protest. As soon as the movement headed into the phase of street protest the reaction of the police became increasingly repressive and brutal. At practically every march and demonstration (by this stage the NICRA leadership in Belfast had little control over the proliferation of marches and demonstrations across the North) the police responded with disproportionate violence. During one of the first civil rights marches in Derry, in October 1969, attended by about 400 people, 'the RUC punched, batoned and pursued civil rights demonstrators in a brutal display of ... concerted violence' (O'Dochartaigh 1997: 5). This initial repression brought about a radicalisation of protest, encouraging further militancy and the formation of more militant groups. Such a group was People's Democracy (PD) which was founded by Belfast university students and others immediately after the events in Derry. In defiance of the NICRA leadership, PD embarked upon a march from Belfast to Derry on 1 January 1969. The march was consciously modelled on the famous Selma-Montgomery march of 1966, an event which in the eyes of one of the organisers of the march to Derry 'had exposed the racist thuggery of America's deep South and forced the US government into major reforms' (Farrell 1976: 249).

The march was ambushed at Burntollet Bridge close to Derry city by groups wearing armbands. The ambush, which resulted in an uncertain number of injuries (the RUC put the number of injured at thirteen but all the evidence points to a significantly higher figure), gave the march a crucial significance in the subsequent dynamic of escalation in movement behaviour. It soon became public knowledge that the RUC had involved itself on the side of the attackers yet members of the Government, including the Prime Minister, were quick to lay the blame at the door of the marchers. Two significant processes were in train: state repressiveness was creating a myth that had the instant effect of delegitimising the State by creating injustice frames (Gamson 1992) and arousing a feeling of absolute injustice (Manconi 1988). In addition, whatever vestige of neutrality the RUC may have enjoyed was dispelled by reports of its collaboration with the attackers. The effect of these events was to give the movement the appearance of an insurrection, and after the beating by the RUC of an elderly man in Derry – who subsequently died from his injuries – in the following April, the question of policing, and by proxy the very legitimacy of the State, had displaced the original reformist agenda of NICRA. As historian Marianne Elliot writes (2000: 416–17): 'Whatever people at the time thought of the Burntollet march – it had been opposed by the main CRM and many student supporters withdrew in its aftermath – it had achieved what some of its more radical leaders had sought. It had shown the bankruptcy of the Northern Ireland state and was a preliminary to its swift disintegration.'

By the beginning of 1969 the conditions for a rapid slide into a violent confrontation between the CRM and the State were in place:

- a blocked political system incapable of reacting energetically and creatively to the reformist demands of NICRA;
- the occurrence of symbolic events which acted as a catalyst for mobilisation;
- an extension of support for the aims and objectives of the CRM into the wider nationalist community and further afield; and
- an increasing focus upon the question of policing and justice leading to direct confrontations with the RUC.

The Stormont administration, crippled by internal divisions, was incapable of pushing through a coherent reform package, which might have defused the situation: it was a clear case of too little, too late. The use of *hard* policing worked to discredit the more moderate NICRA leadership and the tactics of peaceful protest. The RUC, attuned to policing a divided society in a partisan fashion, had no conception of itself as an institution of civil society (Smyth 2002). Indeed, even after the collapse of the RUC as an organised police force in 1969 and the introduction of the British Army in August of that year, the RUC still clung to the traditional interpretation of its role and refused to accept any culpability for the situation which the force had helped create. The Chief Constable in his *Report* for 1969 wrote:

> From its inception in 1922 the RUC played a dual role in the policing of Northern Ireland. Not only was the force required to provide a service of law enforcement ... it had the added responsibility of protecting the Province from subversion from within as well as from outside Northern Ireland ... In later years, and especially during the first eight months of 1969, the police were heavily engaged in a police-keeping role dealing with serious problems of public order on the streets of our cities and towns. (PSNI 1970: vii–viii)

Conclusions

Writing in 1976, Daniel Bell observed that one of the consequences of welfare state legislation was the creation of a multitude of group identities intent on realising the redress of social and economic inequalities in society. The welfare state led to the creation of a public political culture and the mobilisation of groups around new or reconstituted identities. In Northern Ireland, the universalistic principles of the welfare state were directly in conflict with the sectarian particularism of the Unionist State, and it was around this new reality that the CRM emerged by embedding the long-standing grievances of nationalists in the discourse of social democracy.

The CRM shared many of the characteristics of NSMs (Laraña 1994: 7ff.), particularly its middle-class leadership and the focus upon achieving cultural and symbolic change. The very nature of the mode of protest, street demonstrations and marches, challenged the dominant culture's hegemony over the space of Northern Ireland. Seen in a broader historical context, the CRM was not a *new* social movement but a continuation of a type of protest that dominated the political arena in nineteenth-century Ireland. Social movements of one sort or another proliferated, from the mass movement for Catholic Emancipation in the 1820s, probably the first genuine popular democratic movement in Europe. Because of the blocked political system administered from London, Ireland was a defining case of what Laraña (*ibid*: 8) called 'the credibility crisis of the conventional channels for participation in western democracies', and this situation fostered the emergence of social movements such as the Young Irelanders, the Land League (including the interesting case of the Ladies' Land League), Conrad na Gaeilge and Sinn Féin, to mention but a few. The legitimacy crisis which gripped Ireland throughout the nineteenth century was played out on two fronts: reform movements which had limited success and then gave way to some form of violent protest of an agrarian or more overtly political nature.

The CRM was *modern* in context, but followed a well-worn path of protest. New socio economic circumstances led to opportunity and reassessment against the background of a failed and discredited IRA campaign. Tarrow stresses the framing power of nationalism 'lacking the fine mechanical metaphors of class dialectics, nationalism possesses a much greater emotional potential [than socialism]' (1998: 112). Every society has a particular history, what Touraine calls its 'historicity' (Touraine 1981), which forms a background and focus for struggle. The exclusion and misrecognition of the minority population was understood collectively in a historical context, but was lived out under changed circumstances. The success of the CRM lies in the fact that its demands have been realised, and Northern Ireland is a different place for nationalists from what it was thirty years ago. The tragedy is that in took three decades of internal war for this to be achieved.

Notes

1 London: Harvill, 1994.
2 NICRA came into existence with the merger of two groups: the Wolf Tone Society and the Campaign for Social Justice. It was modelled on the British National Council for Civil Liberties. As NICRA tended to follow in the wake of the actions of local ad hoc groups which spearheaded the movement, the movement in general will be referred to as the CRM (Civil Rights Movement).
3 Injustice can be both socio-economic (embedded in the political economic fabric of society) and cultural, or symbolic. The latter involves the devaluing of the culture of a specific group, misrecognition of a group's culture and repression of its symbolic forms: see Fraser 2000.
4 See Gamson (1992).
5 For a general theoretical introduction to social movement theory see Crossley (2002).
6 Both Honneth and Fraser agree that recognition cannot be reduced to redistribution and both, like social movement theorists such as Melucci, stress the importance of cultural factors. The differences between Fraser and Honneth (the latter, true to his Hegelian background, sees recognition as a fundamental overarching category while Fraser sees the two categories as 'co-fundamental and mutually irreducible dimensions of justice') need not detain us here: see Fraser and Honneth (2003).
7 For a discussion of the events surrounding the establishment and consolidation of Northern Ireland see Farrell (1976), Buckland (1981), Bardon (1992), Elliot (2000).
8 Habermas, following J.L. Austin, introduced the interesting concepts of 'preluctionary' and 'illocutionary' into the discourse on mobilisation in the public sphere. Preluctionary speech is coercive and instrumental ('If you accept the union with Britain we will accept you', or the nationalist mirror image: 'If you join a united Ireland we will treat you as an equal') while illocutionary speech attempts to achieve mutual respect and understanding: 'We respect and will represent your needs and values': see Habermas (1984: 289ff.).
9 For a discussion of the tradition of secret societies and violent protest see Roberts (1983) and Donnelly (1983).
10 The centrepiece of the apparatus of legal repression was the Civil Authorities (Special Powers) Bill 1922. This Act (which has been amended since and is now commonly known as the Special Powers Act) gave the Minister of Home Affairs, who directly controlled the RUC, wide powers of arrest, search, questioning, detention without trial and internment. The Act also allowed for flogging as a punishment for political offences. The actions of the RUC, under the Act, were excluded from the scrutiny of the courts through the process of judicial review. The Act also stipulated that the minister (or agents acting on his behalf) could 'legally take all such steps as may be necessary for preserving peace and maintaining order'. This clause effectively gave retrospective legal immunity to the police for 'anything done in good faith in the execution of their duty in Northern Ireland'.
11 During the post-war period the Catholic Church was the most cohesive and influential organisation on the nationalist side. It had broad control over education, health and welfare provisions for Catholics. The provisions of the welfare state threatened this control and the Church fought a long and bitter rearguard action against reforms. It retains control over education, but even here its grip is loosening.
12 An index of unionist unease is given by the fact that Unionist MPs at Westminster voted against welfare state legislation. The Stormont Parliament had little option but accept Britain's largesse (albeit with a considerable time-lag) otherwise it would not

just have caused a constitutional crisis but would have invoked the ire of its own working-class supporters as well as sending them into the arms of the Northern Ireland Labour Party.

13 For an extended discussion of the emergence of the CRM see Purdie (1990) and Ó Dochartaigh, (1997).

14 The idea of a blocked political system has been explored for both Italy and Germany in the 1960s by Bonate (1979).

15 The concept of POS was developed by Tarrow (1989) and defines the field of constraints and limitations that moulds the actions of those involved in protest. The given opportunity structure effects a movement's decision to organise, the effects of collective action and the institutional response.

16 This cognitive framework was made up of traditional elements of nationalist grievance as well as the impact of the welfare state and the example of the black CRM in the US.

Bibliography

Alexander, J. and Lara, M., 1996 'The struggle for recognition', *New Left Review*, 220, 126–37.

Bardon, J., 1992 *A History of Ulster* (Belfast: Blackstaff Press).

Bell, D., 1976 *The Cultural Contradictions of Capitalism* (London: Heinemann).

Bonate, L., 1979 *Dimensioni del terrorismo politico* (Milan: Angeli).

Buckland, P., 1981 *A History of Northern Ireland* (Dublin: Gill and Macmillan).

Buechler, S., 2000 *Social Movements in Advanced Capitalism* (Oxford: Oxford University Press).

Chief Constable of Northern Ireland, Annual Report 1970, Belfast, HMSO.

Clark, S. and Donnelly, J. (eds), 1983 *Irish Peasants: Violence and political unrest 1780–1914* (Dublin: Gill and Macmillan).

Crossley, N., 2002 *Making Sense of Social Movements* (Buckingham: Open University Press).

Della Porta, D., 1995 *Social Movements, Political Violence and the State* (Cambridge: Cambridge University Press).

Eder, K., 1993 *The New Politics of Class* (London: Sage).

Elliot, M., 2000 *The Catholics of Ulster* (London: Penguin).

Ellison, G. and Smyth, J., 2000 *The Crowned Harp: Policing Northern Ireland* (London: Pluto Press).

Farrell, M., 1976 *Northern Ireland: The Orange State* (London: Pluto Press).

Farrell, M., 1983 *Arming the Protestants: The formation of the Ulster Special Constabulary and the Royal Ulster Constabulary* (Dingle: Brandon Press).

Faulkner, B., 1978 (ed. John Houston) *Memoirs of a Statesman* (London: Weidenfeld and Nicholson).

Fraser, N., 1997 *Justice Interruptus: Critical reflections on the 'postsocialist' condition* (London: Routledge).

Fraser, N., 2000 'Rethinking Recognition', *New Left Review*, 3 (May–June), 107–20.

Fraser, N. and Honneth, A., 2003 *Redistribution or Recognition: A political–philosophical exchange* (London: Verso).

Gamson, W., 1988 'Political Discourse and Collective Action', *International Social Movement Research*, 1, 219–44.

Gamson, W., 1992 'The Social Psychology of Collective Action', in Morris, A and

Mueller, C. (eds), *Frontiers in Social Movement Theory* (New Haven: Yale University Press).

Habermas, J., 1984 *The Theory of Communicative Action* (Boston: Beacon Press).

Honneth, A., 1995a 'Integrity and Disrespect', in Wright, C. (ed.), *The Fragmented World of the Social: Essays in social and political philosophy* (Albany: SUNY).

Honneth, A., 1995b *The Struggle for Recognition: The moral grammar of social conflicts* (Cambridge: Polity Press).

Isles K., and Cutbert, N., 1957 *An Economic Survey of Northern Ireland* (Belfast: HMSO).

Kriesi, H. Koopmans, R., Duyvendak, J.D. and Giugni, M., 1995 *New Social Movements in Western Europe: A comparative analysis* (Minneapolis: University of Minneasota Press and London: UCL Press).

Laraña, E., et al. (eds), 1994 *New Social Movements: From ideology to identity* (Philadelphia: Temple University Press).

Manconi, L., 1983 'Movimenti e nuovi movimenti: identitá é negoziazioni', *QuaderniPiacentivi* 8, 75–133

Melucci, A., 1996 *Challenging Codes: Collective Action in the Information Age* (Cambridge: Cambridge University Press).

NICRA, 1978 (Northern Ireland Civil Rights Association) *We shall Overcome: The history of the struggle for Civil Rights in Northern Ireland* (Belfast: NICRA).

Ó Dochartaigh, N., 1997 *From Civil Rights to Armalites: Derry and the birth of the Irish troubles* (Cork: Cork University Press).

Offe, C., 1995 'New Social Movements: Changing boundaries of the political', *Social research*, 52, 817–68.

Pivin, F. and Cloward, R., 1992 'Normalising Collective Protest', in Morris, A. and Mueller, C. (eds), *Frontiers in Social Movement Theory* (New Haven: Yale University Press).

Pivin, F. and Cloward, R., 1977 *Poor People's Movements* (New York: Pantheon Books).

Purdie, B., 1990 *Politics in the Streets: The origins of the Civil Rights Movement in Northern Ireland* (Belfast: Blackstaff Press).

Roberts, P., 1983 'Caravats and Shanavests: Whiteboyism and faction Fighting in East Munster 1802–11', in Clark, S. and Donnelly, J. (eds), *Irish Peasants: Violence and Political Unrest 1780–1914* (Dublin: Gill and Macmillan).

Rose, P., 2000 *How the Troubles came to Northern Ireland* (London: Macmillan).

Rowthorn, B., 1981 'Northern Ireland: an economy in crisis', *Cambridge Journal of Economics*, 5, 1–31.

Rowthorn, B. and Wayne, N., 1988 *Northern Ireland: The political economy of conflict* (Cambridge: Polity Press).

Smyth, J., 1985 'Northern Ireland: a case of terminal decline?', in Musto, S. and Pinkele, C. (eds), *Europe at the Crossroads* (New York: Praeger).

Smyth, J., 2002 'Symbolic Power and Police Legitimacy: The Royal Ulster Constabulary', *Crime, Law and Social Change*, 38, 295–310.

Tarrow, S., 1989 *Struggle, Politics and Reform: Collective action, social movements and cycles of protest* (Oxford: Clarendon Press).

Tarrow, S., 1994, 1998 *Power in Movement: Social Movements, collective action and politics* (Cambridge, Cambridge University Press,).

Todd, J., 1993 'Unionist Political Thought', in Boyce, D. et al. (eds), *Political Thought in Ireland since the Seventeenth Century* (London: Routledge).

Touraine, A., 1981 *The Voice and the Eye* (Cambridge: Cambridge University Press).

6 • Niamh Hourigan

Movement outcomes and Irish language protest

THIS chapter focuses on the media activism of Irish language protesters as a case study in order to explore the question of how *movement outcomes* can be theorised in the arena of social movements. The roots of the Irish State can be traced to a variety of nationalist social movements that populated civil society in Ireland during the late nineteenth and early twentieth centuries. Although many activists involved in these organisations were disappointed with the partition of the island in 1922, the establishment of the Irish post-colonial State could itself be considered an outcome of widespread social protest.[1] With the creation of the State's political and cultural institutions during the 1920s, a number of social movement leaders became part of Ireland's newly formed political elite.

From the outset, the Irish language was a critical dynamic in the institutional development and identity of the independent Irish State. Before independence, the Irish language question was closely allied with the broader political nationalist movement and had served as a key basis of recruitment for nationalist and republican groups. From 1922 onwards, Irish language speakers were represented on almost all sides of the political spectrum and the revival of the Irish language was accepted as the primary cultural objective of the fledgling Irish State (Lyons 1973). After independence, it became clear that the Irish language organisations that became associated with the revolutionary elite and the State (e.g. Conradh na Gaeilge) did not represent the entire spectrum of Irish language speakers on the island of Ireland. As the twentieth century progressed, several new constituencies of language activists emerged from Gaeltacht regions and Northern Ireland. For most of the century, members of these grassroots groups did not enjoy a privileged relationship with the State's political elite and their approach to protest differed radically from their counterparts' in the *national* language movement, which was more closely allied with the State. Although locally based Gaeltacht and national language groups often campaigned on the same issues, the structural differences in their positions within the polity meant that their protests often resulted in very different outcomes.

Irish language protest

The second half of the twentieth century is a particularly interesting period in the history of Irish language activism as Ireland experienced a period of rapid modernisation, which transformed not only the economy but also the shared culture and values within Irish society. Violence in Northern Ireland and the restructuring of the Southern State's priorities around economic imperatives provoked a profound revision in the Irish Government's approach to nationalist issues such as the revival of the Irish language and the reunification of the island of Ireland. Campaigns by Irish language groups for a radio service (1969–73) and a television service (1975–95) exposed some key faultlines in government policy on the language, contributed to the economic transformation of Gaeltacht regions and supported the introduction of new discourses on the position of the Irish language within Irish culture. This chapter seeks to examine the outcomes of the media campaigns of the Irish language movement in the context of the evolving dynamic of competition between specific groups within the language movement. The concept of social capital as an outcome of social protest will be used to examine the fluctuating position of different factions within the Irish language movement during the course of these campaigns as well the impact of relationships with Irish political elites on political decisions and cultural outcomes.[2]

Since the fall of the Berlin Wall, analysts of collective action have devoted increasing attention to the question of social movement outcomes. However, tracing causal linkages from incidents of protest to defined political and social change has proved to be a challenge for many researchers. As Schussman comments: 'Social movements and social movement organisations, these great change-seeking forces in society, are hard to connect to the actual changes they seek' (2002: 1). Mario Diani has proposed adopting a social capital approach to the analysis of movement outcomes, which can provide a potential solution to the causality question. He states: 'The problem of causal attribution will resurface again and again. My suggestion is that we scale down our ambitions for causality claims and focus on the structural preconditions, which may facilitate or constrain movements' attempts to influence both politics and culture' (1997: 133).

Social capital (Bourdieu 1986; Coleman 1990; Putman 1993) can be defined in this context as 'ties which, while they do not necessarily imply the presence of collective identity, are however based on sentiments of mutual trust and mutual recognition among actors involved' (Diani 1997: 130). A social capital approach to an analysis of social movement outcomes promotes an investigation of changes in the structural location of movement actors and organisations in broader social networks. This approach assumes that the more centrally social movement actors are located within movement networks, their social milieu and in terms of relations with political and cultural elites, the greater their impact will be on political decisions and cultural outcomes (Knoke 1990).

In examining the outcome of social capital in terms of the two media campaigns conducted by the Irish language movement during the latter half of the twentieth century, a number of dimensions of the concept will be interrogated: the consequences of social capital during protest will be linked to policy changes; and changes in the structural location will be examined in terms of cultural outcomes such as the mainstreaming of new frames around the Irish language. Rucht (1992) has highlighted the distinction between the impact of outcomes *within* a movement network and the external effects of protest in terms of links between the movement and its broader environment. Internal dimensions of consequences will be examined in terms of the competitive relationship that emerged between Gaeltacht groups and Conradh na Gaeilge as a result of changes in the distribution of social capital within the movement network. The external impact of social capital will be examined in terms of

- changing relations with political elites; and
- what Diani describes as 'the dissemination and diffusion of innovation', a process concerning the creation of 'structural organisational practices by which new ideas are spread and new patterns of behaviour and lifestyles are supported' (1997: 141) – the media services that were created as a result of these campaigns, Radio na Gaeltachta and TG4, can be examined from this perspective.

Relations between the Irish language movement and the State changed dramatically during the time-frame of protest under discussion (1969–95). Between the 1920s and the late 1950s, the relationship between Conradh na Gaeilge and the State remained relatively stable and the privileged position of the Irish language in national cultural ideology went unchallenged. However, from the 1960s onwards, rapid modernisation, economic development, as well as erupting violence in Northern Ireland, shattered these stable ties and led to a period of massive flux where national cultural ideology and the project of nation-building became subject to profound and intense questioning. An analysis of social capital as an outcome of social protest sheds light on the relational consequences of social protest during this period in Irish society.

Social movement outcomes

Although the concept of social capital is relatively recent, analysis of social movement outcomes since the 1960s has devoted some attention to the structural position of movements, relations with elites and the impact of these factors on the outcomes of social protest. Movement outcomes can be defined as the intended or unintended consequences of social protest and movement mobilisation. Outcomes have been theorised in variety of ways within the strands of social movement theory. During the mid-twentieth century, collective behaviour theorists such Herbert Blumer (1951) and Neil Smelser (1962) began to ignore the long-established view that collective action was an irrational form of political expression adopted by the most marginalised members of society. Instead, these theorists argued that the political system in which social movements were located approximated the pluralist ideal of open polity where everyone had equal power to influence political decision-making (*ibid*; Parsons 1964). In this system, political leaders were receptive to the demands of social movements, the avenues of political expression were permeable and there was, therefore, little need to engage in protest outside of orthodox channels.

In tracing the outcomes of protest, Smelser (1962) focused on internal changes to movement structures as organisations evolved from a stage of enthusiastic mobilisation through to institutionalisation. This model of institutionalisation is rooted in the work of Michels (1959) and Weber (1964) and concerns the reorganisation of movement structures around the requirements of political elites and institutions. Thus, social movements tend to move from the margins to the mainstream because they adapt their orientation in order to meet the requirements of established political institutions. The model of institutionalisation has some relevance to recent work on social capital as it focuses on what Simmel (1955) describes as the integrative function of conflict within and among collectivities. Advocates of the social capital approach tend to characterise increasingly close relationships with elites as a positive outcome. Diani comments: 'movement actors' chances to be influential will also depend on the extent and strength of their linkages to their environment, in particular to political and cultural elites' (1997: 136). However, theorists of institutionalisation were much more fearful of the consequences of engaging with elites, arguing that the process of institutionalisation resulted in a loss of radical impetus within a social movement without the achievement of real gains (Zald and Ash 1966: 338).

During the 1970s, resource mobilisation (RM) theorists in the USA began to characterise protest as a political resource and viewed collective action as a rational method of achieving political goals (McCarthy and Zald 1973, 1977; Zald and McCarthy 1979). Consequently, outcomes were examined predominantly in terms of immediate changes to policy and increases in the level of representation within the polity. William Gamson (1975) highlighted the difference between new gains and increased levels of acceptance: 'new gains' refers to tangible changes in public policy on issues raised by protest movements, while 'levels of acceptance' refers to changes movements bring about in the system of interest representation.[3] Again, the focus on levels of representation bears some relevance to the notion of social capital. However, the resource mobilisation perspective focused heavily on the activities of a few highly professionalised social movements which were barely distinguishable from orthodox interest groups. Theorists devoted little attention to less formalised, radical, social movements and argued that these groups had no real capacity to improve their structural position either within movement networks or in terms of relations with elites. Diani comments:

> While more formal SMOs undoubtedly play a key role in a number of movements, restricting the analysis of movement outcomes to this level entails the highly problematic assumption that (a) they are representative of movement sectors as a whole and (b) movement success can be reduced to the degree of formal legitimation and/or policy influence enjoyed by specific organisations (1997: 131).

In Europe, NSM theorists such as Alain Touraine and Alberto Melucci directed less attention to the impact of protest on specific policies or relations with elites. NSM analysts were more interested in tracing the role of collective action in contributing to long-term patterns of social and cultural change (Touraine 1971, 1981; Melucci 1984, 1989). Much attention was devoted to developing models that clarified the exact nature of these changes, such as the post-industrial society, the network society and disorganised capitalism (Touraine 1971; Lash and Urry 1987; Castells 1996). NSM literature on movement outcomes tends to focus on the capacity of social movements to create cultural change and introduce movement ideologies into mainstream politics. The master framing of movement discourses within post-industrial societies is a key focus of critical attention while less emphasis is placed on the institutionalisation of SMOs (Eder 1996). During the late 1990s, there was a flurry of efforts to achieve *synthesis* between the RMT preoccupation with immediate policy outcomes and the NSM focus on long-term cultural change (see e.g. Burstein et al. 1995; Kriesi et al. 1995; Banaszak 1996; Giugni 1998; Giugni et al. 1998; Tarrow 1998; Burstein 1999; Andrews 2001).

Renewed critical interest in outcomes during the 1990s coincided with an increasing conviction among theorists that social movements had the capacity to effect profound political and cultural change. In 1999, Della Porta and Diani commented:

> Debates on the chances of social movements obtaining positive results has become more optimistic recently, although hardly to the point of suggesting that a pluralist position will return to favour in the sociology of social movements. Students of social movements have undoubtedly inherited the scepticism of elitists and neo-elitists concerning the openness of the decision-making processes, social movements are after all, the form of organisation of the weakest groups in society. However, recent research has highlighted the fact that ... many groups once considered particularly deprived of organisational resources and identity (such as women) have improved their relative position, acquiring channels of access to the decision-making process. (1999: 252)

However, despite this new optimism, considerable problems remain within the analysis of outcomes. Apart from the difficulties in creating causal linkages, definitions of *success* and *failure* are problematical. Marco Giugni (1999) notes that the internal impact of specific outcomes on social movements can often be very different from external perceptions of those outcomes. He comments: 'Movement participants and external observers may have different perceptions of the success of a given action. Moreover, the same action may be perceived as successful by some participants but judged as a failure by others' (1999: xxi). Moreover, while a movement may be unsuccessful in achieving its rational goals, participation in protests can have the outcome of collectively transforming the perceptions, consciousness and worldview of activists and thus contributing to long-term cultural change. It is impossible here to address all the problems in the theorising of movement outcomes however, a focus on social capital has emerged as one of a range of solutions facilitating 'a meso level perspective, focusing on changes in the structural location of movement actors (individual and/or organisations) in broader social networks' (Diani 1997: 130). Analysis of changes in the structural position of different factions within the Irish language movement provides particular insight into the complex consequences of the campaigns for Raidio na Gaeltachta and Teilifís na Gaeilge.

Irish language protest

Before examining Irish language protest, it is important to describe the key features that characterise the Irish-speaking community. Irish speakers in the Republic can be divided into at least two groups. 'Gaeltacht' is the term used to describe the peripheral regions of the country where Irish is the primary language used in daily activity. Gaeltacht communities are, by and large, located in the most economically deprived regions of the Irish State.[4] The fishermen and small farmers who form the majority of the Gaeltacht population survive on low incomes.[5] Lack of basic infrastructure such as roads, water schemes and public transport has been a consistent obstacle to economic development in these regions since the foundation of the State in 1922 (MacAodh 1969; Hindley 1990). Gaeilgóirí are Irish-speakers who do not live in Gaeltacht regions, although most of these individuals learn the Irish language from an early age. These Irish speakers are generally middle-class city-dwellers and many are employed in the Civil Service or state-controlled occupations. For many Gaeilgóirí, their commitment to speak the Irish language in a largely English-speaking environment has been linked to their commitment to Irish cultural nationalism (Ó Riagain 1997). Since the 1970s, new constituencies of Irish language speakers have emerged in Northern Ireland and in the new suburbs of cities in the Republic. Many individuals associated with these new Irish language movements, such as the Gaelscoileanna (Irish-medium schools) movement, do not have a Gaeltacht background or share the broader commitment to nationalism traditionally associated with Irish language activism.[6] Their activities bear closer resemblance to the protests of new middle-class activists identified by NSM theorists (Hourigan 2001).

Conradh na Gaeilge (The Gaelic League) is the largest and most powerful Irish language organisation and represents the interests of Gaeilgóirí at national level. Founded in 1893, the organisation provided many recruits for the Irish revolutionary movement. After Ireland achieved political independence in 1922, the interests of Conradh na Gaeilge were represented in the main political parties by former activists such as Eamon de Valera, leader of Fianna Fáil, and Eoin MacNéil, one of the State's first Ministers for Education. These individuals ensured that the revival of the Irish language was enshrined as the primary cultural aim of the new State (Ó Fearail 1975: 9–20). Historian F.S.L. Lyons comments: 'It was accepted in principle, even if practice lagged far behind, that Irish was an essential element in the establishment of a separate national identity and from the moment the first Dáil assembled in January 1919, the revival of the language became a major object of policy' (1973: 635). The loss of many of the most able members of Conradh na Gaeilge to the new political parties resulted in an immediate period of decline within the organisation after 1922 but reaffirmed the movement's strong links with Irish political elites. Akutagawa states that 'after the task of language restoration was taken over by the State, the role of Conradh na Gaeilge became that of criticising the government for lack of implementation of policy' (1989: 129).

Education was the main vehicle for language revival, though by the late 1940s it became clear that full revival was unlikely ever to be achieved (Ó Riain 1984: 45). Brown comments that 'for twenty years, the language revival had in the main, been left in the government's apparently trustworthy hands. In the 1940s, individuals began to sense that responsibility must rest with themselves' (1991: 192). Conradh na Gaeilge experienced a period of brief revival during this period, with a flurry of new publications. However, younger activists felt that the organisation was losing sight of its radical nationalist roots. Some activists formed a breakaway group, Glúin an Bua, arguing that Conradh na Gaeilge had become compromised because of its close links to political elites; however the organisation achieved little success (MacAonghusa 1993: 184).

In the early 1960s, Ireland began to industrialise and modernise, and this process affected Irish language policy. The old revolutionary elite retired from Irish politics and a new modernising group of politicians led by Taoiseach Seán Lemass prioritised the creation of economic prosperity over the nationalist objectives of the re-unification of the island of Ireland and the revival of the Irish language (Lee 1989). Direct links between Conradh na Gaeilge and the main political parties were diminishing. Cohan notes that while 69 per cent of the revolutionary elite had belonged to Conradh na Gaeilge, only 15 per cent of the post-revolutionary elite were members (1979: 60).

There has been considerable debate about the impact of modernisation on Irish language policy. Officially, at least, the State's attitude towards the Irish language remained positive during the 1960s. Brown notes a new realism entering official debate about the language with the establishment of a commission to examine Irish language issues in 1963 (1991: 268). In 1965, the Government reaffirmed the privileged position of Conradh na Gaeilge by providing the organisation with an annual subsidy of £6,500 and new premises in Dublin (Ó Fearail 1975: 55). However, the emergence of the CRM in Northern Ireland in 1969 and the subsequent escalation of the Northern conflict into serious violence provoked a revision of nationalism in the Republic. Public opinion became a crucial factor in the formulation of Irish language policy. Ó Riagáin comments: 'the new emphasis on public attitudes clearly reflected the government view that the major constraint on policy development was the absence of sustained public support and not state action per se' (1997: 23). Therefore, by the mid-1970s it became clear that the privileged relationship which Conradh na Gaeilge had enjoyed with the national political elite for forty years was no longer secure.

Between the 1920s and the 1960s, members of Gaeltacht communities who became involved in social protest developed a different relationship to state authorities. Gaeltacht activists did not play a very active role in Irish nationalism before the foundation of the State, although the regions occupied a hugely important symbolic position within the cultural ideology of Irish nationalism. Because of their language status, the Gaeltachtaí were regarded as the heartland of Irish national cultural identity. Terence Brown states:

> The 1920s saw the confirmation of the west, of the Gaeltacht and particularly of the western islands as the main locus of Irish cultural aspiration. After the War of Independence and the civil war ... the vision of heroic rural life in the Gaeltacht or on a western island served as a metaphor of social cohesion and an earnest symbol of a cultural unity that transcended class politics and history. Islands of Gaelic speaking people in a sea of Anglicisation, the Gaeltacht represented that ideal unity which nationalist ideologues had envisaged and prophesied, but which in reality had failed to provide. (1991: 92)

Despite this privileged position in national cultural ideology, Irish language policy was rarely defined separately for English-speaking and Irish-speaking (Gaeltacht) regions. Michie Akutagawa argues that 'the state's approach became an imposition on the Gaeltacht of the specific function of contributing to the state in its cultural objective ... policy for the Gaeltacht has never been motivated by concern about the Gaeltacht in its own right' (1989: 129).

Levels of extreme poverty in Gaeltacht regions between the 1920s and 1960s meant that Gaeltacht people had few resources to devote to social protest, preoccupied as they were with survival.[7] The sporadic Gaeltacht protest movements which emerged during the first forty years of the State's existence focused on economic rather than cultural issues. Groups such as Muintir na Gaeltachta, established in 1933, argued that land reform, fishing rights and agricultural development were essential to the survival of Gaeltacht communities. Muintir na Gaeltachta was heavily influenced by the socialism which was finding favour among Republican groups during the 1930s and, as a result, the movement was regarded with great suspicion by political elites and Irish language activists in Conradh na Gaeilge.[8] Evidence from Deparment of Justice records at the time indicates that Muintir na Gaeltachta was being heavily watched by police.[9] Indeed, the relationship between Gaeltacht activists and state authorities continued to be marked by open conflict during the subsequent twenty years. A protest at Baile na hAbhann in 1948 where Gaeltacht people demanded fishing rights resulted in the jailing of ten activists for a fortnight while activists were also imprisoned for involvement in a protest demanding a new schoolhouse at Inis Barachán in Connemara (Akutagawa 1989: 65). Therefore, Gaeltacht movements were much less institutionalised than their Conradh na Gaeilge counterparts and did not enjoy a privileged relationship with the State's political elites.

The final thirty years of the twentieth century were dominated by campaigns from all constituencies of Irish speakers for Irish language radio and television services. However, as activists from Gaeltacht regions and Conradh na Gaeilge began to conduct protests on the same issues, clear divisions emerged in their respective tactical repertoire and ideological discourse. The first radio campaign was established in 1969 in the Galway Gaeltacht by a local movement heavily influenced by the Northern Ireland CRM.[10] The protests of the Gaeltacht CRM received considerable press coverage.[11] Activists contextualised their demands in terms of civil rights for members of the Gaeltacht community rather than the needs of the broader Irish population. Almost immediately, Conradh na Gaeilge launched a competing campaign for a national Irish language station oriented to Irish speakers throughout the island rather than inhabitants of the Gaeltacht (Ó Glaisne 1982: 60). Leaders of the Gaeltacht CRM felt that the national Irish language organisation had hijacked their very effective local campaign to request a service which had no relationship to the needs of their community. One activist commented: 'the people of the Gaeltacht did all the work towards the establishment of a radio for the Gaeltacht. We will not allow a group of professional Gaeilgóirí to take over.'[12] However, when state representatives began to negotiate with Gaeltacht civil rights representatives, the latter's lack of experience in dealing with political elites and civil servants became abundantly evident. Gaeltacht activists negotiating through English, their second language, admitted to feeling highly intimidated (Ó Glaisne 1982: 111–14).[13] The relevant government ministers also met with Conradh na Gaeilge representatives, many of whom were members of the Fianna Fáil party and decided to establish a station oriented to a national audience but based in Connemara. Commentators on the new radio service were quick to identity its orientation. Just a year after its establishment, one critic observed: 'Raidio na Gaeltachta is broadcasting for an elite, for a mini elite within an elite. What service does the station provide for teenagers who want to hear pop music, housewives or local farmers and fishermen? Who is the station broadcasting for – Irish language aficionados?' (Ó Murchú 1973: 14).[14]

Despite the new gains achieved by Conradh na Gaeilge during the radio campaign, the organisation's privileged position within the State's broader network of allied social movement organisations diminished in the 1970s. There was growing public resistance to the reified position of the Irish language within the education system, and the escalating political violence in Northern Ireland provoked a move towards a more critical view of Irish nationalism in the South. Politicians and civil servants started to look more favourably on social movements which contextualised Irish language initiatives in terms of the discourse of minority rights favoured by the European Union. In examining this change in national cultural ideology during the 1970's, Watson comments:

> It would clearly have been injudicious for political leaders to oppose Irish bearing in mind its popular support as a core element of Irish national identity (see CLÁR and ITÉ surveys) yet it seems inappropriate to continue with the restoration of the language in the current political and ideological environment. Therefore, one could postulate that the gradual shift towards minority rights is the only possible solution: it is the accepted view in the EU and international circles and being founded on democratic principles, it is an acceptable alternative in the current environment. (1996: 170)

Undeterred by this ideological change, Conradh na Gaeilge launched a campaign for an Irish language television service in 1975. Activists framed their demand for the television service in terms of cultural nationalism. As evidence mounted that this frame was unacceptable to national government, the relationship between Conradh na Gaeilge and Fianna Fáil deteriorated and became considerably more hostile. Conradh activists began to withhold payment of television license fees in protest at the Government's broadcasting policy.[15] Underlining their nationalist position, Conradh na Gaeilge formed a closer alliance with republican organisation Sinn Féin.[16] However, the joint Sinn Féin–Conradh na Gaeilge campaign protesting about government broadcasting policy met with no response from the Government. In 1985, newly elected Conradh President Ité Uí Chionnaith acknowledged that the television campaign would have to be re-framed in terms of minority rights in order to achieve any further gains, although some rank-and-file members strongly resisted this re-framing of their demands.

Perhaps because of the ambiguous outcome of the radio campaign, Gaeltacht activists played little part in the television campaign during the late 1970s and early 1980s. However, the links generated during the radio campaign with senior figures in semi-state organisations, national media and national political parties provided the basis for a form of social capital, which resulted in the gradual recruitment of the core membership of the Gaeltacht CRM to these organisations.[17] Alberto Melucci and Timo Lyyra argue that this is not an uncommon outcome of social protest:

> Collective action is the main channel in the selection of new elites for institutional life ... Areas where movements provide new elites and cultures responding to the needs that arise from the emergence of new uncertainties include today the media system, the education system, corporate life, academic life and non-governmental organisations. These areas, again, are easily connected to the political system or may themselves become a breeding ground for the formation of cosmopolitan elites, creating patterns of circulation on a national and global level. (1998: 220)

Civil rights activists who remained in the Gaeltacht channelled their energies into the cooperative movement and the regional development body Údarás na Gaeltachta. These gradual changes led to the increased centrality of Gaeltacht activists within the Irish language movement and an improvement in their connections with political elites.

In 1987, a new Gaeltacht movement, the Gaeltacht Television Working Group (Meitheal Oibre Teilifís na Gaeilge), was established in Connemara to campaign for a Gaeltacht television service. Some of the leaders of this movement had been involved in the Gaeltacht civil rights campaign and their demand was framed in terms of minority rights. Their protests, which included the establishment of a pirate television service, provoked an immediate and positive response from the State: Taoiseach Charles Haughey allocated £500,000 from National Lottery funds for the Gaeltacht television project.

This time the Conradh na Gaeilge leadership was horrified at what it perceived as the Gaeltacht hi-jack of their campaign. Gaeltacht activists added insult to injury by forming a national television campaign group, Feachtas Náisiúinta Teilifíse (FNT – National Television Campaign), an umbrella organisation for all groups framing the demand for Irish language television in terms of minority rights. This group included Irish language activists from the North, and representatives of the Gaelscoileanna movement throughout the country. FNT activists were immediately invited by the Minister for Communications to enter negotiations about the television project. As Gaeltacht activist Donnacha Ó Ealaithe commented: 'We weren't outsiders anymore – we were insiders.'[18] Conradh na Gaeilge activists were largely excluded from these negotiations.[19] These discussions with government and RTÉ officials resulted in the creation of two research committees to examine the television issue. In response to the findings of these committees, Minister Michael D. Higgins introduced legislation for the establishment of a new Irish language television service, TG4, which began broadcasting in 1996.

A comparison of these two campaigns indicates that there was a profound change in the structural location of the two main groups within the Irish language movement during the final thirty years of the twentieth century. Gaeltacht protesters, who articulated their demands in terms of minority rights, were marginalized in late 1960s. They possessed little social capital and occupied a marginal position in terms of the broader Irish language movement and relationships with political elites However, as the old revolutionary elite retired from Irish politics, Gaeltacht activists began to benefit from the social capital generated during the radio campaign. The increasing centrality of Gaeltacht groups in the Irish language movement seems to be linked to a broader ideological openness to the frame of minority rights at national level during this period. The central and privileged position of Conradh na Gaeilge declined during the same period. Modernisation, membership of the European Union and the outbreak of the Troubles in Northern Ireland resulted in the State adopting a less favourable view of the cultural nationalism which dominated Conradh's ideological position on the language (Watson 1996). This change in the structural location of the two groups led to increased competition within the Irish language movement. The new centrality of Gaeltacht groups in the movement allowed state authorities to grant access to civil servants, broadcasting expertise, etc., to groups articulating demands in terms of minority rights, a discourse more sympathetic to their own ideological preferences during the 1980s and 1990s. Conradh na Gaeilge activists who framed their demands in terms of the failure of the State to achieve nationalist goals of the revival of the language and the re-unification of the island of Ireland were increasingly marginalised. As this form of nationalism became increasingly unpalatable to political elites, Conradh na Gaeilge's leadership was excluded from discussions about the establishment of an Irish language television service.

Social capital and the Irish language movement

A review of the outcome of social capital in terms of the campaigns for Raidio na Gaeltachta (1969–73) and Teilifís na Gaeilge (1975–95) facilitates a focus on changes in the structural position of factions within the Irish language movement that had a profound impact on policy decisions and cultural outcomes. In terms of the campaign for Raidio na Gaeltachta, the combined protests of the Gaeltacht CRM and Conradh na Gaeilge activists succeeded in forcing the Government to establish the radio service in 1973. However, the outcome of the campaign would seem to reinforce Marco Giugni's reference (1999) to the importance of perception in evaluating outcomes. While Conradh activists perceived the campaign to be a success, Gaeltacht activists had a more mixed reaction because the service did not correspond to the local access broadcasting model, which they had demanded. In terms of cultural outcomes, the State had accepted Conradh na Gaeilge's legitimating argument for the establishment of the service, which was rooted in cultural nationalism. Therefore, it appeared that Conradh na Gaeilge maintained its privileged position within the Irish language movement and in terms of relationships with political elites. However, a focus on the social capital outcomes of the protest promotes a different analysis of this campaign. It was the dynamic activists of the Gaeltacht CRM who generated the most significant social capital as a result of protests. During the 1970s, activists from the Gaeltacht movement built on links formed with elites in national political and cultural institutions during the radio campaign, and achieved increasing prominence in the broader Irish language movement. This change in the structural location of Gaeltacht movement actors was coupled with favourable changes within the national cultural ideology as the discourse of minority rights began to find favour with Ireland's modernising elite. New grassroots groups from Northern Ireland and the Gaelscoileanna movement were also deeply attracted to the discourse of minority rights. Therefore, Gaeltacht groups moved to a more central position within the movement network and found themselves articulating the mainstream ideology on the role of the Irish language in Irish culture.

When a second Gaeltacht group emerged in the late 1980s to mount a television campaign, the value of the social capital generated in the aftermath of the radio campaign became abundantly evident. Gaeltacht activists, allied with groups from Northern Ireland and the Gaelscoileanna articulating minority rights, were able to ensure that their interests were routinely taken into account by government and they achieved much greater success with their campaign. Conradh activists became marginalised during the latter stages of the second television campaign as their continued emphasis on cultural nationalism alienated them from the broader network of the Irish language movement and political elites who regarded this discourse as incongruous with modern Ireland.

The subsequent establishment of the Teilifís na Gaeilge service TG4 reflected the improved structural position of Gaeltacht social movements and created a broader positive change in the perception of Gaeltacht culture. Activists succeeded not only in establishing their legitimacy as a linguistic minority but TG4 was an effective tool which was used to challenge any taint of inferiority which might have been linked to Gaeltacht culture. Howell notes that broadcasting is one of the most effective ways to improve the status of a minority language culture, noting:

> Broadcasting seems to invest its contents with status; therefore languages used on air have legitimacy and gain credibility in the minds of audiences. This prestige factor is particularly important to children because they hold the key to a minority languages' future. It is, therefore, easy to understand why

cultural minorities throughout the world place a high premium on gaining access to their nations' airwaves and cable systems. (1992: 196)

It is possible to argue that TG4 was one of the most significant means by which the cultural innovations of Gaeltacht groups were diffused and disseminated. In emphasising minority rights, Gaeltacht activists were seeking to assert the parity of their culture with English language culture. The current output of TG4 with its slogan 'Súil Eile' (another eye) suggests that Irish language culture can provide another equally legitimate perspective on Irish society which reflects the cultural diversity typical of a globalised society rather than cultural nationalism. Steve Coleman has commented on 'the new fashionableness' of Irish-medium education (Gaelscoileanna), clubs like Dublin's Club Sult and the new Irish language television channel TG4. Many of these new forms and channels of expression displayed a cultural and linguistic hybridity which seemed to transcend the narrow confines of an obsessively purist nationalist culture (2003: 176).

Watson argues that the success of TG4 and the general acceptance of the discourse of minority language rights reflect the broad congruence of these initiatives with neo-liberalism that has underpinned Ireland's recent economic success. He states:

> The main context in which TnaG emerged was the shift from a more liberal to a more neoliberal ideology from a more European to a more global environment ... Part of the social rights of Irish speakers is to participate in their own culture, the unique features of which is speaking Irish ... Consuming Irish language programmes according to this argument, is an element of participation in cultural citizenship even if it is culture-consuming rather than a culture-debating public. (Watson 2003: 116–17)

Watson sounds a note of warning here which it would be wise to heed in terms of the application of the social capital outcomes to the campaigns for Raidio na Gaeltachta and Telifís na Gaeilge. Gaeltacht groups succeeded in improving their structural position as well as achieving broad recognition for their status as minority language speakers. However, the marginalisation of the cultural nationalist perspective of Conradh na Gaeilge is troubling. In mounting a cultural nationalist challenge to the State through the television licence campaign with Sinn Féin, Conradh na Gaeilge activists were effectively questioning the replacement of nationalist goals with neo-liberal ideology which was open to diversity and minority rights as long as these rights did not interfere with the smooth operation of the market.

Literature on social capital as a movement outcome devotes little attention to the limitations of this process. Although social capital can be generated in movement networks, political elites have a key role to play in generating social capital. They can grant access to or marginalize groups from negotiations and interest mediation arrangements. This role of gatekeeper allows them to manipulate the location of groups within movement networks and within negotiating structures. In the case of the media campaigns of the Irish language movement, the Irish Government was able to privilege groups articulating their favoured ideological perspective and generate a competitive dynamic to effectively divide the movement network.[20]

Many social movement networks, such as those involving Irish language organisations, operate on the basis of competitive cooperation. Della Porta and Diani (1999) outline this relationship in the following terms:

> In such cases, two (or more) organisations concerned with the same issues are keen to develop joint initiatives, based on compatible definitions of issues and some degree of identity, but at the same time, they find themselves facing stiff mutual competition for the same support base, and for similar sections of public opinion whose interests they wish to represent. (1999: 125)

When one organisation within a competitive network increases its social capital, it is essential to examine how this impacts on the other *challenger* organisations within the network. By allowing political elites to use social capital to manipulate the structure of movement networks, activists risk handing them a very powerful political weapon whereby they, as external sponsors, are able to quash ideologies and tactical repertoires more threatening to the status quo. This manipulation can create highly destructive patterns of competition which distract activists from their real goals. In examining social movement participation in the fourth pillar of national partnership agreements in Ireland, Mullan and Cox have noted that this type of competition has been fruitless and destructive to many Irish social movements:

> In practice what happens is that rather than extending their understanding of structural problems, radicalising their demands and developing broader alliances, movement organisations find themselves immediately in competition with those of their sister organisations who stand closest to them and are thus competitors for funding and influence. Hence the growth of particularism and factionalism, as networks develop around this zero sum politics whose terms are, of course, set elsewhere. (2004: 7)

Therefore, within the literature evaluating the social capital outcome of social protest, there is a need for greater scepticism in examining how improvements in structural location impact on subsequent social protest. While it is clear that social capital can contribute to the creation of policy change and cultural innovation, the spectre of cooptation of movement actors remains. While movement networks offer political elites a range of organisations with which to negotiate, it will always be tempting for them to use social capital to *divide and conquer* a movement network and marginalise dissent within the public sphere.

Conclusion

The experience of Irish language activists involved in Conradh na Gaeilge and the Gaeltacht CRM would seem to confirm some of the optimism of recent theorists of social movement outcomes. It is possible for movements, through social protest, to create policy change and improve their structural position within the broader polity. However, by engaging with political elites in order to achieve their goals, social movement activists expose themselves to some risk. It is clear that the Irish Government had a clear image of the relations of competitive cooperation that existed within the Irish language movement. Political elites also recognised that in their capacity to allocate social capital to various movements they controlled a very powerful weapon which could be used to restructure the hierarchy of organisations within the network. This tool allowed government to create immediate policy change, such as the establishment of an Irish language television service, without seriously addressing the broader ideological critique rooted in cultural nationalism that some activists were articulating during the television campaign. It is clear that by the mid-1980s, Conradh na Gaeilge activists were not only demanding an Irish language television service but protesting about the replacement of nationalist goals, such as the revival of the Irish language, by economic goals focusing on integration into the global economy. However, as the campaign progressed, social capital was used by government to marginalise groups campaigning from this perspective and promote groups campaigning from a position of minority rights, which was less threatening to the State's dominant ideological perspective.

Notes

1 Since the re-emergence of the conflict in Northern Ireland in 1969, many historians have argued that it is problematical to characterise the outcomes of the Irish revolutionary period (1916–22) as successful because they resulted in the partition of the island. However, it is clear that Irish revolutionaries were one of the first groups to successfully break away from the British Empire, creating a model for action which influenced many other separatist movements.

2 An elite, in this context, will be defined as 'a minority group which has power or influence over others and is recognised as such' (Abercrombie et al. 1994: 138).

3 Gamson's seminal work *The Strategy of Social Protest* (1975) attempted to create a clear image of a successful social movement. Jenkins summarised Gamson's findings in the following way: 'In general, successful social movements were bureaucratic, pursued narrow goals, employed selective incentives, enjoyed sponsorship, used unruly methods (including violence) and made their demands during periods of socio-political crisis' (1983: 543).

4 The small Co. Meath Gaeltacht of Ráth Cairn would be an exception. This Gaeltacht was artificially planted by the Irish Government in the rich farm land of Co. Meath in the 1930s.

5 Overall levels of income in the Gaeltacht were low throughout the 1960s. Ó Brudair (1971: 5–7) estimates that from 1960 to 1965, at least 13–15 per cent of overall income

in the Galway Gaeltacht was provided by government transfers and emigrant remittances. MacAodh (1969) estimates that the population of the Gaeltacht was declining at a rate of 1 per cent per annum. During the 1960–69 period, seven primary schools closed in the Gaeltacht. In the Donegal Gaeltacht, 16 per cent of households contained no one of working age. Lack of infrastructure provided the most tangible evidence of Gaeltacht poverty: in 1969, MacAodh found that 95 per cent of households had no adequate water supply; there was no proper sewage system or telephone service and the road system was of poor quality (ibid: 15).

6 The Gaelscoileanna movement was established to represent the interests of children, parents and teachers associated with Irish language schools. A number of these schools are non-denominational and most are based in urban areas.

7 Poverty was the most dominant feature of life in the Gaeltacht for most of the twentieth century. In 1925, Fr S.J. Walsh found that 'the people of Aran have not sufficient food supply to keep them going at present' (Gaeltacht Commission Report 1925). There was very little infrastructure in terms of roads, sewage, electricity, shops, etc. It is estimated that the overall number of Gaeltacht Irish-speakers halved between 1922 and 1939 as a result of emigration. Between 1946 and 1966, the Galway Gaeltacht lost a fifth (9,600) of its population to emigration (Lyons 1973: 149).

8 Conradh na Gaeilge activists were deeply suspicious of Muintir na Gaeltachta. They distrusted the socialist leanings of leaders Máirtín Ó Cadhain and Seán Ó Coisdeala. Muinter na Gaeltachta ran a candidate in the 1935 general election, though this candidate failed to win a seat.

9 Department of Justice files in the Irish National Archives indicate that An Garda Siochána (Irish police) was monitoring the activities of Muintir na Gaeltachta closely. During the 1935 by-election in Connemara, scuffles broke out between Fianna Fáil activists and members of the organisation (File No. JUS 8/414; JUS 8/200).

10 In 1969, Bernadette Devlin, one of the leaders of the Northern Ireland CRM (NICRA) visited the Connemara Gaeltacht. Her visit received huge coverage in the local and national media and she was treated as a celebrity. Seosamh Ó Cuaig, a Gaeltacht journalist, forged links with NICRA after this visit and the Gaeltacht CRM subsequently adopted much of the rhetoric and tactics of the Northern movement (Arthur 1974: 21–51).

11 The Gaeltacht CRM originally aimed to change the political and economic position of the Gaeltacht as well as providing a radio station. The movement's initial programme included a demand for an independent planning and development authority for the Gaeltacht. However, as the radio campaign became more successful, these broader political aims disappeared from the movement's agenda. For further discussion see Hourigan (2001). RTÉ stands for Raidio Telifís Éireann, the state broadcasting corporation which controlled all national television and radio at the time. The organisation employs a large number of Gaeilgóirí.

12 Sean Ó Tuairisc, quoted in the Evening Press, 25 February 1971, p. 7.

13 Only one Gaeltacht activist was employed in the newly launched service. He describes the interview process: 'I wasn't a Gaeltacht person. I was a supporter. Saying that you were interested in the Gaeltacht was not what they wanted to hear. I mentioned the name of a well-known Gaeilgóir who was a friend of the family and that was enough': Michael Healy, former Gaeltacht civil rights activist, interviewed 8 April 1995, Limerick.

14 Despite the failure of Gaeltacht activists to achieve the exact type of service required, Coleman (2003) argues that RnaG subsequently became a tool in the mainstreaming of the local Gaeltacht perspective in the public sphere. He states: 'the case of Raidio

na Gaeltachta – a local station with national and international reach – shows that perhaps the local is not merely a geographical entity; locality is not a physical container for people but a wider set of concrete social relationships' (*ibid*: 184).

15 This tactic was used in order to force state authorities to summon activists to court where they outlined their grievance regarding the lack of Irish on television to the waiting press (Hourigan 1998). Activists would read excerpts from the Government's own broadcasting legislation outlining its commitment to the Irish language and its failure to meet these stated aspirations. A number of high-profile activists, including a mother of thirteen, were jailed as a result of these court appearances, a relatively repressive state response which would have been unthinkable just ten years earlier.

16 Republican activists were also withholding license fee payments in order to highlight the injustices in the way in which Section 31 of the Broadcasting Act was being applied to republican organisations.There was a degree of overlap between republican and Irish language circles and this boosted the numbers protesting in both campaigns. For instance in 1983, Sinn Féin's Lucilita Breathnach could cite both the treatment of the Irish language on RTÉ and Section 31 as reasons for non-payment of her license fee: *Inniu*, 14 October 1983, p. 1.

17 Leader Peader Mac an Iomaire became the Irish language officer for National University of Ireland, Galway. Seosamh Ó Cuaig and Ruairi Ó Tuairisc began working at the national broadcaster RTÉ. A number of other members went to work for the Gaeltacht development authority Údarás na Gaeltachta. For further discussion see Ó Glaisne (1982). Colm Ó Donnacha subsequently ran as a Workers' Party candidate in Galway West. Seosamh Ó Tuairisce became a manager for Údarás na Gaeltachta. Michael Healy became CEO of Aisling Microsystems, a technology company. Piarás Ó Gaora went on to work for the Irish Press Group.

18 Quoted in Watson (2003).

19 Former Conradh President Prionsias Mac Aonghusa was consulted closely by Taoiseach Charles Haughey. He proposed that the service be located near Dublin rather than in the large Galway Gaeltacht of Connemara. This suggestion was greeted with such public derision that he was excluded from all further deliberations.

20 For further discussion on how destructive competition between these two groups was see Hourigan (1998, 2001).

Bibliography

Abercrombie, N., Hill, S. and Turner, B., 1994 *Dictionary of Sociology* (London: Penguin).

Akutagawa, M., 1989 'The State and a Linguistic Minority: the case of the Irish Gaeltacht with specific reference to Connemara', PhD thesis, Trinity College Dublin.

Andrews, K., 2001 'Social Movements and Policy Implementation: the Mississippi civil rights movement and the war on poverty, 1965–1971', *American Sociological Review*, 66:1, 21–48.

Arthur, P., 1974 *The People's Democracy* (Belfast: Blackstaff Press).

Banaszak, L.A., 1996 *Why Movements Succeed or Fail: Opportunity, culture, and the struggle for women's suffrage* (Princeton, NJ: Princeton University Press).

Blumer, H., 1951 'The Field of Collective Behaviour', in McClung Lee, A.(ed.), *New Outline Principles in Sociology* (New York: Barnes & Noble).

Bourdieu, P., 1986 'The Forms of Capital', in Richardson, J.G. (ed.), *Handbook of Theory and Research for the Sociology of Education* (New York: Greenwood Press), pp. 241–58.

Brown, T., 1991 *Ireland: A social and cultural history 1922–1985* (London: Fontana Press).

Burstein, P., 1999 'Social Movements and Public Policy', in Giugni, M., McAdam, D. and Tilly, C. (eds), *How Social Movements Matter* (Minneapolis: University of Minnesota Press), pp. 3–21.

Burstein, P., Einwohner, R.L. and Hollander, J.A., 1995 'The Success of Political Movements: a bargaining perspective', in Jenkins, J.C. and Klandermans, B. (eds), *The Politics of Social Protest* (Minneapolis: University of Minnesota and London: UCL Press), pp. 275–95.

Castells, M., 1996 *The Information Age*, vol. 1: *The Rise of the Network Society* (Oxford: Blackwell).

Cohan, A., 1979 'The Open Coalition in a Closed Society: The strange pattern of government formation in Ireland' *Comparative Politics* 11: 44–65.

Coleman, J., 1990 *Foundations of Social Theory* (Cambridge, MA: Bellknap Press).

Coleman, S., 2003 'The Centralised Government of Liquidity: community, language and culture under the Celtic Tiger', in Coulter, C. and Coleman, S. (eds), *The End of Irish History: Critical reflections on the Celtic Tiger* (Manchester: Manchester University Press), pp. 175–91.

Della Porta, D. and Diani, M., 1999 *Social Movements: An introduction* (Oxford: Blackwell).

Diani, M., 1997 'Social Movements and Social Capital: a network perspective on movement outcomes', *Mobilisation*, 2:2: 129–47.

Eder, K., 1996 'The Institutionalisation of Environmentalism: ecological discourse and the second transformation of the public sphere', in Lash, S., Bszerszynski, B. and Wynne, B. (eds), *Risk, Environment and Modernity* (Thousand Oaks, CA, and London: Sage).

Gamson, W., 1975 *The Strategy of Social Protest* (Homewood, IL: Dorsey).

Giugni, M., 1998 'Introduction: social movements and change', in Giugni, M., McAdam, D. and Tilly, C. (eds), *From Contention to Democracy* (Lanham, MD: Rowman & Littlefield).

Giugni, M., 1999 'Introduction: how social movements matter', in Giugni, M., McAdam, D. and Tilly, C. (eds), *How Social Movements Matter* (Lanham, MD: Rowman & Littlefield).

Giugni, M., McAdam, D. and Tilly, C. (eds), 1998 *From Contention to Democracy* (Lanham, MD: Rowman & Littlefield).

Giugni, M., McAdam, D. and Tilly, C. (eds), 1999 *How Social Movements Matter* (Lanham, MD: Rowman & Littlefield).

Hindley, R., 1990 *The Death of the Irish Language* (London: Routledge).

Hourigan, N., 1998 'Framing Processes and the Celtic Television Campaigns', *Irish Journal of Sociology*, 8, 49–70.

Hourigan, N., 2001 'A Comparison of the Campaigns for Raidio na Gaeltachta and TnaG', *Irish Sociological Research Monographs*, 1 (Maynooth: National University of Ireland).

Hourigan, N., 2003 *Escaping the Global Village: Media, language, and protest* (Lanham, MD Lexington Books).

Howell, W.R., 1992 'Minority Language Broadcasting and the Continuation of Celtic Culture in Wales and Ireland', in Riggins, S. (ed.), *Ethnic Minority Media* (London: Sage).

Jenkins, C., 1983 'Resource Mobilisation and the Study of Social Movements', *Annual Review of Sociology*, 9, 527–53.

Knoke, D., 1990 *Political Networks: The structural perspective* (Cambridge: Cambridge University Press).

Kriesi, H., Koopmans, R., Duyvendak, J. and Giugni, M. (eds), 1995 *New Social Movements in Western Europe* (Minneapolis: University of Minnesota Press).

Lash, S. and Urry, J., 1987 *The End of Organised Capitalism* (Cambridge: Polity Press).

Lee, J., 1989 *Ireland 1912–1985: Economics and society* (Cambridge: Cambridge University Press).

Lyons, F., 1973 *Ireland since the Famine* (London: Fontana).

MacAodh, B., 1969 *Galway Gaeltacht Survey* (Galway: Social Science Research Centre, University College Galway).

MacAonghusa, P., 1993 *Ar Son na Gaeilge: Conradh na Gaeilge 1893–1993* (Dublin: Conradh na Gaeilge).

McCarthy, J.D. and Zald, M.N., 1973 *The Trend of Social Movements in America: Professionalization and resource mobilisation* (New York: General Learning Press).

McCarthy, J.D. and Zald, M.N., 1977 'Resource Mobilisation and Social Movements: a partial theory', *American Journal of Sociology*, 30, 1212–41.

Melucci, A., 1984 'An End of Social Movement?', *Social Science Information*, 23, 819–35.

Melucci, A., 1989 *Nomads of the Present: Social movements and individual needs in contemporary society* (Philidelphia, PA: Temple University Press).

Melucci, A. and Lyyra, T., 1998 'Collective Action, Change and Democracy', in Giugni, M., McAdam, D. and Tilly, C.(eds), *From Contention to Democracy* (Lanham, MD: Rowman & Littlefield), pp. 203–28.

Michels, R., 1959 *Political Parties* (New York: Dover).

Mullan, C. and Cox, L., 2004 'Social Movements Never Died: community politics and the social economy of the Irish Republic', available: www.toolsforchange.ie (6 October).

Ó Brudair, A., 1971 'Forbairt Eacnamuil sa Ghaeltacht', *Comhar*, 4, 5–7.

Ó Fearail, T., 1975 *The Story of the Gaelic League* (Dublin: Conradh na Gaeilge)

Ó Glaisne, R., 1982 *Raidio na Gaeltachta* (Indreabhán: Clá Cois Fharraige).

Ó Murchú, M., 1973 'Raidio na Gaeltachta agus an Eisteoir', *Comhar*, 3, 15.

Ó Riagain, P., 1997 *Language Policy and Social Reproduction: Ireland 1893–1993* (Oxford: Oxford University Press).

Ó Riain, S., 1984 *Pleanáil Teanga in Éirinn* (Dublin: Institutuid Teangolaiocht na hÉireann).

Parsons, T., 1964 'Evolutionary Universals in Society', *American Sociological Review*, 29, 339–57

Putnam, R., 1993 *Making Democracy Work: Civic traditions in modern Italy* (Princeton, NJ: Princeton University Press).

Rucht, D., 1992 'Studying the Effects of Social Movements: conceptualisations and problems', paper presented at the ECPR Joint Sessions, Limerick.

Schussman, A., 2002 'Movement Outcomes: a review and agenda', CBSM Prelim., question no. 4, Conference of the American Sociological Association, 11 October.

Simmel, G., 1955 *Conflict and the Web of Group Affiliations* (New York: Free Press).

Smelser, N., 1962 *Theory of Collective Behaviour* (New York: Free Press).

Tarrow, S., 1998 'Social Protest and Policy Reform: May 1968 and the Loi d'Orientation in France', in Giugni, M., McAdam, D. and Tilly, C. (eds), *From Contention to Democracy* (Lanham, MD: Rowman & Littlefield), pp. 31–56.

Touraine, A., 1971 *The Post-Industrial Society* (New York: Random House).

Touraine, A., 1981 *The Voice and the Eye: An analysis of social movements* (Cambridge: Cambridge University Press).

Watson, I., 1996 'The Irish Language and Television: national identity, preservation, restoration and minority rights', *British Journal of Sociology*, 47:2, 255–74.

Watson, I., 2003 *Broadcasting in Irish: Minority language, radio, television and identity*

(Dublin: Four Courts Press).

Weber, M., 1964 *Theory of Social and Economic Organisation* (Glencoe, IL: Free Press).

Zald, M.N. and Ash, R., 1966 'Social Movement Organizations: growth, decay and change', *Social Forces*, 44, 327–40.

Zald, M.N. and McCarthy, J.D. (eds), 1979 *The Dynamics of Social Movements* (Cambridge, MA: Winthrop).

7 • *Gerard Mullally*

Relocating protest: globalisation and the institutionalisation of organised environmentalism in Ireland?

IN THE twilight of the twentieth century organised environmentalism in Ireland, as elsewhere in Europe, went through significant transformations. In the 1970s, we witnessed the mass mobilisations of the nuclear movement and the extension of a critical focus to the model of industrial development pursued by the Irish State. In the 1980s, we saw the development of a plethora of local environmental groups and, towards the end of that decade, the emergence of national organisations that arguably contributed to placing *the environment* on the national agenda. Throughout the 1990s, the State adjusted its former position of marginalising environmental concern to adopting various stances of accommodation. During the same period a 'modern and coherent national environmental policy' was put in place (OECD 2000). Recently, there has been a growing emphasis on the role of public participation and policy consultation in official discourse on environmental policies and programmes largely under the sway of international agreements and European legislation.

A recurring feature of this emerging trend is a particular emphasis on the potential role of environmental non-governmental organisations (NGOs) in moving towards sustainable development (DoELG 2002). What then have the consequences been for what is generically understood as the environmental movement in Ireland? Despite the near ubiquity of the definition of the concept of sustainable development as 'development that meets the needs of the present without compromising the ability of future generations to meet their own needs' (World Commission on Environment and Development 1987: 46) it remains an essentially contested concept open to interpretation, negotiation and debate. As such the discursive space created has helped 'to loosen entrenched positions and reshape the debate' (McNeill cited in Lightfoot and Burchell 2005: 77). Nevertheless, it is not enough to simply focus on what is being said. Any analysis must also include 'the institutional context in which this is done and which co-determines what can be said meaningfully' (Hajer 1995: 2).

The institutional domain is centrally important here since we are talking about the de-institutionalisation and re-institutionalisation of environmental discourses in contemporary societies and the kinds of social projects which are being furthered under the flag of environmental protection (Hajer 1996: 261). Social movements are not just about changing discourses and culture, but about trying to ensure that their arguments become an effective part of public discourse used by concrete actors in practical situations (Meaderis 2004). As concepts like sustainable development emerge – not just as the rhetorical talisman of global environmental discourse, but as the touchstone for specific government policy programmes and initiatives – what are the choices facing social movement organisations? How have environmental organisations responded to these choices? What has been the implication for environmental organisations that must contend not only with the greening of erstwhile opponents but the charge levelled by a new wave of activism that sees established organisations as part of the problem, rather than offering a solution to the environmental crisis? What happens when, rather than struggle to place issues on the public agenda, movements have to struggle for a stake in the discourse? Do protest, dissent, contestation and critique simply disappear by virtue of being included in politics?

Cultural politics, social movements and globalisation

In a recent essay on the application of political sociology to the Irish context, J. Paddy O'Carroll (2003), points to a situation of widespread fundamental social change wherein globalisation and culture change have created new societal configurations in work, consumerism, lifestyle and the growth of social movements. Although he identifies many different factors that contribute to contemporary social change, e.g. developments in technological innovation, in means of communication and mass media, he pays particular attention to the role of economic globalisation and the growth of global environmental movements in moving conceptions of politics beyond the State to being a potential feature of all social relations. In such a context, he argues that we need to pay much closer attention to the notion of politics as the contestation of cultures.

O'Carroll both invokes and reflects the impact of a broader cultural turn in social theory which latterly has been picked up in the 'new' political sociology. Nash, for example, points out that social movements theory has widely recognised that social movements are engaged in cultural politics 'contesting dominant understandings of events, institutions and their positioning in relation to others in order to construct an oppositional collective identity' (2001: 86). The notion of cultural and political contestation is central to many definitions of social movements. For example, social movements can be defined as 'a sustained and self-conscious challenge to authorities or cultural codes by a field of actors (organisations and advocacy networks) some of whom employ extra-institutional means of influence' (Gamson and Meyer 1996: 283). But what can the sociology of social movements tell us about the widespread fundamental social change to which O' Carroll refers? At one end of the spectrum the sociology of social movements can instruct us on emergent mechanisms and the conditions necessary for the unfolding of organised collective action in contemporary society; at the other, it can question the very nature of social and cultural relationships through an immanent critique of social life (Dubet and Lustiger-Thaler 2004: 557). Dubet and Lustiger-Thaler point out that while we are currently witnessing an explosion of cultural and political conflicts in society, political processes and processes of institutionalisation have become more visible and accentuated (*ibid*). The former can be manifested at the visible pole of collective action in the form social protest (e.g. against waste management facilities, particularly incineration). The latter can be seen in the proliferation of institutionalised modes of resolving or, indeed, pre-empting social conflict on contentious environmental issues (e.g. public hearings, 'round tables' and consensus conferences). Social protest here refers to 'the collective action of social movements that are attempting to alter the representation system, public policies, or general relationships between citizens and the state' (Jenkins and Klandermans 1995: 5–6). Protest is of course only one resource among the repertoires of collective action available to contemporary movements, but it is important here because it is often perceived to be a resource under threat by incorporation in conventional political processes and processes of institutionalisation.

The theme of institutionalisation has been a recurrent feature in recent work on globalisation and social movements (Della Porta and Kreisi 1999; Hamel et al. 2001; Minkoff 2004). More importantly for our purposes here, the presence (formal organisational structures and incorporation in state-related mechanisms) or absence (lack of national organisation) of institutionalisation is often seen as an indicator of the failure of Irish environmentalism to effect lasting social change. This chapter proceeds from the assumption that since environmental movements are not reducible to their formal manifestations as environmental NGOs, it makes very little sense to conceive of institutionalisation as a *totalising* process. A more subtle gradation of the processes of institutionalisation and change is therefore warranted.

Environmental movements, institutionalisation and globalisation processes

At a minimum environmental social movements can be defined as broad networks of people and organisations engaged in collective action in the pursuit of environmental benefits (Rootes 1999: 2). If we are to assume with O'Carroll that global environmental movements have contributed to social change in

Ireland, we must address two fundamental questions:

- How durable are the changes brought about the environmental movement?
- Are these effects mostly positive or negative for society and for the movement itself? (Giugni 1999)

Giugni points out that these two questions have often been posed in terms of the institutional impact of movements and their contributions to democracy (1999: xxix). In an earlier essay on the impacts of social movements on social change he makes a distinction between incorporation and transformation as modalities of social change (Giugni 1998).

Incorporation involves a series of interrelated processes including: changes in power relations (participation in interest intermediation processes, institution-alisation of action repertoire, incorporation in political parties); policy changes (incorporation of movement claims in government agendas, legislation and public policies); and incorporation in public discourse (movement claims are taken up by different sectors of society or public opinion) which sees environ-mental movements or part of them being incorporated within existing institutional arrangements without fundamentally transforming the rules of the game (Giugni 1998: xviii). In contrast, *transformation* means that 'the basic rules of the game or principles of order that characterise a society at a given point in time are transformed' (Giugni 1998: xix). Whereas incorporation tends to be linked to reform-oriented movements demanding policy changes, transforma-tion tends to be linked to revolutionary social movements demanding fundamental social change. In either case, institutional change is not just confined to state or political institutions but may also impact on a social and cultural level (Giugni 1999). The difficulty, however, is one that is well estab-lished in the social movements' literature: namely the problem of establishing a causal link between the public claims and actions of social movements and the eventual outcomes, in both the short and the long term (Tarrow 1994; Tilly 1999). Tilly points out that influences outside the public claims and actions of social movements have a bearing on their contribution to social change (*ibid*: 269). One influence that has attracted increasing attention of late is that of glob-alisation (O'Carroll 2003).

At the same time as many movements have become institutionalised in their national contexts, processes of globalisation have prompted increasing mobili-sation beyond the nation state (Minkoff 2004: 294). This has drawn increasing attention to the impacts of globalisation on and for social movements, creating both new possibilities and new constraints on collective action (Della Porta and Kreisi 1999; Hamel et al. 2001). Hamel et al., for example, suggest that globali-sation, from a social movement perspective, might best be understood as 'a metaphor for a specific body of actions, beyond territorial borders, and the manner in which they become institutionalised, seek institutionalisation or strategically avoid it' (2001: 2). The implication in much of the recent literature is that, in addition to changing the contexts in which social movements operate, globalisation may well be changing social movements themselves. However, as Mol has pointed out in his recent review of the contemporary global environmental movement, the impacts of globalisation processes are historically shaped and contextual, and will be determined by the outcome of social and political struggles (2000: 123). As such, it is important to briefly consider recent Irish scholarship on globalisation before addressing its relevance for Irish environmentalism.

Globalisation and social change in Ireland

Hamel et al. contend that whatever way we understand globalisation, its constant evocation indicates that it has become a powerful metaphor for 'societies in flux and transformation' (2001: 1–3). The experience of globalisation in Irish society can be seen in, and at least partially related to, the transformation of the Irish economy through the 1990s commonly referred to as the 'Celtic Tiger'. Coulter, citing Irish historian J.J. Lee, captures the exuberance associated with this economic transformation in the assertion that the Republic of Ireland had moved from being 'a carthorse to a thoroughbred' in global terms (Lee quoted in Coulter 2003: 3). Meanwhile, the literature on economic globalisation and the Celtic Tiger has been joined by a growing corpus of critical reflection on cultural, social and political aspects of globalisation in Ireland (Kirby 2002; Kirby, Gibbons and Cronin 2002; Coulter and Coleman 2003). In general the Irish sociological literature on globalisation has transcended the notion of 'the global as active and dynamic' in contrast to a 'local seen as a passive and tradition-bound place' (Munck 2003: 87). Yet, much of the available Irish literature on environmental movements, politics and protest retains a narrow view of globalisation as economic. Economic globalisation is seen as the harbinger of environmental protest, whether it is interpreted as a local reaction to the impact of a globalising economy (Curtin and Varley 1995) or as local community opposition to the hazards of globalisation (Allen 2004). The idea that 'local place-bound communities are simply lost in the whirlwind of globalisation' (Fagan 2003), however, risks foreclosing a more constructive relationship between global and local discourse and action. Moreover, it obscures the fact that many of the protests, campaigns and organisations that together constitute Irish environmentalism have had globalising tendencies of their own. Irish groups and organisations have had formal and informal organisational linkages with transnational environmental NGOs, have been part of global networks and have been active on the global stage in trying to move the sustainable development agenda forward (Garavan 2003; Davies 2005).

When reading some accounts of the Irish environmental movement, one could be forgiven for seeing environmentalism in terms of failure: failure to effect *enough* change in environmental regulation (Taylor 2001); failure to mobilise a movement on a national level (Curtin and Varley 1995); or, more recently, failure to protect local communities from the adverse effects of globalisation (Allen 2004). In the case of the latter, institutionalised manifestations of environmentalism in the form of environmental NGOs are seen as distanced from any immanent cultural critique that was carried in former popular and more radical expressions of environmental protest (Allen 2004). Irish environmentalism has variously been characterised as nebulous (Baker 1990), rational but inchoate (O'Neill 1997) and doomed to failure (Allen 2004). Giugni identifies at least three implicit dangers in using the language of failure (and success) when analysing social movements:

1 it assumes that movements are homogenous entities;
2 while there may be objective indicators of success and failure, these are frequently assessed subjectively; and,
3 it over-determines the role of intentionality in relation to outcomes while underplaying the role of unintended consequences (Giugni 1999: xx–i).

Despite the conclusion that Irish environmentalism is somehow a failed entity, several commentators have noted both the persistence of environmental protest and its proliferation over the last decade or so rather than its decline (Mac Sheoin 1999; Taylor 2001; Tovey 2003; Allen 2004). Tovey (2003) has suggested that we might seek explanations for the persistence of protest within changes that have taken place in environmental politics over the last decade, rather than simply in the failure of the environmental movement. To do this we need to locate environmentalism both conceptually and historically by examining the available academic literature; situate contemporary collective action on the environment in the transformation of Irish environmentalism and the transformed context in which it now exists; and explore the nature of its engagement with the processes of globalisation by examining the *cultural politics* of waste in Ireland today.

Locating Irish environmentalism

There is now a small but growing body of literature in Irish social science on environmental politics and protests in the disciplines of sociology, anthropology, political science and different facets of cultural, social and political geography. The field, not surprisingly, is far from unified. Although some of the available literature explicitly begins from within a social movement idiom (Baker 1990; Tovey 1992, 1993; Yearly 1995), by and large, work on different facets of Irish environmentalism tends to be dispersed in fragments across a multitude of other concerns and topics. There is, however, some consensus among different commentators that Irish environmentalism stemmed not so much from the student and counter-cultural movements of the 1960s like their counterparts in Europe and America (Baker 1990; Tovey 1992, 1993; Allen 2004). With the exception of one evaluation that placed environmental social movement organisations at the centre of its analysis (Yearly 1995), Irish environmentalism tends to be perceived as an overwhelmingly local phenomenon based on the historical pattern of mobilisation and protest in environmental controversies. Furthermore, Irish environmentalism tends to be understood primarily as a reaction to the encroachment of external forces: initially as a particular example of dependent development (Baker 1990), and more recently as a response to economic globalisation (Allen 2004).

A seminal contribution to the literature comes from a sociologist who suggested that historically there have been two environmental movements in Ireland (Tovey 1992, 1993). The first is the conservation movement, represented by national organisations like An Taisce – the National Trust, but also made up of academics and experts in the field of environmental management. Tovey labels this 'official environmentalism' because of the recognition afforded to conservation discourse and latterly heritage discourse by the State, and the adaptation of some of its priorities into state policies and programmes. On the other hand, she identifies 'populist environmentalism', which articulates a radical critique of the State's development policy, which she links to one-off siting controversies predominantly located in rural Ireland. This radical strand tends to retain a protest orientation and adopt an oppositional stance to the State (Tovey and Share 2000). This distinction has subsequently been read as a dichotomy between *all* formal environmental organisations (environmental NGOs), and local community-based activism (Allen 2004). It also resonates with a similar distinction in the literature on Irish community politics between 'integrationist' and 'oppositional' tendencies in community development (Curtin and Varley 1995). What these classifications have in common is that they rely on the degree of incorporation of movements within the apparatus of State, and their institutionalisation as formal organisations as a clear faultline within Irish environmentalism. This suggests a definitive division between ideological and strategic orientations in Irish environmentalism that is deeply embedded, enduring and absolute. In contrast, social movement scholarship has shown the modern social movement to be 'a fluid social phenomenon subject to change through institutional pressures, popular innovation and a host of other evolutionary pressures' (McAdam 1998: 229).

The dichotomy between official and populist environmentalism has to a large extent been overtaken by empirical events such as the growing influence of environmental NGOs, like Greenpeace, Friends of the Earth and the Irish Green

Party in the 1980s and 1990s. These organisations are neither official environmentalists (in the strict sense of Tovey's classification (i.e. conservationists), but they are organised formally. Nor indeed are they populist environmentalists (they are not community-based), but at times could be considered radical and oppositional. By the same token it does not adequately account for the emergence of formal organisations out of single-issue campaigns and their persistence over time at the local and regional levels, e.g. Cork Environmental Alliance, Cork Harbour Alliance for a Safe Environment, Foyle Basin Council (Derry and Donegal). In contemporary Irish environmentalism – where (1) individuals have multiple memberships in different environmental organisations; (2) individuals, groups and organisations participate in a diversity of temporary coalitions (the Network of Irish Environment and Development Organisations, Irish Coalition for Sustainability, Earth Summit Ireland); (3) formal organisations join community-based groups in issue-based networks (Zero Waste Ireland); (4) members of environmental and conservation organisations participate in decentralised campaign networks (Friends of the Irish Environment); and organisations like FEASTA: the Foundation for the Economics of Sustainability that transcend all of the above but eschew the label of campaigning organisation or protest group (Garavan 2003) – it makes very little sense to trade in binary distinctions.

Tovey has of course recognised this, and suggested that by 1990 there were already tentative indications of 'a process of re-composition and redrawing of boundaries within Irish environmentalism in general' (1993: 427). Recently, she has offered a more expansive description of Irish environmentalism, indicating a considerably diversified movement containing everything, from the more spiritual dimensions of environmentalism contained in deep ecology to single-issue conflicts over resource use, and involving actors as diverse as officials in government departments and agencies, 'eco-warriors', Green Party activists and the spokespersons of leading environmental organisations (Tovey and Share 2000). These developments are broadly in line with transformations in environmental activism identified in the broader European and global environmental movements (Rootes 1999; Mol 2000).

There are, however, other reasons why the *two environmentalisms'* distinction is best treated as a historically valid, but potentially limited classification in the current situation. Firstly, analysts examining the incorporation of social movement actors in institutional arrangements, e.g. partnerships, tend to focus on exposing the underlying operation of power and illusion as if citizens or social movement actors are not able to understand their own actions. Movements 'contest institutional networks which they contribute to, while using them not only as resources but also as conflictual forms of action' (Maheu cited in Tovey 1999: 46). Therefore, institutional participation may not be the most accurate gauge of radicalism or moderation. Secondly, as research on the Irish community development sector has shown, overdrawing these types of distinction can obscure the fact that movement organisations have the capacity to work through official channels, while remaining critical of their operation and the underlying power relations that sustain them (Powell and Geoghegan 2004). Thirdly, research on Irish environmentalism in the twenty-first century suggests that more radical forms of activism are more likely to find expression in the personal experiences of individuals than in formal organisations contesting the public sphere (Garavan 2003). These forms of activism are to be found in the 'hedge schools' of activist networks (Rogers 1998) and the 'hidden discourses' of movement milieu (Cox 1999), which transcend and are irreducible to particular formal organisations (Garavan 2003).

The final, and most important reason, however, is that adequate attention has not been given to the argument that the two environmentalisms' distinction was designed to sustain – that Irish environmentalism is best understood as a cultural politics of national identity, a contest regarding changes in Irish society carried in environmental debates (Tovey 1992, 1993). As such, the key argument of conservation in Ireland has tended to follow a storyline of cultural modernisation, which acts as a corrective to the official storyline of economic modernisation by re-balancing the relationship between nature and society through management and education. In contrast, the key storyline of populist environmentalism lies in a critical response to the failure of the official storyline of economic nationalism and independence, and is carried in a discourse of dependent development. However, the negotiation of identities carried through environmental debates is not taking place in isolation, because since the early 1990s it has increasingly been implicated in the global debate on sustainable development.

Situating Irish environmentalism

In the Irish literature, conservation environmentalism has been treated as both distinct and distant from more populist and political manifestations of environmentalism (Baker 1990; Tovey 1992, 1993). The explanation offered for this division is linked to the social and cultural basis and concerns of conservation organisations, the campaigns and issues they have adopted (or not adopted) historically and, at times, the perceived moderation of their approach.

Between integration and opposition?

Conservation environmentalism in Ireland is made up of a variety of organisations including Coastwatch Ireland, Conservation Volunteers Ireland, Crann (trans. tree), ECO, Irish Peatland Conservation Council, to name but a few. An Taisce – the National Trust for Ireland – is, however, the most publicly recognisable face of conservation environmentalism.

The key emphasis of An Taisce throughout much of its history has been on consensus and cooperation, scientific argumentation and informed persuasion (Mullally 1998). Nevertheless, in spite of the orientation to institutional modes of action, it should not be forgotten that the organisation emerged from an early example of environmental conflict in Ireland, has been active historically in many of the key environmental controversies of the 1980s and 1990s, and is actively engaged in many of the formal and informal environmentalist networks that exist today.

The origins of the organisation lie in a conflict over controversial plans to establish a tourist resort on North Bull Island in Dublin, which was the first legally established bird sanctuary in Ireland. It was within the context of this conflict that the need for a dedicated conservation organisation was identified, and the demand for the formation of An Taisce emerged. From the period of its foundation in 1948 until the 1960s, An Taisce played a somewhat ambiguous role in Irish public life, but in the early 1960s the organisation was given strong institutional footing when it was included as a 'prescribed body' under the Local Government (Planning and Development) Act 1963. This status was something of a mixed blessing for An Taisce: at the national level, it enhanced the status of the organisation, giving its activities a legitimacy and a unique position among environmental NGOs; at a local level, it has led to public opposition to An Taisce and its activities (Meldon 1997: 43).

In Tovey's account, populist environmentalism is distinct not only from conservation environmentalism, but also from popular expressions of environmentalism elsewhere in Europe. Similarly, it has been argued that the success of the Irish anti-nuclear movement in defeating the introduction of civil nuclear power into Ireland in the 1970s is 'attributable to its ability to draw on and exploit aspects of traditional culture', such as religious belief and Irish neutrality (Tovey and Share 2000: 460). While this is accurate, the anti-nuclear movement was the context in which early manifestations of organised environmentalism and countercultural manifestations of deep ecology were encountered (Baker 1990).

The nuclear debate, centred largely on the opposition to the proposal to build a nuclear power station in Carnsore, Co. Wexford, was the context in which international environmental organisations like Friends of the Earth and Greenpeace became active in Irish environment politics and protest (Baker 1990). One of the key factors distinguishing An Taisce from these newly arrived environmental organisations was the stance the organisation adopted, broadly welcoming civil nuclear power. Yet, at the same time, An Taisce was among the first to challenge the industrial policies of the Irish State on environmental grounds at local level, and were central to fostering demand for a national environmental policy (Allen and Jones 1990). Allen and Jones provide an extensive catalogue of the environmental conflicts and protests of the 1970s and 1980s, documenting community-based opposition to the states industrial development policies. However, alongside intermittent and dispersed local protests, a number of organisations began to emerge as a significant component of Irish environmentalism during a period of high-profile mobilisation (Allen and Jones 1990; Baker 1990).

From populism to professional environmentalism?

The transnational pharmaceutical industry was one among several sectors (chemicals, mining and electronics) to arrive in Ireland subsequent to the Irish State's development strategy of attracting foreign direct investment. The environmental consequences of industrial modernisation became an important theme in a series of grassroots mobilisations against proposed developments by multinational companies, such as Merrell Dow and Sandoz in Cork, Du Pont in Derry and, later, Roche in Clare (Allen 2004). Key campaigns certainly built upon the elements of the cultural tool-kit of populist environmentalism, e.g. family and community, but they also contributed to the extension of both the symbolic and strategic repertoire of Irish environmentalism.

Kitschelt identifies a clear division in movement structures between groups fighting particular projects and facilities and 'efforts to develop and legislate long term environmental policies and that take into account the temporal and substantive complexity of the subject matter' (1993: 26). The experience and the aftermath of the Irish anti-nuclear movement had provided a fruitful context for the emergence of formal professional campaign organisations like Earthwatch (Friends of the Earth Ireland, originally Help Organise Peaceful Energy), Greenpeace Ireland, and even the creation of an Irish Green Party (Baker 1990). Meanwhile, local single-issue campaigns persisted beyond the immediate focus of their concerns and formed into the corpus of an indigenous environmental NGO sector. Taken together, these diverse elements came to constitute a particular type of environmentalism that has been labelled the 'Irish anti-toxics movement' (Baker 1990).

The cumulative picture of the level of environmental protest in the period from the late 1980s into the 1990s, derived from both activist accounts and media analyses, shows an upsurge of protest after a period of relative abeyance in the mid-1980s (Allen and Jones 1990; Mullally 1995; Mac Sheoin 1999). Between 1988 and 1993, there were a number of high-profile environmentalist mobilisations, particularly in the South-West, the West and the North-West of Ireland. These included the campaigns against proposed pharmaceutical facilities in the Republic of Ireland, largely concentrated around Cork Harbour (Baker 1990: Peace 1993, 1998); the development of an interpretative centre in the Burren, in Co. Clare; and the siting of a national toxic-waste incinerator on the Donegal–Derry border in Northern Ireland (Jordan and Gilbert 1999).

Progressively, through the 1980s, there was an increase in the level of formalisation within the environmental social movement sector in Ireland, though we should be careful not to reduce organisational evolution over the period to a crude transition from movement organisations to professional environmental NGOs (Diani and Donati 1999: 25–6). This was not so much an organic evolution of previous mobilisations as it was an attempt to build upon the cultural and political opportunities created in the context of a diverse range of environmental protest actions.

Curtain and Varley point out that the different environmental campaigns in the 1980s and 1990s did not 'comprise a movement in any centrally co-ordinated sense', and could frequently result in division in communities (1995: 394–5). In a strictly formal organisational interpretation, this is certainly true and can be traced through successive failed attempts to unify diverse and fragmented local campaigns through a coordinated national effort (Allen and Jones 1990; Baker 1990). Diani and Donati, note that local protests are not necessarily dependent on, nor coordinated by, central social movement organisations (1999: 25). Gamson and Meyer (1996: 289) suggest that those who create a space in public discourse for new issues and claims-making do not attempt to act as spokespersons; rather, they defer to others who can articulate a shared position without the baggage of accounting for extra-institutional action. Once issues and demands become established in public discourse, however, internal rivalries may re-emerge and undermine such divisions of labour.

Although it is certainly true that tensions between larger professional campaign organisations and local community-based groups have been a persistent feature of movement relationships, there is also some evidence pointing towards a de facto division of labour in Irish environmentalism (Baker 1990). Greenpeace Ireland, for example, operated by supplementing its stable professional core, inert membership and media orientation with a grassroots by proxy, through its involvement in local campaigns. They have been an important catalyst in stimulating coalitions of local groups that subsequently consolidated as formal organisations, e.g. Cork Environmental Alliance (Peace 1998). Many of the central controversies of the period, focused as they were on industries with a high technical component, were conducted within a highly circumscribed legal and scientific discourse (Peace 1993). In the early 1990s, the process of networking between groups such as Greenpeace, Earthwatch, the Irish Women's Environmental Network, Cork Environmental Alliance and An Taisce constituted the basis of a network which allowed Irish environmentalism to build up the capacity to engage in technical debates, while adopting different strategic approaches, ranging from the use of the planning and legal systems to public meetings, lobbying and targeted media campaigns.

A media analysis of environmental issues between 1987 and 1992 indicates an increasing convergence in the public discourse of Irish environmental organisations around the themes of dependent development and the need to modernise the environmental regulatory regime (Mullally 1995). In some respects, this reflects an increased orientation to effecting change by influencing environmental policy by formal organisations, alongside the proliferation of single-issue protests with shorter term goals. What began as a series of localised planning and pollution controversies translated very quickly into questions about democratic decision-making, the locus of political representation, patterns of interest mediation and, perhaps most importantly, the nature of democratic participation. Irish environmentalism was successful in highlighting that, despite the existence of a large body of environmental legislation, there was no coherent national environmental policy and, moreover, that there was an implementation crisis in the area of environmental protection.

The early 1990s also saw an emergent interest in more global issues of sustainable development as many of the organisations active in the anti-toxic movement also began to participate in emergent national networks formed in anticipation of the Earth Summit in Rio de Janeiro in 1992, e.g. the Network of Irish Environment and Development Organisations. Between 1993 and 1995, organisations like Earthwatch, An Taisce and Cork Environmental Alliance increasingly invoked the role ascribed to environmental NGOs in the Earth Summit Agreements to confer legitimacy on their campaigns (Mullally 2001). It is, therefore, reasonable to interpret Irish events in terms of a local reaction to the increased intensity of economic globalisation, while remaining open to the idea that they may also relate positively to wider cultural and political developments in global debates.

Despite the apparent convergence within environmentalism in the early 1990s, renewed attempts at national organisation failed once again. Differences in the organisational cultures and strategic orientations of key organisations may have continued to undermine better coordination within Irish environmentalism. However, the growth of organisational competition and changes in the Irish context leading to the transformation of Irish environmentalism may provide more adequate explanations. The tentative division of labour that emerged in anti-toxic environmentalism was underpinned by a relatively high degree of functional specialisation linked to their national or international campaign structures (in the case of professional organisations), or to the specific issues in local campaigns. If we examine media coverage of environmental issues in Ireland between 1987 and 1992, we gain some insight into the growth of internal competition among environmental organisations. Formal environmental organisations accounted for 9 per cent of the total media coverage on environmental issues over the period, while informal protest networks accounted for a further 4 per cent. What is interesting is that Greenpeace, which dominated the media coverage given to environmental NGOs over the period, was increasingly faced with competition from other environmental organisations for a relatively stable media share. This could simply reflect the increase of environmental NGOs in the late 1980s and early 1990s, but it also indicated a growing propensity for targeted media communication within Irish environmentalism more generally (Mullally 1995). Therefore, having established environmental issues in public discourse, a growing level of internal competition amongst NGOs emerged (Mullally 1995: 48–9; Diani and Donati 1999). In this sense, the *failure* to mobilise nationally may be rooted in the success of establishing environmental issues on the public agenda. However, taken in isolation, this is not an adequate explanation, since the context in which Irish environmentalism was operating was also undergoing a significant transformation.

Allen points out that the critique of the State's industrial policy began to wane in the early 1990s, as the emphasis began to move away from the types of development that had provoked opposition in the previous decade (2004: 20). Mac Sheoin's analysis of protest mobilisations in the 1990s supports this view. Environmental protest through the 1990s shifted from the somewhat integrative focus of anti-toxic environmentalism to an increasingly diversified range of issues centred on indigenous infrastructure developments, particularly in the area of waste management.

Transforming contexts, contextual transformations

The growing formalisation and institutionalisation of Irish environmentalism that had begun in the late 1980s gathered increased momentum in the 1990s. The appearance and consolidation of key environmental NGOs during that period indicates the growing incorporation of environmentalism in society, through the institutionalisation of action repertoires (Giugni 1998). According to Allen (1998), the progressive institutionalisation of the environmental movement in Ireland culminated with the formation of the Green Party in 1988. Was this, as he seems to suggest, the beginning of the end for the Irish environmental movement? Or was it simply the end of the beginning?

Greening politics and policy?

The Irish Green Party has, perhaps more than any other aspect of Irish environmental politics, been the subject of reflection by activists, political scientists and sociologists in Ireland (Farrell 1989; Mullally 1997; O'Neill 1997; Taylor and Flynn 2003). The creation of the Ecology Party of Ireland in 1981 was a conscious decision to access the opportunities opening up on the 'increasingly fluid ground of Irish politics', as coalition governments increasingly appeared to be the norm (O'Neill 1997: 319).

The Irish Green Party's performance in electoral politics could hardly be described as meteoric, with the share of the national vote increasing over two decades from 0.2 per cent in 1982 to 3.8 per cent in 2002. Nevertheless, from the election of the first member of the Dáil in 1989 through to securing six seats in 2002, the Green Party has challenged the perception that it is simply a protest party, and it is now the fourth-largest party in the Dáil (Kennelly and Bradley 2005). Giugni points out that as movement claims are taken up by other sectors of society they become incorporated in public discourse (1998). This observation also rings true in political discourse. For example, in the run-up to the 1989 election, the manifestos of all of the major political parties emphasised the protection of the environment and demanded the creation of a new environmental protection agency. The change in politics was paralleled by a growing demand from the industrial and agricultural policy communities for the modernisation of Irish environmental policy (Taylor 2001). At a more concrete level, the incorporation of movement demands in policy changes followed quickly after the 1989 election. The Fianna Fáil–Progressive Democrat coalition programme for government proposed the creation of a junior ministry for the protection of the environment, and signalled the intention to create an independent environmental protection agency. It is unlikely, however, that the modest success of the Green Party in 1989 had singularly affected these developments; rather it reflected a broader shift in the Irish context. Nonetheless, environmental issues have figured in the political discourse of Irish political parties ever since. The modernisation of Irish environmental policy, however, is best interpreted as the dynamic interaction between local, national and international developments. Politically, it marked the recognition by the Irish Government of a need to accommodate the environmentalist critique of the 1980s, without threatening the free-market ethos that came to underpin the politics of the 'Celtic Tiger' in the 1990s (Taylor 2005).

The decline of organised environmentalism?

If there has been some evidence of a realignment of party politics, as O' Neill suggests, there is even stronger evidence of a realignment within Irish environmentalism. Although always present in the action repertoire of Irish environmentalism, direct action was largely marginalised by more conventional forms of protest action. In the early 1990s, attempts were made to import the direct action strategies of Earth First! to play a more central role in Irish environmentalism but this had little immediate resonance beyond animal rights and animal welfare issues. These types of issues where outside of the campaign structure of larger organisations (Greenpeace Ireland, Earthwatch and An Taisce), and never even approached the scale and intensity of British protests. In the late 1990s, direct action as a strategic orientation enjoyed a brief prominence in protests which largely eschewed formal organisational approaches, e.g. the roads protest in the Glen of the Downs in Co. Wicklow, the anti-pylon campaign in Cobh in Cork, and in the opposition to field trials of Genetically Modified sugar beet. Direct action provided an upcoming generation of activists with an alternative model to the vicarious activism, technical advocacy and scientific argumentation, with which many Irish environmental NGOs had become increasingly associated through the anti-incineration campaigns of the 1980s. The 'new radicals' turned towards direct action in the treetops, among the grassroots, and quite literally went underground by importing the tunnelling tactics used by anti-road protestors in Britain.

Despite a brief surge in direct action protest in 1998, several analyses of protest events indicate that institutionalised modes of acting out conflict and institutionalised modes of interest intermediation remain the dominant forms of action in Irish environmentalism (Mullally 1995; Mac Sheoin 1999; Peillon 2001; Garavan 2003). This does not mean, however, that nothing changed in Irish environmentalism. By 1997, Greenpeace Ireland was closing down, to be replaced by Voice of Concern for the Irish Environment (VOICE); an organisation with a considerably expanded portfolio of campaign issues. In the same year, members of conservation and environmental organisations who wanted to pursue a more active strategy of environmental litigation formed a decentralised campaign organisation called Friends of the Irish Environment. In 1998, FEASTA: the Foundation for the Economics of Sustainability was formed as a network of activists joined together to promote the development of more sustainable world (Garavan 2003). After nearly a decade of campaigning, Cork Environmental Alliance disbanded in 1999, and the remnants of the organisation became affiliated with Friends of the Earth. Whether these new organisations have arisen from disaffection with or the demise of existing organisations, they have tended to build on or, at least, defend the environmental gains of a previous generation of activists. At the same time, more established organisations like An Taisce have recognised the legitimacy of a broader range of roles for environmental NGOs in the Irish context, including direct action (Jeffrey 2001).

Environmentalism incorporated?

The First Environmental Action Programme in 1990 committed the Irish Government to the integration of environmental concerns into all policy areas and to the principle of sustainable development. In the aftermath of the commitments made at the Earth Summit in Rio in 1992, the contemporary debate on sustainable development has shifted away from asserting the existence of an environmental crisis towards 'the nature of environmental responsibility, the predominant focus for that responsibility and the best methods for undertaking it' (Lightfoot and Burchill 2005: 76). Agenda 21 both emphasised the importance of public participation in environmental governance and enjoined environmental NGOs to play a role in moving towards sustainable development

(Mullally 1998). In this context, Irish environmental organisations have been faced with a choice between degrees of selective integration and opposition to participation in interest intermediation channels, which many have sought to resolve by operating on the soft margins of the political system.

By the mid-1990s, with the appearance of new institutional opportunities emerging under the banner of sustainable development, groups like Cork Environmental Alliance had begun to modify their position and re-evaluate the implications of taking an active role in these new arrangements. Earthwatch and An Taisce also began to reposition themselves firmly within the discourse on sustainable development, and become actively involved in partnership projects on waste management and climate change. The period from 1995 onwards provided a seedbed for the emergence of coalitions of environmental organisations and community groups positioning themselves firmly within the discourse on sustainable development. In Cork and Derry, organisations like Cork Environmental Forum and Foyle Basin Council emerged out of the ashes of local incineration conflicts to promote local sustainable development. In other parts of the country, coalitions like Dublin Citizens Agenda 21 and Sustainable Ireland formed to take advantage of perceived opportunities for participation created as part of the Government's implementation of Agenda 21.

The price of participation and partnership has, to an extent, been a demand for institutional isomorphism from more powerful economic and political actors, i.e. the adoption of more formal structures, sectoral representation, peak organisations etc. This has added additional pressures to a social movement sector already characterised by a low level of material resources (Garavan 2003), and structurally weak when compared with its European counterparts (Flynn and Kröger 2003). If anything, the spaces opened up by the discourse of sustainable development have made this problem more acute. For example, at local level environmental groups have been incorporated in some partnership arrangements for sustainable development with local government; at national level in COMHAR the National Sustainable Development Partnership; and at a global level both environmental and community groups were included as part of the Irish Government's delegation to the World Summit on Sustainable Development in Johannesburg in 2002 (Mullally 2004). Meanwhile, the influence of the European Union in Ireland has been reflected in an increased emphasis on public participation and partnership between the State and environmental organisations and community groups (*ibid*).

There is a danger of overstating the degree to which Irish environmentalism has become incorporated in decision-making structures since the 1990s. As some institutional channels for public participation in sustainable development expanded through the 1990s, more conventional routes within the planning and legal system contracted (Mullally and Quinlivan 2004). It has also been argued that sustainable development partnerships operate at a remove from the more decisive setting of neo-corporatist bargaining at the national level (Kennelly and Bradley 2005). The inclusion of environmental NGOs in some partnership structures and their exclusion from others could legitimately be interpreted as reflecting political weakness (Garavan 2003).

Yet, if the purpose of new institutional formations has been to contain environmental controversy and protest in 'theatres of control' (Peace 1993), then they have been a singular failure. The controversy over waste management in Ireland is a case in point. Although the issue of waste and waste management has frequently featured in local environmental controversies, it has become intensely political in the first decade of the new millennium. Fagan (2003) notes that from 2000 to 2001, locals embedded in geographical communities backed by environmental NGOs successfully blocked the development of regional waste management plans.

Irish analyses have variously characterised local protests against waste infrastructure as evidence of the growing individualisation of Irish society, with little connection to wider projects of social transformation, or as examples of not-in-my-back-yard) environmentalism (Taylor 2005). Allen (2004) sees within these protests attempts by local communities to stem the – filthy – tide of globalisation; however, he is equally adamant that they bear little connection to environmental NGOs or global environmentalism. Yet, as Rootes (1999) points out, protesters can develop broader understandings in the course of local controversies and local concerns can become identified with global issues. Fagan argues that far from being about NIMBYism, protesting community groups 'use a discourse of responsibility, of environmentalism, of political rights, while at the same time they develop a multi-scalar political agency' (2003: 80). There is considerably more interaction between formal environmental organisations and local autonomous groups than either conventional wisdom or previous research has acknowledged (Garavan 2003). Furthermore, both local community campaigns and Irish environmental NGOs are becoming increasingly active in international and global environmental networks (Fagan 2003; Garavan 2003; Davies 2005).

Climate change(s): relocating Irish environmentalism

Climate change in this instance refers not to the archetypal global environmental problem, but to changes in the cultural climate, *zeitgeist*, or mood, in which environmentalism operates. The emphasis on climate is essentially about the opening and closing of political space as a result of outside events, or the maturing of internal tensions and contradictions that shake up the working political consensus (Gamson and Meyer 1996). The critique of industrial policy that crystallised as a stark alternative between jobs or the environment in a climate tempered by unemployment, emigration and dependent economic development in the 1980s was successful in levering open a space for environmental issues on the public and political agenda (Coulter 2003). Ironically, successes were achieved by Irish environmental organisations despite a mood of cultural resignation to the politics of failure in 1980s' Ireland, and more environmentally benign forms of development began to feature in both public and policy discourses. As environmental organisations sought to secure a position in the debate on sustainable development through the 1990s, the ground had shifted to sustaining the Celtic Tiger (Taylor 2005). Although there was considerable modernisation of the environmental policy regime in the 1990s, it was by and large unable to keep pace with the rates of change in the economy, both in terms of increased inputs into the environment and increased levels of consumption in Irish society (EPA 2000).

In this context environmental organisations are caught up 'in constant dynamic processes of coalition building with rapidly changing opponents and partners with the aim of maximizing and safeguarding environmental gains' (Mol 2000: 49). Subtle institutional pressures can channel organisations into a limited set of choices for organisational action, and the laws that circumscribe different modes of associational activity can act as additional pressures to take on certain courses of action (Minkoff 2004). This is evidently the case if we accept that there is a certain structural uniformity among formal Irish environmental NGOs (Garavan 2003). Yet, at the same time local protests and NGO campaigns on waste management continue to be played out in the public sphere through the media, while formal channels for statutory consultation are barely used (Davies 2003: 85). 'Environmentalism, in an era of globalisation, supports and stimulates direct horizontal contact between campaigners' through the use of information technology (Fagan 2003: 79). The entanglement of the local and the global in fluid environmentalist networks in the Irish waste debate mirrors the wider transformation of global environmentalism (Rootes 1999; Mol 2000). Fagan sees within this a glimpse of social transformation through the democratisation of knowledge. What the waste debate demonstrates is that this is a fleeting glimpse, a view in microcosm of the wider challenges facing Irish environmentalism. It is worth recalling Mol's observation that the impacts of globalisation on environmentalism will be historically and contextually conditioned and determined by the outcome of specific struggles. Success and failure ebb and flow, and movements and their opponents will adapt accordingly. The locus of political protest has diversified over the last decade or more, as indeed have the institutional contexts in which it is being played out. So too have the formations in which the environmental movement unfolds. Recent scholarship on the waste debate has been valuable in tracing these developments empirically (Boyle 2002; Davies 2003; Fagan 2003). Its real contribution, however, is that it has analysed these events using a cultural politics perspective that takes us beyond making absolutist judgements about the success or failure of Irish environmentalism per se.

Contemporary environmentalism has become entangled in the cultural politics of success in Celtic Tiger Ireland. For the time being, 'jobs versus the environment' has been subsumed in questions of risk, responsibility and public good, as the currency of critical debate and neo-liberalism and sustainable development compete as opposite (though by no means equal) sides of the same globalising dynamic (Boyle 2002; Fagan 2003). In post-exuberant Celtic Tiger Ireland, sweeping pronouncements of the failure of the environmental movement (and therefore its imminent demise) perhaps reflect the current *zeitgeist*, rather than adding anything new to the debate.

Bibliography

Allen, R., 1998 'Tiocfáidh Ar La (Our Day Will Come): pixies reclaiming Ireland', *An Talamh Glas (Green Earth)*, 2:March.

Allen, R., 2004 *No Global: The people of Ireland versus the multi-nationals* (London, Dublin, Sterling, Virginia: Pluto Press).

Allen, R. and Jones, T., 1990 *Guests of the Nation: The people of Ireland versus the multi-nationals* (London: Earthscan).

Baker, S., 1990 'The Evolution of the Irish Ecology Movement', in Rüdig, W. (ed.), *Green Politics One* (Edinburgh: Edinburgh University Press), pp. 47–81.

Boyle, M., 2002 'Cleaning Up After the Celtic Tiger: scalar fixes in the political ecology of Tiger Economies', *Transactions of the Institute of British Geographers*, 27:2, 172–94.

Coulter, C., 2003 'The End of Irish History: an introduction to the book', in Coulter, C. and Coleman, S. (eds), *The End of Irish History? Critical reflections on the Celtic Tiger* (Manchester and New York: Manchester University Press), pp. 1–33.

Coulter, C. and Coleman, S. (eds), *The End of Irish History? Critical reflections on the Celtic Tiger* (Manchester and New York: Manchester University Press).

Cox, L., 1999 'Power, Politics and Everyday Life: the local rationalities of social movement milieux', in Bagguley, P. and Hearn, J. (eds), *Transforming Politics: Power and resistance* (Hampshire: Macmillan Press), pp. 46–66.

Curtin, C. and Varley, T., 1995 'Community action and the State', in Clancy, P., Drudy, S., Lynch, K. and O'Dowd, L. (eds), *Irish Society: Sociological perspectives* (Dublin: Institute of Public Administration), pp. 379–409.

Davies, A.R., 2003 'Waste Wars: public attitudes and the politics of place in waste management strategies', *Irish Geography*, 36:1, 77–92.

Davies, A.R., 2005 'Local Action for Climate Change: transnational networks and the Irish experience', *Local Environment*, 10:1, 21–40.

DoELG (Department of the Environment and Local Government), 2002 *Making Ireland's Development Sustainable* (Dublin: Stationary Office).

Della Porta, D. and Diani, M., 1999 *Social Movements: An introduction* (Oxford and Massachusetts: Blackwell).

Della Porta, D. and Kreisi, H., 1999 'Social Movements in a Globalising World: an introduction', in Della Porta, D., Kreisi, H. and Rucht, D. (eds), *Social Movements in a Globalising World* (Basingstoke and London: Macmillan Press), pp. 3–22.

Diani, M. and Donati, P.R., 1999 'Organisational Change in Western European Environmental Groups: a framework for analysis', in Rootes, C. (ed.), *Local, National and Global Environmental Politics*, special issue of *Environmental Movements*, 8:1, 13–34.

Dubet, F. and Lustiger-Thaler, H., 2004 'Introduction: the sociology of collective action reconsidered', *Current Sociology*, 52:4, 557–73.

EPA, 2000 *Ireland's Environment: A millennium report* (Wexford: Environmental Protection Agency).

Fagan, H.G., 2003 'Sociological Reflections on Governing Waste', *Irish Journal of Sociology*, 12:1, 67–84.

Farrell, D.M., 1989 'Ireland: the Green Alliance', in Müller-Rommell, F. (ed.), *New Politics in Western Europe: The rise and success of green parties and alternative lists* (Boulder, CO: Westview Press), pp. 123–30.

Flynn B. and Kröger, L., 2003 'Can Policy Learning Really Improve Implementation? Evidence from the Irish responses to the Water Framework Directive', *European Environment*, 13, 150–63.

Gamson, W.A. and Meyer, D.S., 1996 'Framing Political Opportunity', in McAdam, D., McCarthy, J.D. and Zald, M.N. (eds), *Comparative Perspectives on Social Movements: Political opportunities, mobilizing structures and cultural framings* (Cambridge: Cambridge University Press), pp. 275–90.

Garavan, M., 2003 'Seeking Transformation Not Confrontation: an overview of the Irish environmental movement', paper presented at the 6th Conference of the European Sociological Association, 23–26 September, Murcia.

Giugni, M., 1998 'Social Movements and Change: incorporation, transformation and democratization', in Giugni, M., McAdam, D. and Tilly, C. (eds), *From Contention to Democracy* (Lanham, MD, Boulder, CO, New York and Oxford: Rowman & Littlefield), pp. xi–xxiv.

Giugni, M., 1999 'How Social Movements Matter: past research, present problems, future developments', in Giugni, M., McAdam, D. and Tilly, C. (eds), *How Social Movements Matter* (Minneapolis and London: University of Minnesota Press), pp. xi–xxxiii.

Hajer, M., 1995 *The Politics of Environmental Discourse: Ecological modernisation and the policy process* (Oxford: Oxford University Press).

Hajer, M., 1996 'Ecological Modernisation as Cultural Politics', in Lash, S., Szerszynski, B. and Wynne, B. (eds), *Risk, Environment and Modernity: Towards a new ecology* (London, Thousand Oaks, CA, and New Dehli: Sage), pp. 246–68.

Hamel, P., Lustiger-Thaler, H., Pieterse J.N. and Roseneil, S., 2001 'The Shifting Frames of Collective Action', in Hamel, P., Lustiger-Thaler, H., Pieterse, J.N. and Roseneil, S. (eds), *Globalization and Social Movements* (Hampshire and New York: Palgrave), pp. 1–18.

Jeffrey, D.W., 2001 'The Roles of Environmental Non-Governmental Organisations in the Twenty-First Century', *Biology and Environment: Proceedings of the Royal Irish Academy*, 101B:1–2, 151–6.

Jenkins, J.C. and Klandermans, B., 1995 'The Politics of Social Protest', in Jenkins, J.C. and Klandermans, B. (eds), *The Politics of Social Protest: Comparative perspectives on states and social movements* (London: UCL Press), pp. 3–13.

Jordan, J and Gilbert, N., 1999 'Think Local, Act Global: discourses of environment and local protest', in Fairweather, N.B., Elworthy, S., Stroh, M. and Stephens, P.H.G. (eds), *Environmental Futures* (Basingstoke and London: McMillan), pp. 39–53.

Kennelly, J.J. and Bradley, F., 2005 'Ireland in the New Century: an opportunity to foster an ethic of sustainable enterprise', *Sustainable Development*, 13, 91–101.

Kirby, P., 2002 *The Celtic Tiger in Distress: Growth with inequality in Ireland* (Hampshire: Palgrave)

Kirby, P., Gibbons, L. and Cronin, M., 2002 *Reinventing Ireland: Culture, society and global economy* (London: Pluto Press).

Kitschelt, H., 1993 'Social Movements, Political Parties and Democratic Theory', in Dalton, R.J. (ed.), *Citizens, Protest and Democracy*, special issue of *Annals of the American Academy of Political and Social Science*, 528, 13–29.

Lightfoot, S. and Burchell, J., 2005 'The European Union and the World Summit on Sustainable Development: normative power Europe in action', *Journal of Common Market Studies*, 33:1, 75–95.

McAdam, D., 1998 'The Future of Social Movements', in Giugni, M., McAdam, D. and Tilly, C. (eds) *From Contention to Democracy* (Lanham, MD, Boulder, CO, New York and Oxford: Rowman & Littlefield), pp. 229–45.

McGrath, B., 1996 'Environmentalism and Property Rights: the Mullaghmore Interpretative Centre dispute', *Irish Journal of Sociology*, 6, 25–47.

Mac Sheoin, T., 1999 'Rural Siting Conflicts in Ireland, 1990–1999', *Irish Journal of Sociology*, 9, 115–20.

Medearis, J., 2004 'Social Movements and Deliberative Democratic Theory', *British Journal of Political Science*, 35, 53–75.

Meldon, J., 1997 'An Taisce and Planning: facing new challenges', *Living Heritage, The Voice of An Taisce: Ireland's Environmental Magazine*, 14:1, 43–4.

Minkoff, D.C., 2004 'Social Movement Politics and Organization', in Blau, J.R. (ed.), *The Blackwell Companion to Sociology* (Oxford: Blackwell), pp. 282–94.

Mol, A.P.J., 2000 'The Environmental Movement in an Era of Ecological Modernisation', *Geoforum*, 31, 45–5.

Mullally, G., 1995 'Entering the Stage: strategies of environmental communication in Ireland', in Eder, K. (ed.), *Framing and Communicating Environmental Issues*, Research Report (Florence: European University Institute–Commission of the European Communities, DGXII).

Mullally, G., 1997 'Treading Softly on the Political System? The Irish Greens in the 1997 general election', *Environmental Politics*, 6:4, 165–71.

Mullally, G., 1998 'Does the Road from Rio Lead Back to Brussels?', in Lafferty, W.M. and Eckerberg, K. (eds), *From the Earth Summit to Local Agenda 21: Working towards sustainable development* (London: Earthscan), pp. 204–37.

Mullally, G., 1999 'Relocating Protest: the institutionalisation of organised environmentalism in Ireland?' paper presented at the 2nd Regional Conference on Social Movements and Change, 'Social Movements in Transition: moving towards the millennium?', Department of Sociology, University College Cork–International Sociological Association, Social Movements, Collective Action and Social Change Research Committee, University College Cork, 16–18 April.

Mullally, G., 2001 'Starting Late: building institutional capacity on the reform of sub-national governance?' in Lafferty, W.M. (ed.), *Sustainable Communities in Europe* (London: Earthscan), pp. 130–52.

Mullally, G., 2004 'Tipping the Scales for Sustainable Development in Ireland: lessons from local and regional Agenda 21', in Lafferty, W.M. and Narodoslawski, M. (eds), *Regional Sustainable Development in Europe: The Challenge of Multi-level Cooperative Governance* (Oslo: ProSus), pp. 90–114.

Mullally, G. and Quinlivan, A., 2004 'Environmental Policy: managing the waste problem', in Collins, N. and Cradden, T. (eds), *Political Issues in Ireland Today* (Manchester: Manchester University Press), pp. 117–34.

Munck, R., 2003 'Debating Globalisation and its Discontents', *Irish Journal of Sociology*, 12:1, 85–97.

Nash, K., 2001 'The "Cultural Turn" in Social Theory: towards a theory of cultural politics', *Sociology*, 35:1, 77–92.

O'Carroll, J.P., 2003 'Aspects of the Changed Political Environment of Applied Social Studies: "you can get there only from here"', in Herrman, P. (ed.), *Between Politics and Sociology* (New York: Nova Science), pp. 121–9.

OECD (Organisation for Economic Cooperation and Development), 2000 *Environmental Performance Reviews: Ireland* (Paris: OECD).

O'Neill, M., 1997 *Green Parties and Political Change in Contemporary Europe: New politics, old predicaments* (Aldershot: Ashgate).

Peace, A., 1993 'Environmental Protest, Bureaucratic Closure: the politics of discourse in rural Ireland', in Milton, K. (ed.), *Environmentalism: The view from anthropology* (London and New York: Routledge), pp. 189–204.

Peace, A., 1998 'Taking on the Transnationals: the politics of an urban environmentalist network in Ireland', *Urban Anthropology*, 27:1, 87–121.

Peillon, M., 2001 'The Constitution of Protest as Sign in Contemporary Ireland', *Irish Political Studies*, 16, 95–110.

Powell, F. and Geoghegan, M., 2004 *The Politics of Community Development: Reclaiming civil society or reinventing governance?* (Dublin: A. & A. Farmar).

Rogers, B., 'Sustainability in the Irish Context', in O'Regan, T. (ed.), 1998 *Landscape Forum Proceedings*, available: www.landscape-forum-ireland.com/proceedings_1998.

Rootes, C., 1999 (ed.), *Environmental Movements: Local, national and global*, special issue of *Environmental Politics*, 8:1.

Tarrow, S., 1994 *Power in Movement: Social movements, collective action and politics* (Cambridge: Cambridge University Press).

Taylor, G., 2001 *Conserving the Emerald Tiger: The politics of environmental regulation in Ireland* (Galway: Arlen Academic).

Taylor, G., 2005 *Negotiated Governance and Public Policy in Ireland* (Manchester and New York: Manchester University Press).

Taylor, G., and Flynn, B., 2003 'It's Green, But Is it of a Light Enough Hue? Past performance, present success and the future of the Irish Greens', in Jordon, A., Würzel, R.K.W. and Zito, A.R. (eds), *'New' Instruments of Environmental Governance? National Experiences and Prospects*, special issue of *Environmental Politics*, 12:1, 225–32.

Tilly, C., 1999 'From Interactions to Outcomes in Social Movements', in Giugni, M. McAdam, D. and Tilly, C. (eds), *How Social Movements Matter* (Minneapolis and London: University of Minnesota Press), pp. 253–70.

Tovey, H., 1992 'Environmentalism in Ireland: modernisation and identity', in Clancy, P., Kelly, M., Wiatr, J. and Zoltaniecki, R. (eds), *Ireland and Poland: Comparative perspectives* (Dublin: University College Dublin), pp. 275–87.

Tovey, H., 1993 'Environmentalism in Ireland: two versions of development and modernity', *International Sociology*, 8:4, 413–30.

Tovey, H., 1999 '"Messers, Visionaries and Organobureaucrats": dilemmas of institutionalisation in the Irish organic farming movement', *Irish Journal of Sociology*, 9, 31–59.

Tovey, H., 2003, Book review: 'George Taylor – *Conserving the Emerald Tiger: The politics of environmental regulation in Ireland*', *Sociologia Ruralis*, 43:2, 185–8.

Tovey, H. and Share, P., 2000 *A Sociology of Ireland* (Dublin: Gill & Macmillan).

World Commission on Environment and Development, 1987 *Our Common Future* (Oxford: Oxford University Press).

Yearly, S., 1995 'The Social Shaping of the Irish Environmental Movement', in Clancy, P., Kelly, M., Zoltaniecki, R. and Waitr, J. (eds), *Irish Society: Sociological perspectives* (Dublin: Institute of Public Administration), pp. 652–74.

New movements in old places? The alternative food movement in rural Ireland

In these alternative actor-networks outside the established hegemony of conventional food networks, food becomes a signifier for political, social and ecological struggles that are otherwise easily ignored. (Goodman 1999: 32)

THE LITERATURE on social movements has little to say about rural or agrarian collective action. Despite the 'rich tradition' of collective action by small farmers, peasants and farm-workers around the world, it has been 'social movements with predominantly urban constituencies [that have] received the most attention by scholars as well as the general public' (Mooney and Majka 1995: xi). NSM theorising in particular has contributed to this neglect by its search for social movements which are the bearers of new societal orders (Clark and Diani 1996): the association of modernity with industrialisation, urbanisation, science and technology constructed the rural not as a significant location of struggles around modernity's futures but as a backward and residual periphery, passively receiving innovations which always take place elsewhere.

In recent years, that perception has been changing. The rural is re-emerging as a key location for resistance, contestation and struggle. Its significance as a location for the production of food and the production of nature, two key concerns for late modern society, is increasingly recognised. 'Many of the best experiments in democratic renewal are taking place in rural areas' (Bell and Hendricks 2003: 17). And as social movement theory moves towards new perceptions of what a 'social movement' is (Crossley 2002), with increasing interest in the 'submerged' and lifeworld dimensions of collective action, the capacity of rural settings to provide *free spaces* for innovations in living, beyond the gaze of the State and the dominant culture, commands more attention.

The re-emergence of interest in the rural is linked to the process of globalisation. Globalisation connects the global to the local, often bypassing the national and its urban centres of power and influence. As food becomes a globally traded commodity, effects at the local level and the responses of local growers to the global food system emerge anew as questions for research. Global environmental crises encourage researchers to turn to local natures and their users in search of new potentialities for sustainable economic practices. Of course, economic globalisation is accompanied by its own global movement of resistance. The anti-corporate globalisation movement attaches great significance to food and agriculture, and to providing an alternative to the corporate and World Trade Organisation (WTO) model of a *global* agriculture and food system, in which agriculture is just a basis for 'a system of global profiteering in food products' (McMichael 2003: 72). Because food 'embodies the links between nature, human survival and health, culture and livelihood, it will, and has already, become a focus of attention and resistance to a corporate takeover of life itself' (*ibid*: 84). Via Campesina, an international network of small farmer associations which started in Latin America and in which, for example, the French peasant leader Jose Bove is deeply involved (Bove and Dufour 2001), offers a vision of a future agrarian order which directly challenges that of the current 'Doha Round' of negotiations over global food trade. Often called the 'agro-ecological' model (Marsden 2003), it envisages a world in which every locality would develop its own appropriate farming, fishing and resource-use practices, recognising the twin demands of ecological sustainability and human welfare. The food sovereignty movement, with its slogan 'Coming Home to Eat', similarly connects peasant producers North and South, and links both to food consumers and food activists in the developed countries, such as the US movement for community agriculture. They share common interests in food security, in sustainable food production and in *the local* as the proper site of food circulation and producer–consumer relations, and a common opposition to the global trading of food and the corporate takeover of the food system, symbolised particularly by genetically modified (GM) foods. Mittal (2004) calls the global food and agriculture resistance movement 'the new civil rights movement of today': it posits as a fundamental human right that of *growing and eating* food which is economically, ecologically, socially and culturally appropriate to local conditions, whereas the WTO posits only a right to *trade* food products globally, unimpeded by social, cultural or ecological *barriers*.

Whether there is in fact a single rural NSM that connects activists North and South is open to debate, as is its effectiveness as a form of resistance. While the local has re-emerged as a key preoccupation of some food activists and food movements, perhaps particularly Northern consumers, for others the focus is rather on rural and agricultural livelihoods, and how these can be sustained against a food industry which devours small producers in its global search for the cheapest or most profitable raw inputs. Food rights – access to nutritious, culturally appropriate, consumption – engage only some specific activist groups (Friedmann 2004).

Both locality and livelihood emerge as preoccupations among the group of 'alternative food activists' in Ireland which are the topic of this chapter. Ireland offers a rich history of rural social movements which have been generally neglected by students of social movements and collective action: the farmers' cooperative movement, the organic movement, movements for rural development, environmental activisms, mobilisations against the genetic modification of food, local exchange trading schemes, language rights movements, religious and spiritual movements, anti-waste and anti-waste-disposal movements, slow food and local food movements, and experiments in sustainable living such as the Village project in North Tipperary, to name but a few. Irish rural sociologists, with the notable exception of Tony Varley (see, for example, 2003a, 2003b), have shared with social movements researchers a blindness to the rural as a location for social movements. Instead, research on Irish rural places tends to be captured by a conceptualisation of rural life in terms of (the presence or absence of) *community*. This affects how we have framed and understood Irish rural development, and the place given within it to food.

Social movements and rural development

Since at least the 1930s, Irish rural places have been understood as places which are/ought to be sites of community, territorially bounded, socially integrated, with their own distinctive values and identity. The assumption that it is the *communality* of rural society which distinguishes it affects our understanding of it in some critical ways. It directs our attention primarily towards forms and problems of rural civil society (see also Bell and Hendricks 2003), but can direct it away from the rural as a site of distinctive forms and relations of production and work.

A focus on community shapes how rural civil society is theorised and researched. Community draws our attention particularly to problems of social reproduction; it has a long history of positioning within a debate over *loss* and *persistence*. Rural community research in Ireland has encouraged a perspective on civil society which roots this in the family and in related *private* spheres, rather than in public, political or democratic civic action; community studies have famously faced problems in grasping diversity in local civil society and in understanding social change in terms other than those of 'loss', 'decline' or 'demoralisation'.

Rural development policy, both Irish and EU-driven, represents rural development action as community action. This is associated with a particular understanding of democracy, in which representation and inclusion of the previously marginalised become the main indicators. Busch calls it 'thin democracy': 'a democracy which requires ceding to others the authority to make decisions' (2003: 25), particularly in relation to economic change. Research tends to focus on the *partnership* between the community as developmental actor and the State, on who participates in community development actions and on whether participation is *empowering* for them. It rarely asks: participation for/in what? A 'thicker' version of democracy would include challenge and contestation, autonomous action and social change. Social movement actors generally do not seek the equalisation of an existing system across territories and social groups; they rather question and challenge that system itself. Utopian actors oriented to change are inevitably to a degree exclusionary or unrepresentative, and are a focus of contention within local society.

It has become fashionable for rural development studies to theorise civil society in terms of social capital, influenced in particular by Robert Putnam (1993, 2001). As 'community' is equated with social capital, particularly at the policy level, its broader meanings shrink to an instrumental interest in what formal organisations of community can contribute to economic growth (Shortall 2004). Cohen accuses Putnam of working with a conception of civil society which is 'theoretically impoverished and politically suspect', and likely to 'play into the hands of social conservatives who aim to re-traditionalise civil life and to substitute local "volunteerism" for the public services and re-distributive efforts of the welfare state' (1999: 265). To revitalise our understanding of civil society 'as a dynamic, innovative source for articulating new concerns, developing projects, forming new identities, and generating and contesting new norms' (*ibid*: 266), she argues for a shift in focus from the private dimensions of civil society to the public sphere, and particularly to 'informal social networks and self-organising social movements, as distinct from more formal voluntary associations and networks' (*ibid*).

The community approach to rural development encourages little interest in the appropriateness to rural places of the forms of economic development being sought. Changing how we think about rural places, from sites of community to sites of social movements, can bring the agrarian dimension of rural places back to our imagination. Rural social movements around food are grounded in the relations between society and nature, and in the socio-economic interests which spring from that. Let us contrast the *official* policy perspective on rural development (RD) with an alternative version which has been articulated by a number of recent writers, particularly Van der Ploeg et al. (2000), Marsden (2003) and Van der Ploeg and Renting (2004); I label it here 'new paradigm RD'.[1] New paradigm RD differs from official RD policy in a number of key respects:

1 It repositions small-scale farming/food production practices at the centre of rural development; rural development is initiated and carried out by rural actors themselves. Its practices try to reshape and recombine all those rural resources which the modernisation paradigm treats as 'increasingly obsolete and external to agricultural production' – land, labour, eco-systems, animals, plants, craftsmanship, networks, market partners, town–countryside relations (Van der Ploeg et al. 2000: 398).

2 It aims to create and particularly to *retain* wealth within agriculture and the related rural economy. New opportunities for employment and income generation at the local level should be those which add value to the primary product, rather than, as in conventional development models, cheapening those products and reducing their value (Marsden 1993: 184; see also Douthwaite 1996). Projects appropriate for rural economic growth are distinctively different from industrial modernisation projects in which the eventual location of the wealth generated is irrelevant to the spatial location of the jobs created.

3 New paradigm RD encourages innovation in the institutions supporting and regulating economic activities: for example, new forms of marketing of food, new relationships between food producers and consumers. This follows partly from the first aim above, but it is also a deliberate effort to bypass and avoid incorporation into global chains of production and supply. New paradigm RD 'diminishes, both symbolically and materially, the dependency on financial capital, agro-industry, the global commodity markets and the big retailers', while 're-grounding' rural economic activities on ecological, social and cultural capitals which are held at the local or regional level (Van der Ploeg and Renting 2004: 233).

4 Finally, its supporters understand new paradigm RD as a form of *emancipation*, leading, on the aggregate level, to new patterns of sustainability, natural and social (see also Lyson 2003). Sustainable social organisation requires a rethinking of gender relations, social and spatial divisions of labour, identities and forms of cooperation: 'Central to the current practices of rural development, then, is that the creation of new wealth, the rise of new institutional patterns and identities, and the shift in power balances, are increasingly being intertwined' (Van der Ploeg and Renting 2004: 233).

New paradigm RD reminds us that *development* is a contested process (McMichael 2000), an important insight which even keen critics of state-endorsed rural development generally do not address. It offers a challenge and an alternative both to the conventional agricultural modernisation model, in which agriculture is given the part of extracting the primary resources from which others outside the rural economy can create wealth for themselves, and to post-agrarian models of rural development in which a declining agriculture creates space for consumption of the countryside, converting agricultural land into recreational facilities, nature reserves, areas for sub-urbanisation, or sites for factories and hotels. But does new paradigm RD really exist; and, if so, how has it arisen? Van der Ploeg and Renting estimate that half or more of European family farmers today are involved in the sorts of practices outlined above; Marsden (1993), less optimistically, argues that the possibilities for its successful realisation are unequally distributed across European rural space, and will never become 'mainstreamed' unless given strong and appropriate state supports. Van der Ploeg and Renting emphasise that new paradigm RD has emerged out of *autonomous* processes, and *in spite of* official attempts at rural development: small to medium farmers' experience of the disastrous effects of trying to integrate themselves into the dominant modernisation model, with its goals of continuous expansion of scale, industrialisation of production and integration into increasingly globalised agro-industrial corporations, force them to find a range of ways to 'jump over' the boundaries that model prescribes for them (2004: 234). Marsden locates the origins of new paradigm RD in state-led 'bottom-up' initiatives to empower rural communities, but those involved then undergo a 'cognitive liberation' (McAdam 1982) which transforms their understandings of the role of agriculture in rural development, moving it from a peripheral and dying to a central activity in rural places. The re-valuation of agriculture has come to be understood by participants themselves as a way to combat 'the severance of society from nature' (Marsden 2003: 178).

Both appear to be describing an NSM for rural development in Europe, yet neither fully theorises it as such. The practices which farmers are evolving to 'jump over' the boundaries of the modernisation model add up to 'a widespread *resistance paysanne*' (Van der Ploeg and Renting 2004): a 'counter-movement' (Marsden 2003) which asserts a new vision of society–nature relationships, reclaims rural places as important and distinctive places for the production of food, and restates the rights and possibilities of rural inhabitants to generate a livelihood for themselves from a sustainable use of the natural, cultural and social resources specific to their own rural locale. Yet both emphasise *aggregate* rather than *collective* change, and functional effects more than utopian intentions. Their interest is not in what actors intend to achieve by altering their livelihood practices, but rather in the effects, often unforeseen, which such changes have for wider institutional networks. At the basis of their theorisation is an assumption that 'peasant resisters' are better understood as rational than as cultural actors.

New paradigm RD assumes that cultural and social capitals are not prerequisites for new economic practices; rather, new livelihood strategies lead to the (re)generation of social and cultural capitals (Van der Ploeg and Renting 2004: 238). In many ways this is a persuasive conclusion about how rural development works: livelihood strategies (if successful) bring new civic and cultural strengths into rural places, whereas attempts at civic and cultural regeneration, especially if externally imposed, will not inevitably produce new livelihoods for rural people. But if we bracket off the social movement dimensions of new paradigm RD – the cultural visions, civic innovations and social networks which carry new practices across time and space – can we understand how new livelihood strategies could become apparent in the first place and how they could be widely taken up?

Social movements around alternative food in Ireland

This chapter combines a new paradigm RD with a social movements perspective to present some material on alternative food activists in rural Ireland. The term 'alternative food movement' has become widely used in rural sociology to identify a range of efforts to resist or bypass the dominant, capitalist, globalised and industrialised system through which food today is produced, processed and circulated. It encompasses more than just 'organic' food, although the organic food movement is seen as central within alternative food activisms (but not all organic producers are 'alternative' – see Buck et al. 1997; Lyons and Lawrence 2001). Alongside its use in relation to movements to produce food in ways sensitive to nature, the term is also used for movements to reconstruct local institutions for food circulation (such as farmers' markets), movements to revalue *traditional* and place-based food specialities, and movements to promote fresh, relatively unprocessed or un-scientised foodstuffs. 'Alternative' refers not just to the product, since both organic and industrial food chains can produce virtually identical products, but to the relationships constructed in the production, processing, distribution and selling of food (Marsden et al. 2000: 426). These include relations to nature, relations to customers and relations in production.

The literature on alternative producers represents them largely as ecologically aware producers, who use nature in a careful and sustainable way (Pugliese 2001). They are also often characterised (Marsden 2003) as 'short chain' or 'local' producers, who characteristically engage in novel forms of marketing such as box systems, off-farm sales and local markets. Producer–customer relations depend on personal knowledge, local reputation, or the construction of what Sage (2003) has called 'relations of regard'. A third aspect, less often referred to, is their tendency to use relations in production which are 'alternative' to conventional capitalist labour relations: domestic or kinship relations, the assimilation of work relations into relations of friendship and their conceptualisation as a form of apprenticeship through which ideologies, knowledge and skills are imparted.

The actors themselves do not, to any marked extent, use the term 'alternative food'. Irish food activists prefer to describe themselves as organic producers or as part of a movement for 'local food'. We can also call them (Tovey 2002) 'alternative entrepreneurs': 'entrepreneur' to emphasise their practices in organising and bringing into relationships with each other the various resources – land, labour, knowledge, techniques, exchange circuits and social relationships – which they need to create and maintain a livelihood; 'alternative' to direct attention to the way in which their entrepreneurial activities are carried out within a worldview which rejects the practices and values of conventional capitalist entrepreneurialism.

The alternative food movement

Resistance and challenge to the conventional food system has a long history, although much discussion treats 'food fear' as a recent phenomenon (Beardsworth and Kiel 1997), a product of living in a late-modern 'risk' society (Beck 1992; Guthman 2003). In Ireland the first known organic farm was established in Kilmurray, Co. Kilkenny, in 1936 (Moore 2003). Moore's historical research into organics in Ireland suggests a movement which has gone through a long struggle to recognise its own place and conditions of existence, and to integrate successive waves of 'incomers' with a slow but steady trickle of indigenous Irish converts. The early period was dominated by Anglo-Irish landowners, influenced by Steiner's biodynamic practices and by leaders in the English organic movement (see Reed 2001). In the 1970s a new wave of activists joined their ranks, many from continental Europe or Britain; in flight from industrial and urban life, they saw rural Ireland as a place of cheap land and relatively unspoilt nature where they could experiment with alternative forms of living (see Willis and Campbell 2004). Moore describes most of these organic activists as 'homesteaders': they wanted to live self-sufficiently, using environmentally sensitive practices. Others, however, both incomers and natives, were already looking at organic food production as a viable commercial enterprise. Gradually, links were built between the different groups. During the 1980s a series of meetings was held, out of which came the setting up of IOFGA (Irish Organic Farmers and Growers Association), the launch of an Irish organic symbol, and in 1989 the establishment of the Irish Organic Inspectorate to manage the certification process. By the end of the decade there were three representative organisations in Ireland, as the Organic Trust was set up alongside IOFGA and the Biodynamic Association. By this point, a complete break from the British representative organisation, the Soil Association, had occurred; but tensions were surfacing within the Irish movement, particularly between those who embraced organic farming as a way of life and those who had more commercial ambitions for it. From 1990 on, as the Irish State slowly began to see commercial possibilities in organic food, tensions around relations between the movement and the State also became more overt. The introduction of the Rural Environmental Protection Scheme (REPS) in the mid-1990s, which included a sub-scheme of funding for conversion into organic farming, brought new organic producers onto the scene. Some were farmers or ex-urbanites who had already been interested in converting and saw in the financial aids offered by REPS a small but possible way of activating their dreams; others were conventional farmers drawn in simply by the additional grants. REPS brought a shift in the basis of the movement. Many of the new actors were Irish livestock farmers, whereas previously production had been almost exclusively horticultural; and at the same time a number of existing 'growers', while still practising organic production methods, began to reject the organic symbol and certification requirements.

It is difficult to estimate the size of the contemporary alternative food movement, and estimates based only on the membership of the three organic certification organisations would severely under-represent actual numbers. But today, networks of alternative food producers, organic and post- or non-organic, can be found in all parts of Ireland. There are important movement institutions in Leitrim (home of the Irish Organic Centre), Tipperary (Ballybrado), Cork (the English Market), and Galway (the Farmers' Market), and local place can shape the ideas and the practices of the actors involved. The discussion here draws on research both with converted organic farmers in the West, Midlands and South-East of the country,[2] and with a group of alternative food activists, not only farmers but also growers, restaurateurs, small food processors (cheese, pork, smoked fish), traders, marketers and distributors in West Cork[3] (see Tovey 1997, 1999, 2002 for further detail). For a variety of conjunctural reasons (a long history of tourism and food tourism, a tradition of incomers settling in the area, the availability of small plots of land at relatively cheap prices, proximity to dynamic and educationally well-serviced urban centres), alternative food networks have developed particularly strongly in West Cork. They are somewhat different from the 'peasant' counter-movement described in the new paradigm RD literature, in which the core actors are farm households seeking to develop their enterprises as farms. Some of the most prominent 'local food' actors, even if they are farmers or growers, see themselves as part of a consumer movement rather than a rural producer movement. Their networks include farm households occupying the same land for several generations, but also settled New Age Travellers from Britain, American, German, Swiss, English and Irish ex-urbanites, women who had married into farming or fishing families, and returned Irish emigrants.

Economic entrepreneurs and livelihood practices

Van der Ploeg and Renting (2004: 235) identify three sets of strategic practices as characteristic of those pursuing a livelihood under the new paradigm RD:

- 'deepening';
- 'broadening'; and
- 're-grounding'.

Deepening practices generate more 'added value' for the product at the local producer stage: for example, returning to the farm food-processing activities which were historically appropriated from it by the food industry (Goodman et al. 1987), such as converting raw milk into butter or cheese, or processing pork raised on the farm into sausages; developing 'quality' products (organic or speciality products associated with the skills and traditions of a particular locality) which can command a higher market price; or creating new, shorter chains through which to market produce such as direct sales from the farm to consumers or at farmers' markets. A wide variety of 'deepening' practices is found among our alternative entrepreneurs, farmers and others. For example, smoking fish allows small local processors to capture for themselves the value added from increasing the 'durability' (Friedmann 1993) of the fish, rather than ceding this to corporate food processors who add preservatives or who apply industrial freezing and drying techniques to fish. Alternative restaurateurs grow a large part of the produce they serve in their restaurant themselves (vegetables, fruits, eggs, chickens and herbs, in one example); vegetable growers bring their produce to trade in a local market instead of selling through supermarkets.

Broadening refers to the creation of new non-agricultural or para-agricultural activities to generate an income for farm household members, such as agri-tourism, biodiversity management or 'the delivery of services within the local economy'. Broadening practices are central to Irish alternative food networks. Organic cattle farmers get together to organise sales of young cattle to organic finishers or to set up organic slaughtering facilities. One household in the West Cork network is a smallholding with a mixed farming regime shaped around the family's own subsistence needs but also generating income through sales of farm produce (turkeys, ducks and milk from the goats), some income from REPS and sales of craftwork to visitors. Here, the husband organises an organic grain delivery service in the region; he buys bulk organic animal feed and stores it on the farm for selling on. Customers come to the farm to collect what they need or he delivers to them, sometimes over quite long distances. He puts customers with small flocks of organic chicken in touch with each other so that they can buy from him in bulk and then share the grain among themselves, saving on costs, travel and time. Finding sufficient grain for feeding organically raised live-stock is a constant problem for many small local producers, so grain distributors simultaneously generate income for themselves and provide services for the local economy. In many cases, women are prominent in developing alternative food enterprises, often drawing on resources held by their husbands (a fish-smoker, for example, is married to a fisherman; some cheese-makers are married to farmers with dairy herds) to develop a new enterprise, which they themselves can direct, and control. Many mentioned the importance of giving women an income of their own in an economy in which resources tend to be held by and pass down through the males, and of drawing women into local economic and civil life as independent actors instead of leaving them in depend-ent roles on often remote holdings.

These 'broadening' practices could, however, be subsumed under the conventional rural development heading of pluriactivity or 'the pluriactive household'. To give them any distinctiveness, they need to be related to the third category, *re-grounding*. Van der Ploeg and Renting explain re-grounding as strategies to end dependence on financial and industrial capitals and replace them with inputs of social and ecological capitals. Re-grounding is at the heart of the claim that this is rural development under a *new paradigm*. It is also the least developed of the three categories they outline. To examine re-grounding, we need to move out from the livelihood strategies of individual households and consider the broader 'moral economy' (Willis and Campbell 2004) which these actors collectively negotiate to create. Without space to cover this in detail, our discussion looks briefly at just two dimensions: informalisation; and a crafts aesthetics of food.

Informalising the local economy – networking, marketing and barter

Both organic farmers and alternative food activists are active civic participators: they take leading roles in many different sorts of formal organisations and institutions, from the Organic Inspectorate to the board of IOFGA, from slow food and anti-GM food networks to community development associations. These more formal memberships generate extensive loose and overlapping networks between activists, which are further reinforced by meetings, festivals, farm walks and mutual visiting, and in particular by relationships established through livelihood practices. As Willis and Campbell (2004) say of their 'neo-peasants' in the Cevennes, it is the day-to-day spatially located livelihood practices and their associated informal networks, rather than organisational memberships, which anchor and sustain the Irish alternative food movement. The moral economy of the alternative food movement is shaped by strong tendencies towards informalisation, both of trading relationships and of regulatory standards.

Customers call informally to producers' houses to buy food or crafts produce or producers sell eggs and vegetables through a box system, delivering bags of produce directly to customers. Selling at stalls at weekly markets brings alternative producers into contact with much larger numbers of people, some of whom are regulars, known by name, who come every week, even in winter when there is less on offer, and who would stop for a while to talk. Informalisation of economic relationships is a reflexive strategy to socialise market relations, to avoid involvement in circuits of financial capital and to create an alternative to labelling and certification:

> The wonderful thing about selling in the street is that you get constant feedback, it's lovely, even if it's only one person in the day who comes back and says 'I like it', and people are prepared to queue for it. I mean I think that's fantastic. And then you're getting that constant feedback. And also sometimes you get it wrong, like the turnips get too big so they're hollow in the middle, and somebody would tell you that, so then you replace it and then we stop harvesting those ones. You know, 'cos what we try to do is eat the vegetables all the time here, but sometimes we don't get round to eating, whatever, for a

couple of weeks and then we wouldn't notice if they'd gone woody. So there's so much more, it's such a social thing. See, it's my social day out. If you just go into a shop, I mean, who do you meet? Hopeless. (West Cork grower and street-trader, 2001)

Knowledge used in production and marketing is circulated through informal networks by word of mouth. For example: 'The other night SC rang up from Dunmanway and told us that MO'F has some seventy free-range pullets for sale and they are in Millstreet if we want them. So the word gets round, you don't actually have to advertise anything' (West Cork grower, 2001). In another case:

E tells SK about a local woman they both know of who has been given a licence to grow hemp. They discuss the benefits of this, and E goes to the hall and comes back producing two whole plants which he got from an existing hemp farm. He asks SK for advice on which machine would be suitable to cut it, then he explains how hemp can be used as green manure by digging it directly into the ground. SK is very interested and E promised to take him to see the place. (Field notes, West Cork, 2001).

Networks for selling produce or animal feed provide opportunities to experiment with other forms of exchange, such as bartering. At a day-to-day level, bartering is used quite extensively for exchanges between producers, but also to acquire goods at local shops or to pay workers and helpers:

In organics it works, it works quite well. Because, especially if you're direct selling to people, and they're producing produce and you're selling them produce as well, more than likely they're going to have something you want, you're going to have something they want. So it seems ridiculous that you're handing over X pounds so they can hand you back Y pounds, there's no point to it ... And certainly, whether it's psychological or whatever, but you barter a bag of chicken feed for a chicken and the chicken just seems to taste better than if you had actually got the equivalent amount of money and gone out and bought that chicken. And of course it saves a lot of hassle. You have less shopping to do, you know where your food comes from, it makes a lot of sense. Some of my customers I'd actually, rather than taking money for the feed I sell them, I'd actually take produce off them, and that needn't necessarily be produce for me. Ok, I might take chickens off somebody or maybe cattle off somebody, in exchange for feed, and I might actually sell those cattle on to a third person or those chickens on to a third person, and realise the money in that way. It works in many different ways, and it shifts produce, you know. I mean, most of the people that I'd be dealing with, if I don't barter with them or if I don't buy produce off them, if they have produce for sale and they're looking for customers I'd always keep an eye out for them for customers. If I don't buy the stuff myself I might know somebody. who does (West Cork organic grain farmer, 2001)

Barter and other informalised exchanges *re-ground* economic relationships in local social capital. Re-grounding in ecological capital is part of a decision to replace industrial values for good food by an aesthetics of craftsmanship.

An aesthetics of *good* food

For organic farmers, part of the experience of going organic is a rediscovery of themselves as producers of food, not just of agricultural commodities. Thinking about oneself as a food producer also means thinking about oneself as a food consumer. As one organic convert said: 'I think more about food now. I also get paid more for food so I am willing to pay more.' Another organic farmer dismissed conventional farmers as uninterested in food: 'The people who grow potatoes [as a commodity] haven't any interest in it at all, they are above that you know.'

Food processors and restaurateurs, however, articulated a highly developed discourse of *good* food. Part of what is alternative in the alternative food movement is the different 'regime of value' (Murdoch et al. 2000; Dixon 2002) it operates in relation to food quality. The industrial food system, and in particular corporate retailing chains, articulate an understanding of *good* food as safe, hygienic, efficiently produced, standardised, inexpensive, and delivered to the customer through a 'quality retailing experience' (Marsden et al. 2000). The West Cork activists, in contrast, talk about good food via an aesthetic discourse, which constantly calls attention to the sensory qualities of the food produced – taste, smell, freshness and appearance:

> This is the last country where there's any appreciable sea fishery for wild salmon. There's estuary fishery but the fish are in a different condition when they've gone into the estuary, they're preparing themselves to go back into the fresh water. Unlike the sea-caught fish, the fat content's better, it's exercised, it's just come swimming from a long, long way away. It's free of any food stuff so there's no problem freezing it as a whole animal, because there's no digestive juices in its tract. I did tastings, I had taken four different tastings of wild salmon from other producers in the country and my own. And I hadn't tasted all the others at that stage, so for them it was an interesting experience because they all taste different. Even though we're all using the same fish, we're all using hardwood smoke and we're all using salt, so it's quite extraordinary that variation in flavours. (West Cork fish-smoker, 2001)

This is also a discourse of craftsmanship, in its fascination with transformative processes and the possibilities of varied outcomes, and its commitment to skills which have been developed through experience and through learning from other masters of the craft:

> Every now and again you meet someone who really gets it, who really gets into the microbiology of cheese making, which is complex, complex, it's an alchemy. With the microbiology of cheese-making, I completely understand

why it was the monks who were the first to make cheese, to distil, to make compost heaps even, fermentation is just, you've got to be in your head, it's fascinating, it's another cosmology ... But the thing about cheese is that it's a very honest depiction, it's so much more than a microbiological process, if you understand and get it right there's going to be something, a personality, and then if it has something, a personality that people like, it will succeed ... We sell, that's our response, it's a taste that people like, it tastes real, it tastes friendly, tastes clean, it's got I don't know how but it's got what it takes and it tastes Irish ... that is, West Cork, it couldn't be anywhere else, there is this fungusy smell of the rind, and that's where it comes from. (West Cork cheesemaker, 2001)

Alternative food is distinctive because it is made by someone who really gets the alchemy, but also because it is local. Small artisan producers recognise the variability of natural inputs and try as crafts-workers to produce from these a food which is unique, place-related, non-standardised and aesthetically appealing and which also contributes to the livelihoods and civic life of the local community.

Working utopias

Informalising practices resonate with Melucci's interest (1989) in the 'latent' and 'submerged' dimensions of social movements – networks as ongoing 'cultural laboratories' in which new lifestyles and forms of social relations can be developed. Crossley (1999a, 1999b, 2002) develops the concept of 'working utopias' to elaborate these dimensions. Movements are 'laboratories of experience' which reveal themselves 'as specific transformations in ways of thinking, speaking and acting, and in forms of social relationships ... that is, they manifest as transformations in social practice' (1999a: 649). Working utopias are the places where a culture of resistance and a habitus for change become practical, *real* phenomena. They 'provide a model of the changes which movements wish to bring about and can thus be made to serve both a symbolic and a cognitive function for movements in their efforts to persuade others of their cause. They can publicly "prove" that the alternative "works"' (1999b: 824).

In terms of the alternative food movement, Crossley's concept most obviously applies to formal education and training centres such as the Organic Centre in Leitrim. But alternative food actors generally seem to treat their place of work, whether it is a restaurant, a farm or a small business, as a working utopia. They understand what they are doing as providing working examples of alternative enterprise, alternative livelihoods, alternative relations with nature, which involve practical, technological experimentation, but also experiments in different ways of living in terms of both household relations and relations within local networks and communities. Willing workers stay on farms to learn and contribute, farm walks are organised for customers and colleagues. The enterprise's survival is attributed a demonstration effect, providing evidence that not only can alternative technical and cultural knowledge be converted into economic capital, but the alternative social arrangements associated with this also convert into social capital.

Working utopians fall easily into pedagogic mode. Practical knowledge, about plant types or veterinary practices, basket-making or herbalism, is passed on within the family to children and outside the family to volunteer workers ('WOOFERS') and customers. Farmers, cooks, cheese-makers and fish-smokers spend hours discussing the techniques, social arrangements and ideas underpinning alternative food production with their workers/apprentices as they work together on the enterprise. Innovation in technical knowledge is important to them, and they engage in various forms of practical experimentation to improve the technicalities of alternative food production. As we have seen, experimentation in new or alternative ways of marketing also takes place – for instance, farm walks construct workplaces as centres of education and sociability; hard-to-come-by knowledge is shared by example. Farms are opened to peers, customers and the general public, who are given tours and the opportunity to ask questions and seek advice. Such 'pedagogic action', Crossley argues, constructs and disseminates a 'resistance habitus': 'People visit them in order to learn how to practise differently; how to perceive, think and act in different ways' (*ibid*: 817).

The other side of the coin is that the utopianism that alternative food activists practice is of the 'nook and cranny' kind (Alexander 2001). They reject attempts to 'totalise' or 'universalise' their ideas, and dislike overt attempts at conversion/recruitment into the movement, arguing that *doing* is far more important than *saying* as a way of converting others:

> I never, ever try to persuade anyone to go organic. It's a complete and utter waste of time, trying to persuade somebody. If somebody wants something they'll come to you and they'll seek the information ... I think the best way of creating awareness for anything is just to do what you do well yourself, and if you do that, that's probably the best advertising that you can do for it. I wouldn't be, to be quite honest, if nobody went organic in the morning or if everybody went organic in the morning, it's not for me to decide (West Cork organic grain farmer, 2001).

Or as a local vegetable grower and trader put it: 'I do in lots of ways believe that, if you want, like it's a little bit like the early Christians, they were told if they wanted to change the world they'd have to live it.'

A single movement?

This account of the alternative food movement in rural Ireland represents it as a loose, informal network of individual entrepreneurs and households organised around a series of movement practices, sites, hubs and local spaces. But should we treat these as all elements of *the same* social movement? Does a shared interest in and concern about food collect these disparate activists into a single movement with a clear collective identity? Or is collective identity less important, in theorising this as a movement, than other features such as networking, mutual acquaintance and sharing of knowledge and worldviews?

Whether even the organic movement can be considered a single social movement has been a lively topic of debate. Lyons and Lawrence (2001) find a bifurcation in Australian organic production between farmers who are increasingly 'conventionalised' and incorporated into large-scale corporate systems, and those who reject conventionalisation and continue to practise organic production on a small scale, for local markets, and often without benefit of certification, relying on local reputation to establish their food's quality. These two tendencies are often labelled 'organic' versus 'post-organic'. Moore, on the other hand, sees the organic movement as a single movement with a 'dual logic': it has always been engaged in 'a transformative dialogue with itself' (2004: 2), always in a sense 'post-organic'. Both interest in and resistance to its own institutionalisation has been a feature of the organic movement since its earliest beginnings: organic activists are themselves keenly aware of the 'dilemma of institutionalisation' (Tovey 1999), the simultaneous embrace of and flight from the State and from global markets, and the historical tensions between 'homesteading' or self-sufficiency ideals, and commercial entrepreneurship revolving around a symbol which 'can travel'.

The activists described here comprise neither a single movement with a 'dual logic' nor different movements in competition with each other. They constitute a series of interconnected and overlapping networks and acquaintances, with common livelihood problems, shared locales and a similar 'cosmology' (Eyerman and Jamison 1991) which integrates nature, work and social organisation. We can find some differences among them. For example, some groups seem more likely to use *agro-ecological* discourses in their talk, while others use *food aesthetics* discourses. Agro-ecological discourse seems most common among farmer converts, particularly from the pre-REPS period. The identity it expresses is that of a producer of healthful, nourishing food commodities, through care for natural resources, particularly care for the soil (land, grassland), maintaining it at high and sustainable levels of fertility, full of earthworms, a source of biodiversity. This discourse often expresses strong criticism and a rejection of agro-industry and in particular the chemicals industry. Agro-ecological converts tend to favour certification; they share a lot of agrarian values with conventional farmers, including the view that their task is to maintain nature and to produce from it healthful, high-quality, food but that what happens to the produce after it leaves the farm gate is not particularly their concern. They link organic farming not just to maintaining the soil but also to better incomes for farmers, the retention of farmers in the rural locality and the provision of rural employment.

The food aesthetics discourse, on the other hand, is used most by incomers with no previous farming background, and by restaurateurs and food-processors. This is a discourse about consumption as much as production. Its users express interest in the consumption qualities of the food they produce, identify themselves as food consumers as much as food producers and, as we have seen, emphasise the aesthetic qualities of food, particularly the distinctive taste which they associate with using natural processes to create food in specific and distinctive locales. Many of them use organic standards in production, but do not seek certification. They see the organic symbol as destructive to the education of the food consumer, who is encouraged to place blind trust in a label instead of developing their own knowledge and taste. They prefer to emphasise local production and local exchange of food, mediated by personal knowledge. Their critique of the industrial food system focuses less on agribusiness and more on global distribution and retailing, specifically supermarkets. Despite their emphasis on local food, local social and economic sustainability, local wealth generation and retention, and the provision of employment opportunities for local women, their values are cosmopolitan rather than agrarian, and the communities in which these food activists root themselves are trans-local communities of taste and interest, including tourists, internet customers and European organisations and movements (Eurotocques, Slow Food) as well as local.

While such differences are present, and of interest, they need not bar us from treating Irish alternative food activists as a collectivity, given their 'nook-and-cranny' style of utopianism and their insistence that there are many different ways of being *alternative*. On a global level, too, as McMichael points out, the new agro-ecological and food sovereignty movements have different historical, cultural and philosophical origins or goals; but they still 'express a certain unity in rejecting or re-framing the discursive claims and material practices of the global corporate food regime. Arguably, the counter-movements are unified around reversing the marginalisation of rural culture and the extreme commodification of a life force such as food' (McMichael 2003: 83).

Alternative food movements and the 'crisis of development'

McMichael describes globalisation, the late modern version of the project of 'development', as currently in crisis. The crisis arises, at least in part, because of the impacts of globalisation on everyday life, particularly on food which is wrenched by the corporate system out of nature and culture. This produces a counter-movement that tries to resist corporate globalisation by reconstructing links between food, local ecology and local cultures. Proponents of new paradigm RD suggest that European farmers are being increasingly drawn into this counter-movement – not so much, or not only, by joining the formal organisations associated with it or by taking part in protests, demonstrations and World Social Forum meetings, as by evolving new strategies to develop and protect their livelihoods which disengage them from global capitalism and re-embed them in local nature and in local and regional networks and institutions.

The alternative food movement in Ireland is part of that counter-movement. Actors' accounts of their practices resonate with global counter-movement ideas about agro-ecology, food sovereignty and local food. And it does appear to be an *autonomous* emergence in the Irish countryside, and to be engaged in attempts to *re-ground* Irish rural living. But looked at in this context, it has some odd or ambiguous aspects.

First, this is not a *mobilised* movement. Historically, mobilised agrarian movements have adopted a variety of tactics to express resistance, from boycotts to squatting, from the formation of cooperatives for production, marketing or inputs purchasing, to rent strikes and withholding product from the market, and from setting up new political parties to protests, lobbying and the formation of alliances with third parties such as the labour or environmental movements (Mooney and Majka 1995). The Irish movement uses few of these tactics and is characterised by an orientation to informalisation rather than to organisation and institutionalisation. Its preferred mode of resistance appears to be 'exit' rather than 'voice' (Hirschman 1970). Like most farmers, before agricultural modernisation enmeshed them in the bonds of financial and state regulations, alternative food entrepreneurs retain the possibility of retreating from market relations into a self-sufficiency tempered by barter and other non-financial exchanges. Their utopianism emphasises demonstration more than active persuasion, practice more than critique, and distance from formal association. They believe, with Melucci (1989), that the form is the message, rather than a means to an end. 'Exit' can be variously interpreted, however, as disengagement from participation in the wider society or as a deliberate turn towards local civil society and its reconstruction. The second interpretation suggests we see rural Ireland at present as a 'cold spot' in the global resistance movement (Willis and Campbell 2004: 319): not as a 'hot spot' of formal and collective protest, as in Seattle and Genoa, but a place which 'stands largely outside the formal economy and is inhabited by participants who, while never formally mobilising politically, are drawn into a set of practices that have a distinctly alternative or experimental quality'. Cold spots seek to put 'development' projects in crisis by treating them as irrelevant, but are easily themselves treated as irrelevant in return.

Second, it is not unambiguously an agrarian movement, although it is not coincidental that it has emerged in rural Ireland. Earlier agrarian movements in Ireland, such as the cooperative movement in its first decades (see Tovey 2001), shared similar concerns for rural civil society and community, for quality and craftsmanship in food production, and for egalitarianism and the retention of surplus in the local rural economy. But they were rooted in a clear vision of the interests of farmers and of the countervailing interests against which they had to contend. Social movements are defined by *the enemy*, what they are against, as much as by what they are for (Della Porta and Diani 1999), and the Irish alternative food movement interprets its enemy variously. Sometimes this is the agro-industrial system, particularly the chemical inputs industries which corrupt both farmers and nature; sometimes it is the global food system, particularly the retailing corporations which destroy good food and mis-educate consumers. Although it values and celebrates *thick* rather than *thin* democracy, it is very rarely concerned with justice, access and food rights. From some aspects the movement is a consumer movement, from others a producer movement. It is a hybrid movement, reflecting the hybridity and the cultural complexity of rurality in the contemporary world.

Notes

1 Confusingly, it is generally referred to in the literature simply as 'rural development', although Marsden (2003) sometimes refers to it as 'real rural development' or 'agrarian-based rural development'. My use of the label 'new paradigm RD' follows Van der Ploeg and Renting (2004).

2 Interviews were collected with twenty organic farmers during the summer of 1997. My thanks to Brian McMahon for conducting the interviews and to the Arts and Social Sciences Benefactions Fund of TCD for contributing to funding the work.

3 This research, which combined interviews and participant observation, was carried out between 2000 and 2002. I am very grateful to Annette Jorgensen for her magnificent work in collecting the data and to the Trinity Foundation for funding the project.

Bibliography

Alexander, J., 2001 'Robust Utopias and Civil Repairs', *International Sociology*, 16:4, 579–91.

Arensberg, C. and Kimball, S.T., 2001 *Family and Community in Ireland*, 3rd edn (Ennis, Co. Clare: Clasp Press [1940]).

Beardsworth, A. and Kiel, T., 1997 *Sociology on the Menu* (London: Routledge).

Beck, U., 1992 *Risk Society: Towards a new modernity* (London: Sage).

Bell, M.M. and Hendricks, F., 2003 'Introduction', in Bell and Hendricks (eds), *Walking Towards Justice: Democratization in rural life* (Oxford: Elsevier), pp. 1–19.

Bove, J. and Dufour, F., 2001 *The World Is Not For Sale: Farmers against junk food*

(London: Verso).

Buck, D., Getz, C., Guthman, J., 1997 'From Farm to Table: the organic vegetable commodity chain of northern California', *Sociologia Ruralis*, 37:1, 3–20.

Busch, L., 2003 'Democracy: the missing element in the market celebration', in Bell, M.M. and Hendricks, F. (eds), *Walking Towards Justice* (Oxford: Elsevier), pp. 23–34.

Clark, J. and Diani, M. (eds), 1996 *Alain Touraine* (London: Falmer Press).

Cohen, J.L., 1999 'Does Voluntary Association Make Democracy Work?', in Smelser, N. and Alexander, J. (eds), *Diversity and its Discontents* (Princeton, NJ: Princeton University Press), pp. 263–91.

Crossley, N., 1999a 'Fish, Field, Habitus and Madness: on the first wave mental health users in Britain', *British Journal of Sociology*, 50:4, 647–70.

Crossley, N., 1999b 'Working Utopias and Social Movements: an investigation using case study materials from radical mental health movements in Britain', *Sociology*, 33:4, 809–30.

Crossley, N., 2002 *Making Sense of Social Movements* (Buckingham: Open University Press).

Della Porta, D. and Diani, M., 1999 *Social Movements: An introduction* (Oxford: Blackwell).

Dixon, J., 2002 *The Changing Chicken: Chooks, cooks and culinary culture* (Sydney: UNSW Press).

Douthwaite, R., 1996 *Short Circuit: Strengthening local economies for security in an unstable world* (Dublin: Lilliput Press).

Eyerman, R. and Jamison, A., 1991 *Social Movements: A cognitive approach* (Cambridge: Polity Press).

Friedmann, H., 1993 'After Midas' Feast: alternative food regimes for the future', in Allen, P. (ed.), *Food for the Future* (New York: Wiley).

Friedmann, H., 2004 'Remembering Livelihood: why agriculture is key to the future of the world system', symposium presentation, International Rural Sociology Association's 11th World Congress of Rural Sociology, 'Globalisation, Risks and Resistance', Trondheim, Norway, July.

Goodman, D. 1999 'Agro-Food Studies in the Age of Ecology: nature, corporeality, bio-politics', *Sociologia Ruralis*, 39:1, 17–38.

Goodman, D., Sorj, B. and Wilkinson, J., 1987 *From Farming to Biotechnology: A theory of agro-industrial development* (Oxford: Blackwell).

Guthman, J., 2003 'Eating Risk: the politics of labelling genetically engineered foods', in Schurman, R.A. and Kelso, D.D.T. (eds), *Engineering Trouble* (Berkeley: University of California Press).

Hirschman, O., 1970 *Exit, Voice and Loyalty* (Cambridge, MA: Harvard University Press).

Lyons, K. and Lawrence, G., 2001 'Institutionalisation and Resistance: organic agriculture in Australia and New Zealand', in Tovey, H. and Blanc, M. (eds), *Food, Nature and Society* (Aldershot: Ashgate).

Lyson, T.A., 2003 'The Civic Community and Balanced Economic Development', in Bell, M.M. and Hendricks, F. (eds), *Walking Towards Justice* (Oxford: Elsevier), pp. 103–20.

McAdam, D., 1982 *Political Process and the Development of Black Insurgency 1930–1970* (Chicago, IL: Chicago University Press).

McMichael, P., 2000 *Development and Social Change: A global perspective*, 2nd edn (Thousand Oaks, CA: Pine Forge).

McMichael, P., 2003 'The Power of Food', in Almas, R. and Lawrence, G. (eds),

Globalisation, Localisation and Sustainable Livelihoods (Aldershot: Ashgate), pp. 69–85.

Marsden, T., 2003 *The Condition of Rural Sustainability* (Assen, NL: Royal van Gorcum).

Marsden, T., Flynn, A. and Harrison, M., 2000 *Consuming Interests: The social provision of foods* (London: UCL Press).

Melucci, A., 1989 *Nomads of the Present* (London: Hutchinson Radius).

Mittal, A., 2004 'Food Sovereignty: a new farm economy to challenge economic globalisation', plenary presentation, International Rural Sociology Association's 11th World Congress of Rural Sociology, 'Globalisation, Risks and Resistance', Trondheim, Norway, July.

Mooney, P.H. and Majka, T.J., 1995 *Farmers' and Farmworkers' Movements: Social protest in American agriculture* (New York: Twayne Publishers).

Moore, O., 2003 'Organic Organisations and Movement Bifurcations: collective identity or otherwise in the organic movement in Ireland 1936–1991', paper presented at the European Society for Rural Sociology 20th Conference, Sligo, Ireland, August.

Moore, O., 2004 'Farmers' Markets and What They Say About the Perpetual Post-Organic Movement in Ireland', paper presented at the International Rural Sociology Association's 11th World Congress of Rural Sociology, 'Globalisation, Risks and Resistance', Trondheim, Norway, July.

Murdoch, J., Marsden, T. and Banks, J., 2000 'Quality, Nature and Embeddedness: some theoretical considerations in the context of the food sector', *Economic Geography*, 76:2, 7–25.

Peace, A., 2001 *A World of Fine Difference* (Dublin: University College Dublin Press).

Pugliese, P., 2001 'Organic Farming and Sustainable Rural Development: a multifaceted and promising convergence', *Sociologia Ruralis*, 41:1, 112–30.

Putnam, R., 1993 *Making Democracy Work* (Princeton, NJ: Princeton University Press).

Putnam, R., 2001 *Bowling Alone: The collapse and revival of American community* (London: Simon & Schuster).

Reed, M., 2001 'Fight the Future! How the contemporary campaigns of the UK organic movement have arisen from their composting of the past', *Sociologia Ruralis*, 41:1, 131–46.

Sage, C., 2003 'Social Embeddedness and Relations of Regard: alternative "good food" networks in South-West Ireland', *Journal of Rural Studies*, 19:1, 47–60.

Shortall, S., 2004 'Social or Economic Goals, Civic Inclusion or Exclusion? An analysis of rural development theory and practice', *Sociologia Ruralis*, 44:1, 109–23.

Tovey, H., 1997 'Food, Environmentalism and Rural Sociology: on the organic farming movement in Ireland', *Sociologia Ruralis*, 37:1, 21–37.

Tovey, H., 1999 '"Messers, Visionaries and Organobureaucrats": dilemmas of institutionalisation in the Irish organic movement', *Irish Journal of Sociology*, 9, 31–59.

Tovey, H., 2001 'The Co-operative Movement in Ireland: reconstructing civil society', in Tovey, H. and Blanc, M. (eds), *Food, Society and Nature* (Aldershot: Ashgate), pp. 321–38.

Tovey, H., 2002 'Alternative Agriculture Movements and Rural Development Cosmologies', *International Journal of the Sociology of Agriculture and Food*, 10:1, available: www.ryerson.ca/~isarc40.

Van der Ploeg, J.D., Renting, H., Brunori, G., Knickel, K., Mannion, J., Marsden, T., de Roest, K., Sevilla Guzman, E. and Ventura, F., 2000 'Rural Development: from practices and policies towards theory', *Sociologia Ruralis*, 40:4, 391–408.

Van der Ploeg, J.D. and Renting, H., 2004 'Behind the "Redux": a rejoinder to David Goodman', *Sociologia Ruralis*, 44:2, 233–42.

Varley, T., 2003a 'A Region of Sturdy Smallholders? Western nationalists and agrarian politics during the First World War', *Journal of the Galway Archaeological and Historical Society*, 55, 127–50.

Varley, T., 2003b 'Populism, the Europeanised State and Collective Action in Rural Ireland', in Blanc, M. (ed.), *Innovations, Institutions and Rural Change* (Luxembourg: Office of Official Publications of the European Communities), pp. 127–68.

Willis, S. and Campbell, H., 2004 'The Chestnut Economy: the praxis of neo-peasantry in rural France', *Sociologia Ruralis*, 44:3, 317–31.

Anti-racism in Ireland

THE DEVELOPMENT of anti-racism as a discourse and practice of social movements differs from country to country in terms of the specific historical conditions under which racism and resistance to it take shape and along different time-scales that demonstrate the various stages at which racism and anti-racism take on significance across societies. Ireland, a country of relatively recent immigration, yet with a long history of emigration, represents an interesting case for examining the impact of the evolution of anti-racism in the context of social movements theory. It demonstrates both how racisms and anti-racisms mirror and *copy* their manifestations in other settings and how attention to historical specificity is essential for making sense of the development of a phenomenon in any given society. With regard to racism, this work of historicisation within a particular context serves as a means of explaining how it successfully takes on various guises that depend on both place and time.

Anti-racism cannot be unproblematically thought of as the mere opposite of racism (Bonnett 2000). The tendency to do so has meant that anti-racism has been subject to little scholarly attention, either by students of social movements or by those interested in the construction of political discourse. In my research into racism and anti-racism in Europe (A. Lentin 2004), I have attempted to redress this gap. I suggested that, given that our understanding of *race* and racism, in the post-war era, is almost entirely shaped by the work of scholars coming from an anti-racist perspective, it is essential to conceptualise *anti-racism* itself in order to examine its emergence and submit it to a critique which will ultimately further our understanding of the persistence of racism in contemporary societies. As anti-racism in Ireland is a relatively recent development, growing exponentially with the diversification of the Irish population due to immigration over the last decade, I propose a timely examination of some of the key characteristics of Irish anti-racism that intends to assist those interested in making sense both of the 'specificity of Irish racism' (McVeigh 1992), and of the place of anti-racism among the array of social movements that have emerged in recent years in Ireland.

This chapter argues that although the phenomenon of anti racism in Ireland displays some of the characteristics of NSMs, it cannot be adequately analysed *solely* within a deterministic interpretation of social movements. It also demonstrates how the term 'social movement' has been inappropriately applied to explain a whole range of social and political issues in contemporary societies, such as anti-racism, and questions its use as a blanket term. Fundamentally, the phenomenon of anti-racism in Ireland demonstrates the limits of the NSM paradigm as it was initially developed in European social theory.

This chapter intends, therefore, to provide both a theoretical discussion of social movements and a specific analysis of anti-racism in Ireland, based on empirical research into the conceptualisation of racism in the Irish context. It is divided into three parts. The first makes some theoretical remarks on the treatment of anti-racism from an NSM theory perspective. It examines the primacy of identity to the conceptualisation of the NSM phenomenon and points out the confusion often made between anti-racism and 'identity politics' by many authors. In contrast, I outline an alternative theoretical framework for making sense of anti-racism, which emphasises the complexity of the phenomenon and warns against unproblematically equating anti-racism with the struggle of minority ethnic groups for equal recognition in multicultural societies (Taylor 1994). The second part of the chapter examines the emergence of Irish anti-racism in relation to the main forms taken by racism in the society. The memory of colonialism and emigration, the divisions created by the problem of Northern Irish sectarianism and the specificity of anti-Traveller racism, upon which nascent anti-racism in Ireland was based, are discussed with regard to the types of anti-racism that emerged in response and the problems they have faced. It is argued that Irish anti-racism is structured around the idea of a *warmth of community* that unwittingly mirrors the interrelationship of nationalism and racism at play in the Irish context. The final section looks at some alternative approaches to anti-racism in Ireland, focusing mainly on direct-action groups and the self-organised anti-racism of migrants, asylum seekers and other racialised groups. In conclusion, the success of such radical anti-institutional groupings in challenging both Irish racism and the hierarchical structures of anti-racism are questioned in relation to current policy which, in line with that of the European Union as a whole, makes the future of the non-Irish, non-white and non-Catholic uncertain.

Questioning the identity paradigm: anti-racism and NSM theory

Anti-racism has often been thought of as an example of what have come to be known as NSMs (see, e.g., Wallerstein 1989). Whereas a focus on NSMs, a specific movement-type emerging in the late 1970s – principally peace, women's, ecological and local-autonomy associations (Cohen 1985) – dominated the study of collective action by the 1980s, it became necessary to question the extent to which the concept adequately covers contemporary left-wing activism[1] in general and anti-racism in particular.[2] Nevertheless, the NSM paradigm certainly provided a useful framework for understanding the novel nature of the organisations emerging in the 1970s that broke with class-based and nationally specific movements such as trade unions and political parties. As discussed in the Introduction to this volume, approaches have been taken to the study of NSMs which tend to emphasise either the mobilisation of resources or the operationalisation of identity as central to their activity. The identity-oriented paradigm in NSM theory is particularly problematical in trying to conceptualise anti-racism in terms of an approach to social movements more generally. The shared identity of NSM members as the very raison d'être for their action has been emphasised by many authors (see Dalton 1994; Klandermans 1989), who see it as the essential characteristic that divides NSMs and OSMs. In NSMs, members construct a common identity based upon their shared vision of how they wish the world to look. The identity constructed, for example, in green movements around environmentally aware, non-consumerist, lifestyles takes on a universalistic quality because it is advocated by the movement as a way of life that ideally should be adhered to by all. NSM identity, therefore, is not pre-ordained, but is rather constructed within the movement and then diffused.

However, identity as it has been theorised with regard to politics has more commonly been associated, not with an identity under construction, but with a reified, pre-determined and supposedly *authentic* identity. 'Identity politics' is the term used to describe what Charles Taylor (1994) has called the 'politics of recognition', most often associated with the claim of so-called 'minority' groups within multicultural societies for recognition and a respect for their *difference*. Identity politics, as it has come to obtain mainly in the North American context, has, as a concept, often been conflated with anti-racism. Taylor, in his theorisation of the politics of recognition, turns to Fanon (1963) to conceptualise authenticity, which he sees as crucial to the development of arguments around identity and recognition. Authenticity can be understood as the notion that there is a true essence of individual and/or group identity. The idea is important both in nationalist ideology and in anti-colonial liberation movements that sought to reinstate the culture of the colonised, suppressed by colonial domination. Taylor misconceptualises Fanon's ambivalent relationship with negritude, the name given to the movement for black authenticity by anti-colonial thinkers such as Aimé Césaire and Léopold Senghor. Fanon saw negritude, not as constituting a claim to authenticity, but at best as a last resort in the struggle to overthrow colonial domination. Taylor's failure to read Fanon's ambivalence with regard to negritude is emblematic of the way in which the fight against racism has been conflated with the purported need of minorities in society to assert their uniqueness.

Anti-racism

In effect, the ease with which anti-racism has often been placed under the heading of identity politics has much to do with the interpretation of the role of anti-racism, since the advent of multicultural policy-making in the 1980s, in particular in Anglo-American settings. Since the early 1980s, there has been a tendency, particularly in Britain and North America, for governmental institutions charged with responding to racism to focus on *culture* as the primary framework for making sense of racist exclusion and reacting to it (Anthias and Yuval-Davis 1992; Gilroy 1992; Vertovec 1996). As a result, emphasis was placed on the *community* and on projects that focused on *intercultural* communication or the valorisation of minority culture. This reification of minority ethnic *communities*, rather than being based on demands for a recognition of their authenticity by the members of such communities themselves, often led, in the British context for example, to the undermining of local anti-racist initiatives that emphasised the racism of the State's institutions and the far-right, and which united members of different ethnic groups as well as white people.

While it has been unproblematically accepted that identity politics emerges from a claim to a shared authentic identity under attack (e.g. that of ethnic or sexual minorities, the disabled, etc.), in reality, the emergence of identity politics has rarely followed a bottom-up process, particularly when related to the fight against racism. On the contrary, the implementation of multicultural strategies in policy-making has led to an emphasis by states on culture and identity which, in turn, has been welcomed by many community leaders who do not necessarily represent the internal heterogeneity of the groups they claim to represent (Vertovec 1996). Such strategies have hindered the anti-racism of the civil rights and autonomous, self-organised, movements of the 1960s and 1970s that highlighted the institutionalisation of racism and critiqued the search for solutions at the level of attitudes promoted by the advocates of multiculturalism.

These distinctions are important because the focus on identity in NSMs theory may lead to a conflation with so-called identity politics and, as a result, with anti-racism. In effect, anti-racism has rarely been the object of study from within an NSMs perspective, yet it is often listed as exemplary of NSMs in the literature. This grouping of anti-racism under the heading of both identity politics and NSMs, despite their starkly different nature and the problems associated with both as conceptual categories, is a result of the paucity of research into anti-racism I began by pointing up. What research into anti-racism in Europe reveals is that anti-racism is a heterogeneous phenomenon that employs a variety of discourses and collective action practices to further its cause. Consequently, any conceptualisation of anti-racism within a framework of NSM theory must take into account that, perhaps more than other forms of political and social contestation, it contains within it a particularly complex relationship with the State.

The varieties of anti-racism, as both discourse and practice of movements in Europe, may be thought of as existing along a continuum of proximity-to-distance from the public political culture of the nation state (A. Lentin 2004). Public political culture may be thought of as made up of a set of 'familiar ideas' (Rawls 2001: 5) that shape political thought for the members of democratic societies. Many of the ideas that form public political culture may also be associated with the principles of anti-racism, for example democracy, solidarity, freedom, equality, tolerance, respect, etc. My research (A. Lentin 2004) revealed that what creates the anti-racist continuum of proximity-to-distance from the public political culture of the nation state is the extent to which various anti-racist discourses conceive of these principles as inherent to the liberal democratic nation state. At one extreme of the spectrum, there are anti-racist organisations that tend towards a universalist or mainstream orientation that put forward the claim that the full and equal implementation of principles contained within the ideology of the State will lead to an eradication of racism. For example, a representative of the French anti-racist organisation SOS Racisme, which describes itself as having a *generalist* outlook that sees as counter-productive the grounding of anti-racism in the experiences of the racialised, claimed that 'it was simply the application of the Republic that could stop the process of ghettoisation in the neighbourhoods' (quoted in A. Lentin 2004: 202).

At the other extreme, rather than stressing the principles associated with anti-racism that are also contained within public political culture, anti-racism conjures up notions such as emancipation, empowerment, resistance, liberation and self-determination. These notions, inspired by the anti-colonialist movement and employed by anti-racisms in the West, 'denote a critique of the state's readiness to guarantee freedom and equality, justice and fairness' (*ibid*: 2). In other words, an anti-racism that stresses these notions distances itself from public political culture and, rather than seeing an application of its principles as a solution to racism, insists upon the institutionalisation of racism at the State's core. Beyond these two extremes, anti-racism also displays a high degree of variance along the continuum, taking into account constraints such as funding sources, political alliances and activist profiles, to name but a few. Therefore, it is impractical to think of anti-racism as a unitary or easily categorisable social movements phenomenon. Moreover, its heterogeneity creates a significant degree of conflict between anti-racisms that, in many contexts, makes it impossible to speak of an anti-racist movement as defined by early formulations of NSM theory. Rather, there are a number of competing, or overlapping, organisations, networks, publications, research teams, advocacy or advice workers, direct-action groups and others that make up the panoply of discourses and practices that set out to resist racism, often from radically different points of view.

The specificity of Irish anti-racism

In 1992, Robbie McVeigh published an article entitled 'The Specificity of Irish Racism' which identified five interacting processes as determining the nature of racism in Ireland:

- the impact of British racism;
- Irish involvement in colonialism;
- the Irish diaspora experience;
- the link between racism and sectarianism/nationalism; and
- endogenous anti-Traveller racism.

Over a decade later, it would certainly be possible to add the recent experience of migrants, asylum seekers and refugees into Ireland as shaping the specificity of racism in the country, particularly as it interacts with the Irish emigrant experience. My intention in this section is to revisit what I consider to be the three central factors pointed to by McVeigh (1992) – the diaspora experience, the impact of sectarianism and anti-Traveller racism – and discuss how they have shaped the development of Irish anti-racist responses. Throughout, I build upon research I carried out on anti-racism in Ireland between 1999 and 2002 and relate it to secondary sources that discuss nascent anti-racisms prior to this period.

The Irish diaspora experience

The experience of Irish people as emigrants and the construction of an Irish diaspora are crucial for understanding both anti-Irish racism and Irish racism (McVeigh 2002a). It has also been fundamental, therefore, to the construction of anti-racist discourse in two ways: Firstly, because the Irish experience of racism, most significantly in Britain, led to the involvement of Irish emigrants abroad in the anti-racist movement who later contributed to the establishment of anti-racism in Ireland. Secondly, as I discuss at greater length in the third part of the chapter, the experience of the Irish as emigrants has been used by anti-racists to counter the contemporary racism against immigrants to Ireland who point to the hypocritical nature of such a stance.

The Irish experience of emigration has deeply impacted on the national psyche. This is undoubtedly due to Ireland's history under British colonial rule and the fact that such a large proportion of emigration was to Britain itself, constantly reminding both émigrés and those at home – due to its very proximity to Ireland – of that domination. Ní Shúinéar (2002: 177) suggests that Irish racism today is strongly influenced by the Irish experience of colonialism which produced in them a 'self-loathing and scapegoating'. As in the immigration experiences of numerous colonised and formerly colonised peoples, Irish emigration may be interpreted as a continuation of the colonialist experience, brought about, as it was in the post-war period, by continued economic dependence on the former colonial power.

Anti-Irish racism has a longer history, dating back to colonial times and to the first wave of Irish emigration to the 'new world'. McVeigh (2002a) and Ní Shúinéar (2002) describe how anti-Irish cartoons in the nineteenth century simianised Irish people in much the same way as Africans were caricatured as sub-human. McVeigh also demonstrates how anti-Irish language has entered into British English, with phrases such as 'taking the mick' unquestioningly used to this day. He points out, however, that the definition of this as anti-Irish racism came about in the context of the Irish emigrant experience and, more specifically, with the involvement of Irish people abroad such as he himself in anti-racism, particularly in Britain.

In this context, during the 1980s, the *ethnicisation* of the language of politics led to the possibility of the Irish in Britain being identified as an ethnic group, in line with other racialised communities. For many anti-racists, furthermore, the Irish could be considered politically 'black' (Sivanandan 1983), thus engendering solidarity between black and Irish people involved in left-wing and anti-racist arenas. As McVeigh writes of his own experience, despite his arrival in London in the early 1980s as 'a kind of socialist unionist' (2002a: 137), he quickly became influenced by anti-racism through his African–Caribbean friends. His politics gradually turned to republicanism due to his experience of anti-Irish racism and his belief in the symmetry of black, Asian and Irish experiences in the UK. This experience, therefore, led him to develop a secure Irish identity, to become aware of anti-Irish racism but also, due to his involvement in anti-racism in Britain, to commit to condemning Irish racism upon his return to Ireland. As McVeigh himself points out, the experience of anti-Irish racism, led him 'to adopt a broader approach to racism – if I was going to challenge anti-Irish racism, I couldn't ignore Irish racism' (*ibid*: 138).

For many Irish anti-racists, the involvement of the Irish in the multiculturalisation of British urban spaces had an important impact upon their vision of the type of society they envisaged for Ireland. For example, a representative of Sport Against Racism in Ireland spoke of Liverpool as

> the Healing City, because it's got such a melting pot of different cultures. You know, it's the oldest Chinatown in Europe, big Chinese community, big West African community, you know going back generations to the slave trade – a slave city. You had Irish – 30% of the population has Irish background, Welsh, there's very few English in Liverpool, it's like an independent republic. (SARI, quoted in A. Lentin 2004: 133).

However, the diaspora experience and the meeting with other formerly colonised populations also creates an interesting overlap between anti-racist and nationalist politics that is unique in Europe to the Irish context, due to the historical links between republicanism and the Third World anti-colonialist movement. As a result, contemporary Irish anti-racism sees a marked participation by individuals close to the republican movement as well as, more formally, by the nationalist party Sinn Féin. For example, Residents Against Racism (RAR) counts several active members with close links to Irish republicanism, as the following two interview extracts attest:

> There will be a Sinn Féin speaker as well ... they had a meeting on anti-racism in the ITGWU last year and it was myself and Davina Gael, the Sinn Féin TD, speaking. And that's very encouraging because they draw the parallels between the way nationalists were treated in the North ...

> ... D, an RAR member who had been involved in republican politics for many years and has a background in republican activism.

It is of significance that the potentially problematic strong association created in anti-racist milieux between resistance to racism and republicanism is not generally pointed to. While clearly the Irish republican movement has its roots in the anti-colonial struggle, to what extent is it relevant today for anti-racists and other progressives to claim a nationalist stance, particularly in the Republic of Ireland, which has been an independent state for over 80 years? It is undeniable that Irish nationalism is long since the hegemonic political ideology. In this conjoining of Irish nationalism to anti-racism, there is no questioning of the political interlinkages between nationalism and racism in general nor of the racism that may emerge from the specific configuration of Irish Catholic nationalism. In short, the possibility for Irish people abroad, through their involvement in anti-racism, to recognise, theorise and act upon anti-Irish racism, as McVeigh (2002a) reminds us, is open to criticism without a parallel commitment to fighting Irish racism.

The sectarianism–racism nexus

Closely linked to the discussion of the problematic relationship between Irish anti-racism and diasporic nationalism is the question of sectarianism and its relation to racism. In both Northern Ireland and in the Republic, there has been a direct link drawn by anti-racists between anti-sectarian activism and anti-racism. McVeigh (2002a) points to the usefulness of comparing racism and sectarianism in order to further our understanding of both and to help to see sectarianism as more than just a problem of inter-religious conflict. The parallels drawn by those concerned with countering both racism and sectarianism have engendered a large degree of crossover of those involved in anti-sectarian work to anti-racism in the Irish Republic. Initiatives such as Co-operation North, which organised dialogue between Protestant and Catholic youth from both the North and the South in the 1980s, are cited as precursors for anti-racist work developed in the 1990s.

The work of Sport Against Racism in Ireland, for example, was very much influenced by anti-sectarian youth work, which itself had been shaped with reference to anti-racism in the UK. The following indicates how these influences merge in the work of the organisation:

> So, I looked at the situation in Northern Ireland by conflict resolution and how models that were developed in Liverpool in terms of anti-racism could be applied to the Irish anti-sectarian pattern. And, I found that really interesting because as a kid I used to travel over to watch Liverpool. And I'd be standing in the cockpit by the goal and the guy next to me would have a big King Billy tattoo on his arm and would be shouting for the same team as me. It just didn't make sense that, you know, here we were from the Shankhill Road in Belfast and I was from the inner city in Dublin, coming from those completely different backgrounds, but the same class background, and we had this in common. (SARI, quoted in A. Lentin 2004: 153–4)

The parallels drawn between racism and sectarianism connote a specifically Irish approach to anti-racism that builds upon the particularities of the Irish experience of colonialism and inter-ethnic conflict, and attempt to apply them to a contemporary analysis of racism in the Irish context. This approach recognises that the lines around racist thought and practice are blurred, rarely tracing the simple 'colour line', but rather acting at a number of different levels and affecting different groups at different times. The interplay of anti-Irish racism with Irish racism against non-Irish others, as well as sectarian divisions and their intersection with both of these dynamics, is exemplary of this multidimensional nature of racism, a reality recognised by many Irish anti-racists. However, as remarked upon by the representative of SARI, this multifacetedness is not always accepted beyond the national context by an anti-racism that insists on the primacy of the divide between black and white:

> Some of our colleagues in the likes of Kick it Out and to a lesser extent the Show Racism the Red Card.[3] [t]hey would have a problem with that. When we raise the issue of sectarianism, for example, and the anti-Irish stuff, like the likes of Paul McGrath being called a black Irish bastard or something like that, and they're saying no. No, for them it's not. It's black and white purely. Purely black and white, that's the issue ... (*ibid*: 154–5)

The foundational impact of anti-sectarian work on anti-racism in Ireland would need to be revisited today in light of the marked changes in the societal configuration brought about by increased non-European immigration and the specific racisms that have emerged in reaction to it. Sectarianism does not resonate very strongly for those in the Republic of Ireland for whom it has not been a daily reality. Therefore, while it has been used analytically by anti-racists in their formulation of a response to racism, it may not have currency for the public at large and, more specifically, for the actual or potential victims of racism themselves who experience a racism that does not differ radically from that across 'fortress Europe'.

Anti-Traveller racism

Anti-Traveller racism represents the most important impetus for the development of anti-racist strategies in Ireland. The significance given to racism against Travellers is unique to Ireland, the only country, despite the dramatic problems faced by Roma people throughout Europe, in which Traveller concerns are at the heart of the discussion of racism. The focus on Travellers from a specifically anti-racist perspective was brought about by a shift, during the late 1980s and early 1990s in the discussion of Traveller rights, from a focus on settlement to one on ethnicity. The recognition of Travellers as an indigenous Irish 'minority ethnic' group allowed Travellers and their supporters to theorise their discrimination in terms of racism. The processes by which Travellers were racialised in Irish society could be brought to the fore. Court (1985), for example, remarks on how the terms 'dirty' and 'clean' as well as 'black' and 'white' were applied to differentiate Travellers from 'settled' Irish people.

While the issue of anti-Traveller racism, as a specifically Irish form of racism, has – uniquely – driven the development of anti-racism in Ireland, this has not been without detriment to the development of anti-racism as a whole. At the forefront of the recognition of Travellers as an ethnic group and of their discrimination as racism was one organisation in particular, the Dublin Travellers' Education and Development Group (now called Pavee Point), set up in reaction to virulent racism against Travellers in the Dublin area of Tallaght in 1983 (McVeigh 2002b; Tannam 2002). The anti-racist work of the Traveller Support Movement built on the community development approach and the model of partnership developed by its advocates. It has been recognised (McVeigh 2002b; Tannam 2002; R. Lentin 2004) that the partnership model recreates the dependence of Travellers upon 'settled' Irish people who act on their behalf.

The model is based on the idea that, due to the discrimination suffered by Travellers, they have not benefited from the education and skills that would allow them to represent themselves. They are, therefore, assisted by 'settled' people, for example in the management of finances and public representation. This has led to the situation in which most Traveller organisations in Ireland are not, in fact, run by Travellers themselves, despite the long years of experience of many Travellers in the movement. The tokenistic nature of the partnership model has been recognised by Travellers themselves, such as Martin Collins from the organisation Pavee Point (cited in Tannam, unpublished: 6) who remarked that: '[H]aving four Travellers at a table and having four settled people, it's dangerous to suggest that partnership is taking place there because there can be a huge power imbalance in terms of settled people having had all the opportunities re. education, training – they have a far superior vocabulary.'

As McVeigh (2002b) notes, the tokenism of the 'partnership' model has problematic implications for the way in which anti-racism as a whole has developed in the Irish context. The overrepresentation of white, 'settled' people acting on behalf of Travellers has had a spill-over effect on the anti-racist arena due to the influence of the Traveller Support Movement on the fight against racism more generally:

> The failure to transfer power and resources to minority ethnic people was itself the symbol of 'partnership'. This model became even more dangerous when it began to inform work with refugees and other minority ethnic groups. These groups could be brought into partnership and here too their non-involvement at a leadership level could be excused as an example of partnership. (McVeigh 2002b: 221)

These dangers can be directly witnessed in the application of partnership principles to work with other minority ethnic groups in an anti-racist perspective. For example, in the case of the Bosnian community's women's project Žena in Dublin:[4]

> Most of the time it's actually Irish people who are running refugee projects ... Most of the time you'll have refugees, say, working in a project as part time or very smaller positions only to give those projects credibility but they are not given themselves a chance. And very often the argument is that there aren't educated refugees around which is not a good argument because there are plenty with university degree and experience. (Žena Project, quoted in A. Lentin 2004: 251)

Tokenism, as the partnership model engenders it, has been witnessed in anti-racism across all national contexts. It impacts significantly on the extent to which anti-racism is seen as a principle to be generalised and, therefore, equally owned by all, or, in contrast, as an act of resistance that, although not exclusive, must be grounded in the lived experience of the actual or potential victims of racism themselves.

The centrality of the issue of anti-Traveller racism to the defining of the Irish anti-racist agenda creates a further problem for the construction of a unitary movement. With the birth of a variety of organisations during the late 1990s by recently arrived 'immigrants', such as the now defunct Pan-African Organisation or the Association of Refugees and Asylum Seekers in Ireland, the primacy of anti-Traveller racism began to be challenged. In addition, the work of associations, comprised mainly of Irish people, that specifically targets the Government's policy of deportation of refused asylum seekers, such as RAR, enlarges the focus of anti-racism in Ireland from so-called indigenous minorities, principally Travellers, to the victims of state racism more generally.

There is a danger that the advent of such initiatives, which during the period covered by my research were relatively new, may lead to the construction of a hierarchy of victimhood and competitiveness between groups within the anti-racist arena. For example, although certainly not representative of the Traveller Support Movement as a whole, an interview with some members of the National Traveller Women's Forum[5] revealed unease with regard to the treatment of Traveller concerns following the construction of organisations by new immigrants. With regards to the public reception of the issue of racism, the representatives claimed that the experiences of Travellers, who it is believed have had enough 'airtime', are no longer taken into consideration. Racism is now purportedly seen as merely a black-and-white issue and the work done by Traveller organisations to put racism on the agenda has, in those organisations' view, been ignored. By talking about racism in the general sense which includes that experienced by all racialised groups, the NTWF representatives felt that the importance of racism against Travellers was being diluted. While they stated the importance of working in solidarity with other organisations, they expressed a fear that these organisations were being voyeuristically exploited by the media and that this leads both to the overlooking of Traveller concerns and to a neglect of the amount done by the Traveller movement to positively influence government policy.

The problems engendered by the construction of such hierarchies of victimhood are common to anti-racist arenas in all countries. The phenomenon of 'pulling up the ladder', namely the belief of some former immigrants that contemporary migration must be limited due to 'scarce resources' or the purported influence it may have on the rise of racism, cannot be denied. However, it is necessary to question the extent to which this approach is not, in the case of the Irish Travellers, brought about by the degree to which their struggle itself has been made into the symbol par excellence of Irish anti-racism by the settled people who initiated the Traveller Support Movement on their behalf. The construction of the Irish anti-racist movement around Traveller concerns by settled Irish people, based on a principle of – often unequal – partnership, may have created an a priori hierarchy of 'discriminated groups' that hinders the building of networks of solidarity between them.

The 'warm community' of Irish anti-racism

McVeigh's path-making paper on the specificity of Irish racism proposes the notion of 'warmth of community' as a means of conceptualising a specifically Irish way of being. This concept denotes a cosiness and familiarity that is common to Irish self-conceptualisations as an outgoing and friendly people. When related to racism, as McVeigh intends, the concept of the warmth of community separates the Irish from outsiders, extending only as far as to what can be comfortably included in a definition of Irishness: undoubtedly white,

Catholic and settled. The three factors I see, following McVeigh, as central to an understanding of both Irish racism and the anti-racism discussed above – the diasporic and colonial experiences, the impact of sectarianism and anti-Traveller racism – are intimately connected with the construction of a warm community of Irish insiders. The warmth of community extends to include all those descended from the Irish emigrants forced to leave the ancestral home-land. It is constructed in opposition to Britain as the colonial dominator and importer of Protestantism. Lastly, it resists the notion that the Irish are not in reality a *pure* people untainted by internal differences, so that the Irishness of Travellers, Jews, Protestants and blacks is negated. Therefore, the Irish commu-nity is constructed in opposition to all that differs from the self-conceptualisation of the essence of Irishness. The warmth generated by the community may (to extend the metaphor) be seen as a weather front that blocks itself off from what cannot be conceived as assimilable to it. While it warms and comforts its insiders, it may coldly reject those who seek to enter it.

McVeigh opposes Irish anti-racism to the pathologising of out-groups entailed by the creation of an Irish warmth of community. He proposes that anti-racism in Ireland has served as a means for tackling a range of problems inherent to Irish society, notably around gender, class and sexuality, the open discussion of which has been hindered by the hegemony of the notion of the warmth of community within which such differences would be unimaginable. For McVeigh, the anti-racism arena allows for the discussion of other differ-ences inherent to Irish society by displacing the oppression experienced by the Irish themselves, thrown into relief by the focus on the discrimination faced by others. However, while Irish participation in anti-racism may certainly have had the effect of challenging the closure with regard to the discussion of sensitive social topics, this does not mean that the particular course taken by Irish anti-racism should go uncriticised.

Indeed, rather than challenging the warmth of community, the Irish anti-racist arena has, to a large extent, recreated its own warm community that mirrors the hegemonic notion of community McVeigh critiques. In particular, the anti-racisms initiated by Irish people on behalf of racialised groups, such as the Travellers, often emerging from the experience of emigration or of develop-ment work in the Third World, recreate the notion of a uniquely Irish way of doing things, applied successively to the anti-racist domain. Implicit in this anti-racist discourse is the notion that, due to the Irish history of colonial oppression and dispersal, the anti-racism of Irish people in Irish society itself avoids the pitfalls of tokenism and paternalism often present in anti-racisms that do not base themselves on the lived experience of the actual or potential victims of racism.

As McVeigh (1992) rightly points out, the observation of anti-Irish racism has often engendered the belief that the Irish are incapable of racism. Irish anti-racists, therefore, by building on both the Irish experience of racism and anti-colonial resistance, propose an anti-racist version of the warmth of community that equalises the experience of the present-day victims of racism with that, historically, of the Irish. When added to the failure by many Irish anti-racists to create spaces for the autonomous organisation of anti-racism by those who face racism themselves, this can result in a paternalistic approach which denies its being so on the basis of past suffering. The 'warmth of community' created by Irish anti-racists therefore appears to promote the idea that there is no need, in the Irish context, for self-organisation by the racialised because of the 'disingenuous use of the "racism = power plus prejudice" equation to argue that Irish people, like Black people, have no power to be racist' (McVeigh 1992: 151). However, as has been pointed out by Gilroy (1987) and Bourne (2001), the equation of racism to 'power + prejudice' construes 'racial groups' as fixed and 'race' as definitive of identity along the same lines as nationality, a view that denies the impact of racism on the definition of 'races' and the role of state racism – in Ireland as elsewhere – in perpetuating racialisation.

Challenging the race State

As in other contexts, in Ireland the continuum of proximity-to-distance from the public political culture of the nation state, which I propose characterises the diversity of anti-racisms, can be gauged by the extent to which organisations base their discourse upon a critique of the State. The community development approach which has been critiqued for reproducing patterns of paternalism by not allowing space for self-organised anti-racism, is largely government-funded. Projects relying on such funding are limited in their ability to critique the actions of the State in promoting racist practice and instituting discriminatory policies. Furthermore, the strong links between various Irish community development organisations in the anti-racism sphere and European Union-supported bodies creates a further inability to challenge immigration and asylum policy as they are being increasingly consolidated at EU level. The advocates of the community development approach and other anti-racist organisations that may be termed mainstream, such as the National Consultative Committee on Racism and Interculturalism (which is fully funded by the Department of Justice), promote a discourse built upon institutional language. Therefore, for example, rather than emphasising the relationship between government immigration policy and the institutionalisation of racism, arguments are based on the importance of *integration* for a *multicultural* society. Rarely does such discourse question the terms under which integration takes place, the role played by Others in defining multiculturalism or the paradox of promoting 'diversity' on the one hand while deporting unwanted 'illegals' on the other.

In contrast, reacting to the steady institutionalisation of racist policy since the start of significant immigration into Ireland in the mid-1990s, several organisations were active during the period in which my research was carried out. These are mainly organisations of Irish people, increasingly joined by refugees and migrants, emphasising direct action against the criminalisation of immigration. Three issues emerging from an analysis of these anti-racist groups inform us further as to the range of anti-racisms characterising the development of this form of collective action in the Irish context. They are:

1 the stance of independence taken vis-à-vis the State, seen as the instigator of racism;
2 the development of a discourse opposing that characterised by the 'warmth of community'; and
3 the challenge posed by the principle of black and minority ethnic representation to such groups.

A central dividing point among different forms of anti-racism relates to the degree to which it is thought that relying on state (and supra-state) funding influences the independence of an organisation. Organisations such as the National Federation of Anti-Racist Campaigns (NFARC) and RAR, interviewed for my study, believe that receiving government funding would influence the degree to which state policy could be publicly criticised. This position is illustrated by the following remark:

> We feel that we would then be beholden to the State [if we accepted state funding] and we're criticising the State ... It's state racism that Residents Against Racism ... That's our particular agenda because we feel that if racism is endorsed by the State it gives every petty little racist ... you know, they feel justified in the nasty things that they do. (RAR member)

A representative of the NFARC also commented that were the organisation to seek state funding, 'it would be hard for us to go and get core funding from a government agency so that we can challenge government policy right down the line'. The reason for which maintaining independence is seen either as a matter of principle or as a result of the critical stance adopted by these organisations is bound to their interpretation of institutional racism in Ireland. NFARC, for example, critiques the belief, promoted by the State, that immigration policy is unrelated to racism, compounded by the Government's investment in anti-racism:

> [We are] trying to identify in a very public way the level of state xenophobia and the contribution that promoting an anti-immigrant policy has in terms of the emergence of racism in the country; i.e. we always try to pull it back to it's not that racism is a separate thing out there and then you have the anti-immi-

grant policies over here. The two are so closely connected because in order for a government to effect a policy of deportation or exclusion in effect, in order to effect a policy like that, they cannot paint asylum seekers in Ireland in a very positive light because in order to deport them you must ensure that levels of public sympathy for them remain low. (NFARC, quoted in A. Lentin 2004: 286)

The emphasis placed on institutionalised racism, demonstrated by the independent stance taken by these organisations, relates to the second issue raised by the discussion of this form of anti-racism in Ireland, namely the critique of the notion of 'warmth of community' as theorised by McVeigh (1992). The organisations have undertaken a project of sensitisation of the Irish public to the problems associated with assuming, on the basis of past suffering, that the Irish are incapable of racism. NFARC, for example, has used Irish emigration as a means of reminding Irish people of their own experiences of racism in order to stress the hypocrisy of racism against present-day immigrants to Ireland:

We've done protests at the airport on, maybe, the day before Christmas Eve when all Irish emigrants are coming back ... I do think it jogged people's memories a little bit to make connections between the lunacy of us welcoming home all these Irish emigrants at Christmas time, most of whom – in fact probably all – were economic migrants in one form or another, and probably less entitled to the description 'economic migrant' than many of the people who have come to Ireland. Making people recognise the lunacy of that type of behaviour that we can, on the one hand welcome people, our people, home – many of whom were illegal elsewhere, particularly in the United States – welcoming people back and at the same time dragging people through the airport to stuff them on planes and push them out of the country.

The organisations recognise the divide created in public opinion between purportedly legitimate asylum seekers and others construed as economic migrants disguised as 'bogus refugees'. Irish emigration for economic purposes is stressed and used to illustrate the relative absence of choice in migration whatever the reason motivating it.

Despite the focus on state racism and on what is seen as the hypocrisy of Irish racism, these organisations have not been very successful in involving actual or potential victims of racism themselves in their activities. Therefore, while the pitfalls of 'partnership' are avoided because organisations such as NFARC and RAR do not claim to speak on behalf of those targeted by racism, they have not largely been able to promote real co-operation with immigrant groups. According to Residents Against Racism, this difficulty is brought about by the fear faced by most asylum seekers and migrants: 'It's difficult when you're a refugee to go public' (RAR). This is backed up by NFARC, emphasising the onus on Irish people to speak out where those facing racism feel they cannot, as the two following remarks attest:

There's no threat to my position by doing this. I will not face a harsher interview in the Department of Justice than some people possibly have because of
being vocal in their opposition to the policies of the government, I mean
someone coming from an ethnic minority or asylum seekers background. I
still think that, as an Irish person, I am perfectly entitled in my own right – or
we are in our right – to challenge the policies of the Irish Government, which
are enacted on our behalf. (NFARC, quoted in A. Lentin 2004: 259–60)

Conclusion: the erosion of Irish anti-racism

This paper set out to theorise the development of anti-racist social movements
in Ireland in light of the specificity of racism in the Irish context. It has largely
been based upon primary and secondary resources gathered over the course of
the 1990s and early 2000s. In order to adequately conclude this chapter and
make some remarks about the future prospects for this form of collective action
in Ireland, it is necessary to turn now to the contemporary situation facing anti-
racists in the Irish Republic.

The singular most significant challenge faced by those committed to opposing racism in Ireland has been the passing in 2004 of the citizenship referendum.
The referendum, held in June 2004, asked citizens to vote on whether or not
birthright citizenship – a foundational principle of the Irish Constitution since
the establishment of the Irish State in 1922 – should be revoked in the case of
children born to non-Irish nationals. Support for the change was registered by
a vote of four to one, meaning that migrants' children born in Ireland will not
have birthright citizenship. Prior to the referendum, as a result of a Supreme
Court ruling in January 2003, migrant parents of children born in Ireland (and
therefore citizens) were deemed not to be entitled to residency rights in Ireland,
as has been the case since the 1990s. As a result, some 11,000 migrant families
face deportation and their Irish-citizen children face being forcibly removed
from Ireland.

In light of the extremity of the Irish electorate's rejection of immigrants – and
of Irish children born to immigrant parents – the anti-racist cause appears to
have suffered a severe blow. The possibilities open to anti-racist action are
increasingly limited under the general government-promoted consensus,
according to which the problems faced by immigrants are irrelevant because
their presence in the country is temporary. Nevertheless, the reality of immigration cannot be denied due to the simple fact that some 250,000 immigrants
arrived in Ireland over the course of the 1990s (many of them returning Irish
emigrants, including labour migrants essential for the continuation of economic
growth), adding to other 'minorities', including the 24,000–strong Traveller
community (R. Lentin 2004). The only way in which their presence as well as
their needs may be accounted for, under present conditions, is through an integrationist paradigm that denies the right to immigrants, black people and

minority groups to define their own agendas. Furthermore, the only way to fight mass deportations of migrant parents of Irish-citizen children seems to be through legal channels, all political avenues having been explored and having failed, as is evident from the work of the Coalition Against Deportation of Irish Children (CADIC), a coalition of human rights, children's rights, migrant support, and refugee support organisations, which came into being in July 2003, at the request of AkiDwA – the African Women's Network (see CADIC 2003).

Although a myriad of migrant-led and local community groups, representing the interests of various groups committed to anti-racism, do exist, the funding available to them has been radically cut, leaving them to compete for scarce state and European funding with Irish-led organisations (A. Lentin 2004: 6). The emphasis placed on integration denies the racism of the State's policy on immigration, separating it from the need to cater for those already admitted during less harsh times. The integration policies promoted by the State are based on an unproblematised multiculturalism that ignores the uneven power relations necessarily defining the positioning of refugees and immigrants with regard to the State. Denied the possibility of adequately representing themselves due to cuts in funding and the change in the charity laws, bringing about curtailed permission to hold demonstrations, immigrant organisations are increasingly forced to rely on integration programmes that cannot but reinforce their exclusion.

Few of the organisations originally interviewed for my research are still in existence in more than just name. Residents Against Racism has been at the forefront of the Campaign Against a Racist Referendum (CARR), and continues to lead an avowedly radical anti-institutional stance of critique of Irish state racism. However, as their representative clearly pointed out: 'We're not funded at all. We just get by by the skin of our teeth from people sending us £2 membership.' Despite the growth in Ireland, as across the world, of the movement for a globalisation from below, the strong presence of an anti-war campaign and the development of a range of other progressive debates in civil society, it appears that anti-racism is in decline. A re-analysis of its emergence, as has been proposed in this chapter may, it is hoped, be of use in reassessing where it may go in the future.

Notes

1 It is of interest to note that, generally, the NSMs paradigm has not been widely applied to the study of movements to the right of the political spectrum.
2 Most notably, the proliferation of a 'movement of movements' calling for a globalisation from below, since the Seattle protests of 1999, has radically changed the character of collective action. While the NSMs, with their purported identity-oriented, transnational and alternative characteristics may be said to be a precursor to the networks making up the global movement of today, they also display marked

contrasts – not least their rootedness in the North – which beg the question of whether they still constitute a useful analytic framework. For example, the institutionalisation of many NSMs, in particular the environmental and women's movements, and the emergence from within them of a professionalised NGO 'sector' may signal the end of the NSM as it was theorised in the 1980s and 1990s (see Cohen 1985; Touraine 1988; Melucci 1989).

3 Both are campaigns against racism in football, originating in the UK.

4 The Žena Project has ceased to exist due to the halting of its funding by the Irish Refugee Agency, a body established by the governmental Department of Foreign Affairs to provide for so-called 'programme refugees', including the Bosnian community. The reason for its disbanding was given as the inability of the Bosnian project coordinator to adequately run the project according to 'community development' practices, a criticism which reveals the rejection of practices developed by the community itself due to their lack of 'fit' with fore-ordained strategies developed under the uniquely Irish 'community development' perspective.

5 This unrecorded interview was carried out in Dublin on October 10, 2000.

Bibliography

Anthias, F. and Yuval-Davis, N., 1992 *Racialised Boundaries: Race, nation, gender, colour and class, and the anti-racist struggle* (London and New York: Routledge).

Balibar, E., 1991 'Racism and Nationalism', in Balibar, E. and Wallerstein, I. (eds), *Race, Nation, Class: Ambiguous identities* (London: Verso).

Bonnett, A., 2000 *Anti-Racism* (London and New York: Routledge).

Bourne, J., 2001 'The Life and Times of Institutional Racism', *Race and Class*, 43:2, 7–21.

CADIC, 2003 'Information for Migrant Parents of Irish Citizen Children', leaflet, September.

Cohen, J., 1985 'Strategy and Identity: new theoretical paradigms and contemporary social movements', *Social Research*, 52:4, 633–716.

Court, A., 1985 *Puck of the Droms: The lives and literature of Irish tinkers* (Berkeley: University of California Press).

Dalton, R.J., 1994 *The Green Rainbow: Environmental groups in Western Europe* (New Haven, CT: Yale University Press)

Fanon, F., 1963 *The Wretched of the Earth* (New York: Grove Press).

Gilroy, P., 1987 *'There Ain't No Black in the Union Jack': The cultural politics of race and nation* (London: Unwin Hyman).

Gilroy, P., 1992 'The End of Anti-Racism', in Donald, J. and Rattansi, A. (eds), *'Race', Culture and Difference* (London: Sage).

Goldberg, D.T., 2002 *The Racial State* (Malden, MA, and Oxford: Blackwell).

Klandermans, B. (ed.), 1989 *Organizing for Change: Social movement organizations in Europe and the United States* (Greenwich, CT: JAI Press).

Lentin, A., 2004 *Racism and Anti-Racism in Europe* (London and Ann Arbor, MI: Pluto Press).

Lentin, R., 2004 'The Racial State and Crisis Racism: migration and integration in Ireland', paper presented at the British Council seminar 'Migration: philosophies and practices of integration', Cork, 20–5 June.

McVeigh, R., 1992 'The Specificity of Irish Racism', *Race and Class*, 33:4, 31–45.

McVeigh, R., 2002a 'Nick, Nack, Paddywhack: anti-Irish racism and the racialisation of Irishness', in Lentin, R. and McVeigh, R. (eds), *Racism and Anti-Racism in Ireland*

(Belfast: Beyond the Pale).

McVeigh, R., 2002b 'Is There an Irish Anti-Racism? Building an anti-racist Ireland', in Lentin, R. and McVeigh, R. (eds), *Racism and Anti-Racism in Ireland* (Belfast: Beyond the Pale).

Melucci, A., 1989 *Nomads of the Present: Social movements and individual needs in contemporary society*, ed. Keane, J. and Mier, J. (London: Hutchinson Radius).

Ní Shúinéar, S., 2002 'Othering the Irish (Travellers)', in Lentin, R. and McVeigh, R. (eds), *Racism and Anti-Racism in Ireland* (Belfast: Beyond the Pale).

Rawls, J., 2001 *Justice and Fairness: A restatement*, ed. Kelly, E. (Cambridge, MA, and London: Belknap Press of Harvard University Press).

Sivanandan, A., 1983 'Challenging Racism: strategies for the '80s', *Race and Class*, 25:2, 1–11.

Tannam, M., 2002 'Questioning Anti-Racism in Ireland', in Lentin, R. and McVeigh, R. (eds), *Racism and Anti-Racism in Ireland* (Belfast: Beyond the Pale).

Taylor, C., 1994 *Multiculturalism* (Princeton, NJ: Princeton University Press).

Touraine, A. 1988 *Return of the Actor: Social theory in postindustrial society* (Minneapolis: University of Minnesota Press).

Vertovec, S., 1996 'Multiculturalism, Culturalism and Public Incorporation', *Ethnic and Racial Studies*, 19:1, 49–69.

Wallerstein, I., with Arrighi, G. and Hopkins, T.K., 1989 *Antisystemic Movements* (London: Verso).

10 · Laurence Cox[1]

News from nowhere:
the movement of movements in Ireland

IN 1999, 60,000 protestors shut down the World Trade Organisation (WTO) meeting in Seattle (Charlton 2000; Cockburn et al. 2000), a shock to the ruling institutions of the New World Order which is often seen as the start of the movement against capitalist globalisation. These events, however, barely registered on the awareness of a supposedly global Ireland, caught up in celebrating its new status as the 'Celtic Tiger'. Even Irish activists remained on the margins, with no organised involvement.

Just five years later, a new 'movement of movements' had come out of the shadows to shake this complacency. On 15 February 2003, opposition to war on Iraq involved over 100,000 people in the largest demonstration for two decades. That July, the World Economic Forum (WEF) was forced to cancel its planned regional meeting in Dublin in the face of planned protests. On Mayday 2004, 5,000 protestors faced down riot police defending the EU Summit from the largest libertarian event the country had ever seen. The next month, George Bush's visit was so unpopular that it had to be protected by tanks, nearly 4,000 Gardaí, 2,000 Irish military and 700 US Secret Service agents (Sheridan 2004). Where Clinton's visit ten years back had seen him surrounded by 250,000 supporters in Dublin, now Bertie Ahern was reduced to pleading with people not to protest against Bush.

The movement appeared in Ireland so suddenly that it caught most commentators, journalists and academics on the hop: ill informed, and so unprepared that they could barely identify who to speak to on the subject.[2] To such elites, it seemed to come out of nowhere. It sidestepped the issues of parties and tribunals which usually occupy the public sphere to propose alternative means of organising politics; 'reclaimed the streets' in an era when SUVs had become status symbols for Ireland's nouveaux riches; and raised the slogan 'No Borders, No Nations' in the same month when 80 per cent of the electorate voted for race as a criterion for citizenship.

Yet seen from below, the movement of movements was building on an unofficial reality of social movements and campaigns which long preceded it but

which rarely attract much attention, and developing long-standing countercultural critiques of the Irish mainstream. Thus it took the issue of tolerance for
diversity beyond liberal demands for legal change into the direct action of squats
and street parties; it went beyond conventional calls for public debate and
top–down theories of 'educating people for citizenship' to building alternative
institutions of bottom–up information and discussion such as Indymedia and
social forums; and it challenged the rhetoric of neutrality with direct action
against the US military's use of Shannon for its Third World wars.

In the twilight years of the Celtic Tiger (Coulter and Coleman 2003), this new
movement against capitalist globalisation became a significant force in Irish
politics and society. But the 'business as usual' perspective of professional
commentators seeking to force it into their traditional frameworks – whether
tabloid hysteria, official blandness or 'critical' worthiness – offers little in terms
of actual understanding. How did the movement develop so rapidly, coming
from near-invisibility to push EU summits and US wars out of first place in the
news and forcing the State to militarise Shannon Airport and the Phoenix Park?
Why should it have developed at that point, rather than 5 years earlier or 10
years later? And where is the movement heading?

Studying the movement of movements

Essays often start with definitions, appealing to authority to define what a word
or phrase *really* means. Social – and linguistic – reality, however, work in the
opposite direction: people create new words, and give new meanings to old
ones, in everyday usage (Williams 1983). Dictionaries and researchers then
struggle to catch up with the changes.

In the case of the movement of movements, the meanings are themselves a
site of struggle. There is no one authority deciding what is and is not part of the
movement. The many different names given to the movement are ways in which
different political actors try to draw boundaries around it that include those
groups, issues and strategies which they want to highlight and exclude others.

What's in a name?

The 'anti-globalisation movement' is used by journalists (e.g. Sansonetti 2002)
to imply that the movement is mainly opposed to opening borders. Yet this
highly international movement typically contrasts its demand for the free movement of people and ideas to the freedom for capital and trade promoted by
neo-liberal institutions.

- The 'anti-capitalist movement', a tag often used by socialists (e.g. Bircham
  and Charlton 2001; Dee 2004), embodies a wish that the movement *should*

become so, because the aims of the movement – to bring about social justice and end a purely exploitative form of globalisation – cannot be met within capitalism. However, not all participants share this analysis.

- The 'anti-corporate movement', by contrast, is used by some US writers (e.g. Klein 1999) to narrow the movement to opposing large-scale corporate capitalism (the world of Nike, Coca-Cola and Esso), implying support for local, national or family capitalism. Yet this approach is a minority one within the Irish movement and globally.

- The 'global justice movement' is how some development NGOs and Catholic activist groups describe the movement, side-stepping political strategy to focus on desired results. Social justice, though, is only one theme within a movement that also includes opposition to war, challenges to state power and ecological alternatives.

- The 'movements against capitalist globalisation' is a phrase used to stress both that the movement opposes a particular phase of capitalism, and that it favours an alternative globalisation based on human need rather than profit and power. However, capitalist globalisation provokes multiple forms of resistance and opposition, not all of which belong to the same movement. For this reason, this chapter uses the phrase in the plural.

- The 'movement of movements' (Mertes 2004) is used in this chapter to highlight the structure of the movement as a coming together of different groups, campaigns and individuals which have realised that their different areas of concern – racism and war, economic exploitation and environmental destruction, patriarchy and state power – are interlinked. This way of seeing things fits with the definition of a social movement as a network of interactions between multiple groups engaged in a political or cultural conflict and sharing a collective identity (Diani 1992).

These last two phrases – 'movements against capitalist globalisation' – and 'movement of movements' – highlight different aspects of the movement: the 'top–down' processes of global neo-liberalism to which it responds and the 'bottom–up' processes of movement networking and identity-building which constitute the movement as a movement. As this chapter suggests, an understanding of both elements is crucial to understanding the movement.

Movements against capitalist globalisation and the movement of movements

Arguably, capitalism has been global since its birth in the Renaissance (Arrighi 1994). It continually remakes societies in its own image, destroying older ways of life and creating new forms of poverty and wealth (Marx and Engels 1998). Unsurprisingly, this continually provokes resistance on the part of the dispossessed (Linebaugh and Rediker 2000). In this sense, Ireland, as one of Europe's first internal colonies and a key site of capitalist experimentation, has seen movements against capitalist globalisation from Elizabethan times. Here as elsewhere, these movements combined elements of particularism (defending the status of a single group under threat) and solidarity (building links with other dispossessed groups).

In a narrower sense, capitalism entered a new period from the 1970s onwards (Harvey 1989) in which, firstly, welfare states in the West were dismantled under the hegemony of neo-liberal economics and, secondly, starting from the late 1980s, the model was generalised to the rest of the world as *globalisation*.[3] Following the defeat of earlier movements of opposition to capitalism (Cox 1999a), the movements against capitalist globalisation have come into being as resistance to the effects of globalising neo-liberalism has itself become global (Cox 2001). Since the 1990s, a new wave of 'anti-systemic movements' (Arrighi et al. 1989) has been developing around the world. This movement wave brings together various strands.

Firstly, opposition within the majority world to neo-liberal economics, starting from the 1980s' 'IMF riots' in Africa and Latin America against the International Monetary Fund's imposition of cuts on state provision for basic needs (Alexander 2001). In the 1990s and early 2000s, the Zapatistas and other movements in Latin America offered large-scale organised challenges to neo-liberal economic agendas (Marcos 2001). And across the global South, from India to Brazil, social movements of the dispossessed, the poor peasants and indigenous peoples under threat from capitalist agriculture, have been organising and taking direct action against forms of development which destroy their means of existence (Polet and CETRI 2004).

Subsequently, the summit meetings where the institutions of neo-liberal globalisation take decisions directing world economics have become foci for activists from around the world, objecting both to the decisions taken and to the undemocratic nature of these institutions. Meetings of the Group of 8 wealthiest nations (G8), the WTO, the WEF, the General Agreement on Trade and Services (GATS), the EU, the IMF–World Bank (WB), the North American Free Trade Agreement (NAFTA) and other such bodies have been challenged directly by activists from the global South, Northern trade unionists, environmental activists, and others affected by neo-liberalism. Protests have aimed both to outline alternatives and to shut down these bodies (Anon. 2001a; Starhawk 2002; Harvie et al. 2005).

Since 9/11 the US-led 'war on terror', intended in part to demobilise and criminalise the movement as 'terrorist', has led instead to its development and radicalisation, including the protests of 15 February 2003 (Sauermann 2003) – probably the single largest worldwide event ever organised by ordinary people rather than governmental, commercial or media bodies.

Thus the development of the movement has two aspects. On the one hand are the top–down processes of capitalist globalisation (the expansion of neo-liberalism, the development of a New World Order and its militarisation against all opposition). On the other hand is the growth of opposition to these processes: direct resistance, developing connections between activists and an increasing ability to coordinate and communicate.

This movement naturally attracts comparison with other movement 'waves' or 'world-revolutionary moments' (Katsiaficas 1987) such as 1989–90 in the Soviet bloc, 1968 globally, or the European Resistance of 1922–45. At the same time, it is unusual in that such a scale of opposition to the status quo has neither been repressed nor developed into full-blown revolutions (outside Latin America). Although communication is much faster and coordination much deeper than ever before, the length of time during which the movement has faced off directly against the state is remarkable for the post-war period, showing a degree of interconnectedness, rootedness in local struggles and breadth of vision which marks it out as bearing comparison with those previous periods.

A Marxist perspective on the movement of movements

This chapter develops a Marxist perspective on the movement. Although Marxism developed out of the experience of the eighteenth- and nineteenth-century democratic and socialist movements, it is often misunderstood as providing an abstract 'theory of society'. An alternative reading, which this chapter draws on,[4] is that Marxism is a theory of socially situated collective action which treats overall social structure (such as capitalist globalisation) both as the *result* of past social movements and as the *object* over which present movements struggle.

Conventional social science, by contrast, takes the structure of the social world for granted and organises itself accordingly, with separate disciplines (political science, economics, sociology, etc.), and within those separate, institutionally defined sub-fields (the sociology of the family, the study of political parties, social movement studies, etc). In this context, 'social movements' are understood as a particular type of institution, operating within an essentially given social structure (despite the fact that successful movement processes consist of *change* in that structure).

Marxism as a theory of social movements sees the social world in terms of socially situated human action as liable to develop as collective behaviour. It also famously sees the social world as contradictory, and so expects conflict as a normal part of social interaction. From a Marxist point of view, therefore, social movements (in the sense of collective action in conflict) are the norm rather than the exception, and operate not only in semi-informal ways but equally within the shell of institutional forms (trade unions, political parties, churches, etc.), which are themselves the product of past social movement struggles. In other words, Marxism as social movements theory is not a *sub-theory* related to a specific kind of social institution; it is a theory of how society as a whole works, in whatever forms.

This collective action comes from above as well as from below, and a moment's reflection will make it clear that collective action from above is normally more powerful than that from below, and can be expected to be more consistent, better institutionalised, and to look like *normality* and *routine*. Marxist approaches to social movements, then, involve a reflection on the power relations built into institutional structures, how they have been constructed and how they can be deconstructed, rather than taking movements from above for granted.

Marxism is interested in the relationships between different forms of social movements: not only in the conflict between movements from above and from below, but also in interaction between different movements from above or different movements from below, and in the differing *levels* of social movement action, from localised muttering and go-slow in a single workplace to occasional moments of worldwide revolutionary upsurge – both of which fall outside the range of most social movement studies.

Marxism does not involve believing (as is sometimes thought) that all social movements are movements of a single class. Classes do not start as coherent historical actors (Thompson 1966). Rather, the process of social movement (sometimes) has the result that people form themselves into a *class-for-itself.* Equally importantly, social movements are often spaces of contention between different classes, as in the French Revolution. What *is* characteristic of Marxism as a theory of social movements is its expectation that people's needs and perspectives will be socially situated, so that class, gender, ethnicity, etc., are always present in the process of movement formation.

Marxist theory is geared towards the practical needs of movement activists, derived in large part from the reflections of past generations of social movement participants. This *unity of theory and practice* gives it its characteristic shape, in which propositional statements are linked to proposals for action (Barker and Cox 2002; Nilsen 2004a).

Finally, as a result of the above, Marxist writing on social movements rarely consists of *applying* a theory from outside to a particular *case*, and refuses the separation between *theory* (as a list of Great Texts) and *empirical data* – as if the latter could be seen independently of our informal theorising about the nature of the social world (starting with our assumptions about what a social movement looks like). Instead, the goal of Marxist writing is to achieve a dialogue between what we think and what we see, which results in a more integrated approach to writing.

Most of the systematic thinking about the movement of movements, in fact, has come from outside conventional social movement studies, from activist or activist–academic writers and researchers (see e.g. Brecher et al. 2000; George 2005; Hardt and Negri 2000, 2004; McNally 2004; Notes from Nowhere 2003; Marcos 2001; Pianta 2001; Solnit 2004).

Conventional social movement theory has had little to say about the movement despite Mario Diani's claim in the Foreword to this volume. Thus there are very few monographs within anything like a conventional social movement perspective (exceptions are Starr 2000 and Della Porta 2003). There has, however, been a sudden flurry of collected articles under headings such as 'transnational movement networks' or 'global movements' (Keck and Sikkink 1998; Smith and Guarnizo 1998; Della Porta et al. 1999; Cohen and Rai 2000; Guidry et al. 2000; Hamel et al. 2001; Della Porta and Tarrow 2005), belatedly discovering that social movements operate outside and across national boundaries (the first socialist International was founded in 1864.)

One reason for this silence is that social movement studies have fetishised 'civil society', privileging movements that do not challenge the power of states or the capitalist economy they protect. Since the most obvious fact about the movement of movements is that it does just that, it has been hard to fit the movement within existing frameworks. As I have suggested elsewhere (Cox 1999b), another way of putting this is that social movement studies are defined by the defeat of the movements of 1968. Having assumed a basic institutional continuity, they find it hard to respond to movements that involve counter-institutional actors operating outside the system and mobilising some of the poorest people on the planet.

From a Marxist perspective, social movements from below bring together people who experience their needs as being threatened or constrained by movements from above, such as capitalist globalisation. Starting from local campaigns around specific issues (such as bin charges, opposition to incineration, solidarity work with immigrants, resistance to the US military use of Shannon or opposition to the Rossport pipeline), they come to recognise each other as responding to crises caused by the same drives within the system and start to reach out to other activists and movements at home and elsewhere. In so doing, they articulate visions of alternative social possibilities and create alternative institutions: political forums, independent media, countercultural networks and economic alternatives to the dominant system.

The discussion in this chapter rests above all on my own participatory action research in this movement and on involvement in the process of activist theorising (Barker and Cox 2002) developed within that movement. In other words, it is a distilled form of the ideas, experiences and struggles of activists within Ireland as they attempt to 'build another world'.

The movement of movements in Ireland

Opposition to capitalist globalisation in Ireland has existed for as long as the process itself. In Ireland, the worldwide rise of neo-liberalism and its new phase as globalisation overlaps with a specific local history of opening up to investment by foreign multinationals from 1958 onwards, the politics of recession in the later 1970s and the early 1980s, the process of partnership geared towards 'international competitiveness' from the late 1980s onwards and the development of the 'Celtic Tiger' in the latter half of the 1990s.

This process had losers as well as winners: jobs were lost, farms were no longer able to support farmers, businesses went under, poor people were excluded from the new worlds being created for the privileged, other and older ways of life were being destroyed, and working-class communities felt all the negative impacts of 'development'.

Thus there has been a long-standing community-based opposition to multinational industries (Allen and Jones 1990; Allen 2004). The socialist left has fought both the specific and the general subordination of workers' interests to multinational agendas. Working-class communities have organised to resist their own marginalisation in the 'brave new world' of consumer capitalism (Powell and Geoghegan 2004). And a complex counterculture has resisted the McDonaldisation of Irish ways of life and proposed alternatives (Cox 1997).

The recent Irish movement of movements grows out of a long process of attempts at networking and building links within and around these different movements and campaigns, reaching back at least to the Mustard Seed gathering of 1976 and the Carnsore Point protests of 1979, if not before. Activist festivals and gatherings, an extensive alternative press, attempts at party-building, the creation of 'free spaces', and more than anything else involvement in shared campaigns and projects combined to develop what was rightly called an 'alternative Ireland' (Alternative Ireland Directory Collective 1982), now three decades old.

When speaking of the Irish movement of movements, then, it is important to be clear that it represents a small, albeit important, part of these broader and more diffuse movements and campaigns. Much of its strength lies in its ability to draw on these existing traditions and connections. Against this wider background, its specific characteristics are its character as a network of (some of) these diverse movements, its explicit self-positioning in opposition to neo-liberalism as such and its connection to the broader global movement of movements.

Explaining Irish developments

Probably the first substantial appearance of the Irish movement of movements was participation in opposition to the IMF–WB meeting in Prague in September

2000, and in simultaneous Dublin events highlighting issues raised by the Prague counter-summit. However, this was still a very small-scale participation and largely limited to existing left groups and development NGOs. How did the movement grow from this point – a few dozen individuals meeting in the Temple Bar Music Centre – to the point where it could challenge the State at Shannon and on the streets of Dublin in 2003 and 2004?

The short answer has to do with the increasing incapacity of the Irish State to maintain social consensus in the context of neo-liberalism. Symbolically, while opposition grew at home, the great peacemaker Ahern's attention was focused on the EU Presidency and issues around accession, the new EU constitution and appointing a Commission President.

The Irish State has traditionally been able to maintain its legitimacy and isolate dissent by its ability to distribute sectoral rewards, the fruits of office or the benefits of growth (Breen et al. 1990; Allen 1997). It therefore faces a specific kind of difficulty as it enters into neo-liberal arrangements under which the State is increasingly prevented from subsidising the popular classes. Put another way, once it is committed under the Nice Treaty to privatising transport, health and other public services, and has to operate within EU budgetary constraints, Fianna Fáil has fewer of the spoils of office to distribute. Neo-liberalism, then, tends to undermine the political arrangements on which its power resides.

The anti-capitalist movement and the anti-war movement

A longer answer has to highlight more specific aspects of the conditions under which Irish people have moved into participation in the movement of movements. Growth in popular participation has been primarily linked to opposition to the US-led 'war on terror' and to Ireland's de facto support for that war. Although there was significant Irish participation in the Genoa protests of July 2001, it was not until the war on Afghanistan that this translated into major protests in Ireland.

Patriotism, according to Dr Johnson, is the last refuge of the scoundrel, and 9/11 was a great boost for the Bush administration as well as a blow for the US movement against capitalist globalisation. Yet while the US administration and EU summits developed strategies after 9/11 to criminalise already existing protest movements under new 'anti-terrorist' legislation, in Ireland popular support for neutrality made the use of Shannon by the US military and CIA a political liability for the Irish Government.

This was highlighted by the development of non-violent direct action protests at Shannon by Mary Kelly, the Catholic Workers' and the Grassroots Network Against War– the last of which led to the bizarre spectacle of the Irish Army being deployed to protect the US military from 300 non-violent activists – and of course by the massive protests of 15 February 2003, co-organised by the

Irish Anti-War Movement, the NGO Peace Alliance and the Peace and Neutrality Alliance.

Opposition to the Bush visit of June 2004 was similarly organised primarily around themes of opposition to the 'war on terror', the torture of prisoners and Israeli occupation policies. In supporting the military face of the New World Order, the Irish Government managed to place itself at odds with the large majority of the population. In Ireland, therefore, anti-war themes have been central to the development of the movement of movements. Put another way, the Irish State's collusion with the more unpalatable aspects of the New World Order has been one key reason for the growth in dissent.

Policing the crisis or producing the crisis?

If neo-liberalism has undermined the State's ability to secure consent, its turn to coercive solutions has further distanced it from many citizens. In theory, states have the alternative of governing through coercion or consent. In practice, consent is sought where support cannot be coerced; and when legitimacy breaks down force is used (Gramsci 1977). The movement of movements, this chapter argues, is made possible by the decreasing ability to secure consent. The Irish State has accordingly resorted to force in its response to the movement, thus further weakening its legitimacy for many people.[5]

The policing of Shannon has already been mentioned. The most significant example, however, is the police riot at the Reclaim the Streets protest on 6 May 2002. This event, in which policemen baton-charged a peaceful crowd, including bystanders, and hospitalised over a dozen people, was highly visible, leading to the remarkable spectacle of tabloid newspapers defending protestors against police. It also marked a stepping-stone in the criminalisation of the movement. Traditionally the policing of protest – other than republican protest – has been low-key in Ireland, for reasons that have to do with the conflict in the North. From the police attacks on protestors at the 'public–private partnership' summit at the Burlington in October 2001, however, the movement of movements has increasingly been perceived as threatening by the police.

In all probability, this derives less from the Irish situation (Garda 'intelligence assessments' were shown to be woefully inadequate on May Day 2004) and more from the previously mentioned European context, in which protest groups are (as in the 1970s) seen as falling within the same bracket as terrorism and subjected to the same kind of surveillance.

The high point to date of this militarisation of policing was around the May Day weekend and the Bush visit, both in 2004. For the May Day weekend, 5000 Gardaí and 500 soldiers were used, with the deployment of armed detectives, riot squads, 'non-lethal weaponry' and water cannons. Dublin was in effect placed under martial law, with the effective banning of Dublin Grassroots

Network's planned march to the EU Summit in Farmleigh House (Dublin Grassroots Network 2004).

In the event, the ban almost certainly boosted the numbers of those protesting in defence of civil liberties, and the march came within a mile of the summit despite a supposed 4–mile exclusion zone. This ineffectiveness was coupled with a massive scare campaign about a threat of violence which failed to materialise – from initial claims of '20,000 anarchists' supposedly travelling from the UK, the final comment in the *Garda Review* spoke of '20 activists ... intent on trouble' (Caldwell 2004). In fact, the majority of those arrested (all on very minor charges) were young Irish people, many of them students. It is difficult not to conclude that the purpose of the policing was less to respond to real threats and more to impress European partners.

The militarisation of policing has led to the use of the mainstream media as PR auxiliaries, given the inability of the Garda Press Office to do so after May Day 2002. The run up to May Day 2004 saw, as Harry Brown wrote, 'some of the most atrocious journalism in living memory' (2004b), with claims of secret armies, arms dumps, gas attacks (respectively Conlon 2004, Anon. 2004 and Jolly 2004) – and supposed infiltration of secret meetings which turned out to be publicly advertised and open to all (Boyle 2004). It should be noted, however, that only some sections of the media – typically those most dependent on Garda sources for news – were willing to adopt the police line in full.

Another result is the development of more antagonistic protest strategies – the refusal to give Gardaí advance notice of protests, the use of deliberate disruption and direct-action techniques, and the development of masking and 'black bloc' tactics (Anon. 2001b). Undoubtedly some activists would have supported these in any case, but the shift away from the tradition of mild policing of protest massively accelerated this trend. Here, as more generally, the State's turn towards coercion has resulted in a radicalisation of the movement.

The decline of state-centred organising strategies

Another key development has been the decline in state-centred ways of organising. The fifth Grassroots Gathering (GG), held in Dublin in June 2003, in the run up to the planned WEF meeting, was said by one experienced observer to be the largest libertarian gathering in Ireland since the 1970s. Libertarian, in this context, means strategies that are not geared towards taking state power, whether by electoral or revolutionary means; movements organised on a bottom-up or non-hierarchical basis; and a preference for direct action over tactics (such as petitions and demonstrations to the Dáil) geared towards lobbying the powerful.

In the event, the planned opposition by the Irish Social Forum and GG was apparently enough to cause the cancellation of the WEF meeting. The summer's mobilisation was not wasted, however, in that the movement's ability to organise a full-scale summit protest in May 2004 – and the 5,000 people who participated in the different events of that weekend – undoubtedly drew on those previous activities.

Anti-authoritarian organising is not new to Ireland, but (with the important exception of community activism) it has always been a minority trend within a political scene dominated by authoritarian, state-oriented traditions. As the movement of movements has developed in Ireland, however, the initiative has increasingly moved away from conventional protest to direct action; from top-down committee politics to bottom-up DIY organising; and from the left political parties and the NGOs to the anarchists, the counter-culture and the radical ecologists.

Among activists, the gradual disappearance of external points of reference for a top-down left solution – whether of a social-democratic or a Leninist nature – plays a role in this shift, as does the rising significance of the Internet, which makes it easier for small groups to organise effectively without controlling a printing press or a newspaper (Graeber 2002).

On a wider scale, the change reflects various trends. The increasing political power of neoliberalism restricts the effectiveness of left parties within the Dáil and local government; the constraints of EU membership and subordination to American foreign policy mean that NGO lobbying produces fewer and fewer returns; and the integration of Ireland into wider economic and political contexts makes the mirage of a liberal (let alone radical) alternative in government seem less and less plausible.

Partnership and its discontents

In effect, then, the growth of the new movement and the rise of anti-authoritarianism within it are both responses to the same process of capitalist globalisation, which produces simultaneously a declining ability of the Irish state to maintain popular consent and a declining credibility of political strategies which aim to work within 'the system' or to capture that system intact. The margins of manoeuvre, both for the state and for its traditional opponents, are getting narrower.

In this sense, the rise of the movement of movements is part of the same story as the rising social inequality brought about by the 'Celtic Tiger', and more specifically of the discontents of Ireland's remarkable system of social partnership. In a period when most European states were dismantling neo-corporatist arrangements of centralised political and economic decision-making involving employers, unions and the state (Lash and Urry 1987), Ireland was developing its own model for consensus, bringing first employers, unions and farmers and subsequently community and voluntary groups 'into the fold' – both for the distribution of the fruits of economic growth and for 'participation' in the decision-making process (Community Workers' Cooperative 1996).

However, the results of these arrangements have been to restrain wage demands while employers have seen profits rise massively, with a consequent redistribution in favour of the wealthiest in Irish society and a growing social inequality seen in housing, health and education (Allen 2000). As a result, while the Irish Congress of Trade Unions has itself remained committed to partnership, its member unions and even more their own members have been increasingly restive, with a growth in wildcat strikes and opposition to partnership (Irish Socialist Network 2003). This has been equally true among community groups, which despite their dependence on state funding have been more and more sceptical of the process of partnership (Powell and Geoghegan 2004).

As the institutionalised consensus mechanisms of Irish politics come under strain in the context of capitalist globalisation, it is hardly surprising to see the growth of a new movement against neo-liberalism and operating not just outside but also against those institutions and that consensus. In so doing, the movement is highlighting the needs of those sectors of society that lose out even in periods of neo-liberal growth, but also the costs of neo-liberalism to the environment and in its wars abroad.

Understanding the movement of movements: the goals of the movement

What are these global actors, in Ireland or elsewhere, seeking to achieve? One primary focus is opposition to capitalism's tendency to commodification, to turn the resources and activities needed to meet human needs into sources of profit (Offe 1984); and to its tendency to externalisation, to turn the costs of production (unemployment as factories are moved, pollution and waste production) into costs for states or individuals rather than for producers.

On a micro scale, this opposition can be seen in challenges to the privatisation of water in Cochabamba in Colombia (Notes from Nowhere 2003), or the introduction of bin charges in Dublin and elsewhere in Ireland (Workers' Solidarity Movement 2005); and equally in opposition to incinerators in Ringaskiddy or to road-building through archaeological monuments. On a medium (meso) scale, it manifests itself in challenges to multinationals the operations of which depend on extreme exploitation and violence against trade unionists in majority world countries (Klein 1999).

On the macro scale, it develops into full-scale resistance to the summits where world economic and political leaders shape the policies and institutions which structure and support this process, whether in Dublin in 2003 and 2004 or in Seattle, Genoa or Prague. It also entails opposition to the military and police face of this New World Order, the increased use of coercion – whether the tens of thousands of deaths in the Middle East or the slow erosion of civil liberties in Ireland (Dublin Grassroots Network 2004).

'Another world is under construction!'

At the same time, the movement represents the construction of an alternative kind of social order, even if only in fragmentary ways and on a relatively small scale. In its most general terms, it means large numbers of ordinary people building institutions geared to prioritising human and environmental needs over profit, and which operate on a voluntary and communicative basis (Habermas 1987) rather than being structured around the logics of the market or the state.

This alternative social order is not simply a 'temporary autonomous zone' (Bey 1991): it is a direct challenge to the existing social order in various ways. Public confrontations such as summit protests and counter-summits, where alternative models to dominant social and political policies are discussed, set out directly to challenge the legitimacy of the summits at which, in a globalised world, the policies which affect us all are agreed on (Yuen et al. 2001; Klein 2002; Castellina 2003).

This has proved perhaps the biggest success of the movement, in that the democratic legitimacy of the key summits and international organisations is highly questionable. Even the EU, one of the least undemocratic, is far removed from direct popular control, with the European Parliament being the weakest of its core institutions, the Nice Treaty having been rejected by the Irish electorate and the EU constitution by the French and Dutch. Other institutions – G8, WTO, GATS, WEF – can claim even less of a popular mandate.

Much like the French monarchy's retreat from Paris to Versailles, the movement of movements has forced political and economic elites to meet not just behind closed doors but behind barbed wire, 10-foot fences, sealed-off city centres and massive deployments of security forces – in the face of large and noisy popular opposition. Increasingly, then, the movement is making visible the new legitimation crisis at the core of neo-liberal politics.

Along with these, the development of counter-summits, activist networks and forums such as the World and European Social Forums, represent the beginnings of alternative political structures. Together with their ability to mount massive protests, shut down summits and prevent world leaders from 'bathing in the crowd', activists are debating alternative policies, creating new techniques and theories of cooperation, and contesting the direction of the movement. These are not yet 'dual-power institutions', but they are considerably more significant than simple meetings of specialist NGOs (De Sousa Santos 2003; Sen et al. 2004).

Lastly, the movement is connecting with new socio-cultural milieu (McKay

1996), which challenge the routines that have moulded everyday life in Fordist societies (Lichterman 1996). Whether the issue be cycling rather than driving, vegetarianism rather than meat-eating, Indymedia rather than Sky News, or – even more powerfully – political participation rather than a passive withdrawal, acting for public good rather than private gain (Jasper 1997; Szerszynski 1997), social movements create alternative ways of living (Melucci 1989). In an Ireland traditional routines which (from Mass attendance to the Gaelic Athletic Association) were themselves moulded by earlier social movements, this is of particular relevance.

Conclusion: what future for the movement of movements?

By definition, social movements seek to *move* beyond the present and beyond the status quo (Touraine 1981). In conclusion, then, it is appropriate to ask about the possible futures for the movement of movements, in Ireland and beyond, while being aware that movement practice is creative and liable to make such comments outdated sooner rather than later.

This chapter has argued that capitalist globalisation has a constant tendency to generate opposition, that neo-liberalism undermines the consent on which it is based, and that repression has so far been counterproductive. It is very likely, then, that movements against capitalist globalisation, in Ireland and elsewhere, will continue to appear in the near to medium-term future. In isolation, however, no single movement has the capacity to seriously upset the process.

The key question is thus the relationship between movements against capitalist globalisation in general and the movement of movements, in other words the extent to which new and existing movements are likely to find allies in each other, develop networks of cooperation and a sense of shared identity. How far can the current movement of movements develop alliances and strategies beyond its existing reach? At the time of writing, for example, the Irish movement is trying to move beyond the core participant movements of the left and the counterculture to connect with other social forces such as the women's movement, community activism and ethnic minorities.[6]

The central difficulty here is the much greater involvement of these latter movements with the State (Mullan and Cox 2000; Geoghegan 2006). The more a movement is reliant on the state for finance and access to political power the less likely it is to threaten that position (Piven and Cloward 1977). Much the same is true within movements, in that trade union officials, environmental NGOs or development organisations are much less likely to participate in the movement than shopfloor union activists, the direct-action wing of the ecology movement or Third World solidarity groups.

In these contexts, the problem is structural. Elites in state-centred organisations exist in a symbiotic relationship with state power and cannot easily restructure their organisations, even when state funding is declining and offers of 'consulta-tion' and 'participation' in decision-making turn out to have little substance in reality (Community Action Programme 2000; Murray 2004). It is therefore more likely that neo-liberal policy will undermine the grip of these elites over their own movements and open up possibilities for activists privileging mass mobilisation, confrontation and radical demands than that these elites will be able to execute a radical shift in policy and bring their organisations along with them.

In this sense, movements, organisations and activists are currently making decisions (not always consciously) about the significance or otherwise of the movement of movements. Some are in effect betting on the status quo and investing in the continuation of links with the State (Anon. 1998). Others are in effect betting on the movement of movements and investing in the development of links with other activists. These are often highly conscious processes, and activists generate a substantial amount of formal and informal theory in making these decisions (Barker and Cox 2002).

Much depends on these theories and decisions. Social movements – organ-ised human agency – have the capacity to remake the world, and at times do so. At present, capitalist globalisation – a highly organised movement from above – is engaged in the process of reshaping the planet in its own image. The question of whether it will be successful, or whether the movement of movements will succeed in constructing its 'other world', remains an open one.

Online resources

The best primary sources for the Irish movement are online; the following are useful
   starting points:
bluegreenearth magazine: www.bluegreenearth.com
The Dublin Grassroots Network site: www.geocities.com/eufortress
The Grassroots Gathering site: http://flag.blackened.net/infohub/grassrootsgathering
Irish Indymedia, at www.indymedia.ie
The Struggle site: http://struggle.ws
My own pages on the movement: www.iol.ie/~mazzoldi/toolsforchange/revolution.html

Notes

1 Thanks to Robert Allen, Chekov Feeney, and other activists for comments on an
   earlier draft.
2 See Raftery (2004) and Brown (2004a) for critiques of some of the misinformation in
   the mainstream media.
3 This chapter takes neo-liberalism to be the guiding economic *theory* enshrined in the
   policies of institutions such as the IMF, WB, WEF, WTO, GATS, etc. The social *prac-tice* of extending and imposing neo-liberal rules globally, and the resulting regime of
   accumulation, is capitalist globalisation (Sklair 2002). Finally, the *military* and inter-national relations structures within which this occurs can be described as a 'New
   World Order'.

4 This project, outlined in Cox (1999b), is currently being developed with Alf Nilsen (2004a, 2004b); see Nilsen and Cox (2005) for a fuller statement.
5 There is little published research on the recent change in policing in Ireland, although, when published, James Porter's work should remedy this. A number of authors have studied the policing of protest, most usefully Della Porta (1995) and Waddington (1996); see also Della Porta and Reiter (1998). Academic analysis of the policing of the movement of movements has been limited; Oskarsson and Petersson (2001), however, produced a paper designed to help the Swedish police after they shot three activists at Göteborg.
6 See, for example, the programmes for the 5th (June 2003) and 9th (April 2005) Grassroots Gatherings, available online: http://grassrootsgathering.freeservers.com /fifth.htm and www.indymedia.ie/newswire.php?story_id=68675 respectively, or Dunne's (2006) research on Rossport Solidarity Camp.

Bibliography

Alexander, P., 2001'Globalisation and Discontent', *African Social Review*, 5:1, 55–73.

Allen, K., 1997 *Fianna Fáil and Irish Labour* (London: Pluto).

Allen, K. 2000 *The Celtic Tiger* (Manchester: Manchester University Press).

Allen, R., 2004 *No Global* (London: Pluto).

Allen, R. and Jones, T., 1990 *Guests of the Nation* (London: Earthscan).

Alternative Ireland Directory Collective, 1982 *Alternative Ireland Directory 1981–82* (self-published).

Anonymous, 1998 'Tiocfaidh ár lá', *Do or Die*, 7, 100–8.

Anonymous, 2001a *On Fire* (London: One-Off Press).

Anonymous, 2001b *Bloc Book* (Rome: Stampa Alternativa).

Anonymous, 2004 'May Day Arms Stash', *Ireland on Sunday*, 4 April, p. 2.

Arrighi, G., 1994 *The Long Twentieth Century* (London: Verso).

Arrighi, G., Hopkins, T. and Wallerstein, I., 1989 *Anti-Systemic Movements* (London: Verso).

Ballymun Community Action Programme, 2000 *On the Balcony* (self-published).

Barker, C. and Cox, L., 2002 'What Have the Romans Ever Done for Us?', in Barker, C. and Tyldesley, M. (eds), *Eighth International Conference on Alternative Futures and Popular Protest* (Manchester: Manchester Metropolitan University).

Berger, P. and Luckmann, T., 1967 *The Social Construction of Reality* (Harmondsworth: Penguin).

Bey, H., 1991 *T.A.Z.: Temporary Autonomous Zone* (Brooklyn, NY: Autonomedia).

Bircham, E., and Charlton, J. (eds), 2001 *Anti-Capitalism*, 2nd edn (London: Bookmarks).

Boyle, D., 2004 'Absolute May-Hem', *Irish Star*.

Brecher, J., Costello, T. and Smith, B., 2000 *Globalization from Below* (Cambridge, MA: South End).

Breen, R., Hannan, D., Rottman, D. and Whelan, C., 1990 *Understanding Contemporary Ireland* (Dublin: Gill & Macmillan).

Brown, H., 2004a 'Consenting to Capital in the Irish Media', *Irish Journal of Sociology*, 13:2, 128–41.

Brown, H., 2004b 'Garda Plan May Trigger Trouble', *Evening Herald*, 23 April, p. 14.

Caldwell, J., 2004 'May Day', *Garda Review*, May, 31–5.

Castellina, L. (ed), 2003 *Il cammino dei movimenti* (Napoli: Intra Moenia).

Charlton, J., 2000 'Talking Seattle', *International Socialism Journal*, 86, 3–18.

Cockburn, A. and St Claire, A., 2000 *Five Days that Shook the World* (London: Verso).

Cohen, R. and Rai, S. (eds), 2000 *Global Social Movements* (London: Athlone).

Community Action Programme, 2000 *On the Balcony* (self-published).

Community Workers' Cooperative, 1996 *Partnership in Action* (Galway: CWC).

Conlon, D., 2004 'Anarchist Army Plot Bloodbath in Ireland', *News of the World*, 4 April, p. 7.

Coulter, C. and Coleman, S., 2003 *The End of Irish History?* (Manchester: Manchester University Press).

Cox, L., 1997 'Towards a Sociology of Counter Cultures?' in McKenna, E. and O'Sullivan, R. (eds), *Ireland* (Belfast: Queens University).

Cox, L., 1999a 'Structure, Routine and Transformation', in Barker, C. and Tyldesley, M. (eds), *Fifth International Conference on Alternative Futures and Popular Protest* (Manchester: Manchester Metropolitan University).

Cox, L., 1999b 'Building Counter Cultures', Ph.D thesis, Trinity College Dublin.

Cox, L., 2001 'Globalisation from Below?', paper presented at the 2nd William Thompson Weekend School, Firkin Crane Centre, Cork.

Cox, L., 2003 'Eppur si muove', in Barker, C. and Tyldesley, M. (eds), *Ninth International Conference on Alternative Futures and Popular Protest* (Manchester: Manchester Metropolitan University).

De Sousa Santos, B., 2003 'The World Social Forum', available: www.ces.fe.uc.pt/bss/documentos/wsf.pdf.

Dee, H., 2004 *Anti-Capitalism* (London: Bookmark).

Della Porta, D., 1995 *Social Movements, Political Violence and the State* (Cambridge: Cambridge University Press).

Della Porta, D., 2003 *I new global* (Bologna: Il Mulino)

Della Porta, D., Kriesi, H. and Rucht, D. (eds), 1999 *Social Movements in a Globalizing World* (London: Macmillan).

Della Porta, D. and Reiter, H. (eds), 1998 *Policing Protest* (Minneapolis: University of Minnesota Press). Della Porta, D., and Tarrow, S. (eds), 2005 *Transnational Protest and Global Activism* (New York: Rowman and Littlefeld.

Diani, M., 1992 'The Concept of Social Movement', *Social Review*, 40:1, 1–25.

Dublin Grassroots Network, 2004 'Fortress Dublin?', available: www.geocities.com/eufortress/pr/fortressdublin7may.html.

Dunne, T., 2006 'Rossport Solidarity Camp', in Barker, C. and Tyldesley, M. (eds), *Eleventh International Conference on Alternative Futures and Popular Protest* (Manchester: Manchester Metropolitan University.

Geoghegan, M. 2006 'Consensus, Conflict and Community', in Barker, C. and Tyldesley, M. (eds), *Eleventh International Conference on Alternative Futures and Popular Protest* (Manchester: Manchester Metropolitan University).

George S., 2004 *Another world is possible if . . .* (London: Verso).

Graeber, D., 2002 'The New Anarchists', *New Left Review*, 13, 61–73.

Gramsci, A., 1977 *Quaderni del carcere*, 2nd edn (Torino: Einaudi).

Guidry, J., Kennedy, M. and Zald, M. (eds), 2000 *Globalization and Social Movements* (Ann Arbor: University of Michigan Press).

Habermas, J., 1987 *Theory of Communicative Action* (Cambridge: Polity Press), vol. 2.

Hamel, P., Lustiger-Thaler, H. and Roseneil, S. (eds), 2001 *Globalization and Social Movements* (Basingstoke: Palgrave).

Hardt, M. and Negri, A., 2000 *Empire* (Cambridge, MA: Harvard University Press).

Hardt, M. and Negri, A., 2004 *Multitude* (New York: Penguin)

Social movements and Ireland

Harvey, D., 1989 *The Condition of Postmodernity* (Oxford: Blackwell).

Harvie, D. et al. (eds), 2005 *Shut Them Down!* (Leeds/Brooklyn: Dissent!/Autonomedia).

Irish Socialist Network, 2003 *Parting Company* (self-published).

Jasper, J., 1997 *The Art of Moral Protest* (Chicago, IL: University of Chicago Press).

Jolly, L., 2004 'We'll Gas Bertie', *Irish Sun*, 24 April, p. 1.

Katsiaficas, G., 1987 *The Imagination of the New Left* (Boston, MA: South End).

Keck, M., and Sikkink, K., 1998 *Activists Beyond Borders* (Ithaca, NY: Cornell University Press).

Klein, N., 1999 *No Logo* (London: Flamingo).

Klein, N., 2002 *Fences and Windows: Dispatches from the front lines of the globalization debate* (London: Flamingo).

Lash, S. and Urry, J., 1987 *The End of Organized Capitalism* (Cambridge: Polity Press).

Lichterman, P., 1996 *The Search for Political Community* (Cambridge: Cambridge University Press).

Linebaugh, P. and Rediker, M., 2000 *The Many-Headed Hydra* (Boston, MA: Beacon Press).

Marcos, S., 2001 *Our Word Is Our Weapon* (London: Serpent's Tail).

McKay, G., 1996 *Senseless Acts of Beauty* (London: Verso).

McNally, D., 2002 *Another World Is Possible* (New York: Arbeiter Ring).

Marx, K., 1852 *The Eighteenth Brumaire of Louis Bonaparte*, available: www.marxists.org/archive/marx/works/1852/18th-brumaire/index.htm.

Marx, K. and Engels, F., 1998 *The Communist Manifesto* (London: Verso).

Melucci, A. 1989 *Nomads of the Present* (London: Hutchinson).

Mertes, T. (ed.), 2004 *A Movement of Movements* (London: Verso).

Mullen, C. and Cox, L., 2000 'Social Movements Never Died', paper presented at the ISA–BSA conference 'Are Social Movements Reviving?', Manchester Metropolitan University.

Murray, M., 2004 'Waste Management in Ireland', unpublished PhD thesis, National University of Ireland, Maynooth.

Notes from Nowhere, 2003 *We Are Everywhere* (London: Verso).

Nilsen, A., 2004a 'Practical Experience, Knowledge Production and Theoretical Understanding', paper presented at the 'Politics and Knowledge' conference, University of Bergen.

Nilsen, A., 2004b 'Against the Anti-Politics Machine', paper presented at the 'Education, Knowledge and Development' conference, Norwegian Association for Development Research, University of Bergen.

Nilsen, A., and Cox, L., 2005 'At the Heart of Society Burns the Fire of Social Movements', in Barker, C. and Tyldesley, M. (eds), *Tenth International Conference on Alternative Futures and Popular Protest* (Manchester: Manchester Metropolitan University).

Offe, C., 1984 *Contradictions of the Welfare State* (London: Hutchinson).

Oskarsson, M. and Peterson, A., 2001 'Policing Political Protest', paper presented at the 5th ESA Congress, Helsinki.

Pianta, M., 2001 *Globalizzazione dal basso* (Roma: Manifestolibri).

Piven, F. and Cloward, R., 1977 *Poor People's Movements* (New York: Pantheon).

Polet, F. and CETRI (eds), 2004 *Globalizing Resistance* (London: Pluto).

Powell, F. and Geoghegan, M., 2004 *The Politics of Community Development* (Dublin: A. & A. Farmar).

Raftery, M., 2004 'Disturbing Reflections on Gardaí', *Irish Times*, 13 May, p. 18.

Sauermann, B. (ed), 2003 *2/15* (New York: AK/Hello).

Sansonetti, P., 2002 *Dal '68 ai no-global* (Milano: Baldini & Castoldi).

SchNews, 2001 *Monopolise Resistance?* (Brighton: SchNews).

Sen, J. et al. (eds), *World Social Forum* (New Delhi: Viveka).

Sheridan, K., 2004 'What Does it Take to Protect This Man?', *Irish Times*, Weekend, 19 June, p. 1.

Sklair, L., 2002 *Globalization*, 3rd edn (Oxford: Oxford University Press).

Smith, M. and Guarnizo, L. (eds), 1998 *Transnationalism from Below* (New Brunswick, NJ: Transaction Publishers).

Solnit, D. (ed.), 2004 *Globalize Liberation* (San Francisco, CA: City Lights).

Starhawk, 2002 *Webs of Power* (Gabriola Island, Canada: New Society).

Starr, A., 2000 *Naming the Enemy* (London: Zed Books).

Szerszynski, B., 1997 'Voluntary Associations and the Sustainable Society', in Jacobs, M. (ed.), *Greening the Millennium* (Oxford: Blackwell).

Tarrow, S., 1998 *Power in Movement*, 2nd edn (Cambridge: Cambridge University Press).

Thompson, E.P., 1966 *The Making of the English Working Class* (Harmondsworth: Penguin).

Thompson, E.P., 1977 *The Poverty of Theory* (London: Merlin).

Touraine, A., 1981 *The Voice and the Eye* (Cambridge: Cambridge University Press).

Waddington, P., 1996 'The Other Side of the Barricades', in Barker, C. and Kennedy, P. (eds), *To Make Another World* (Aldershot: Avebury Press).

Williams, R., 1983 *Keywords*, 2nd edn (London: Fontana).

Workers' Solidarity Movement, 2005 'The Campaigns Against the Bin Charges', available: http://struggle.ws/wsm/bins.html.

Yuen, E., Katsiaficas, G. and Burton Rose, D. (eds), 2001 *The Battle of Seattle* (New York: Soft Skull).

Index

abortion 3, 71, 72, 75, 81, 100
  Green Paper (1995) 70
  information and right to travel
    66–7, 70, 74
  referendum 9, 70
Adams, Jonathan 106
Afghanistan *see* anti-war movements
Ahern, Bertie 210, 218
AkiDwA (African Women's Network)
  207
alternative food movement 168–86
  added value 176–7
  bartering 179, 185
  Eurotocques 184
  informal networking 178–80, 181,
    183, 185
  institutionalisation of 183
  livelihood 169
  locality 169
  marketing 172
  opposition to genetically modified
    foods 160, 169, 170, 178
  organic movement 8, 170, 174,
    175–6, 177, 179, 180, 182, 183
  restaurateurs 177, 180, 184
  Slow Food 178, 184
  West Cork 176
  women 176, 177, 184
  working utopias 181–2, 184, 185
Andersen Mary 69
animal rights 45
An Taisce 151, 153–4, 156, 157, 159,
  160, 161
Anti-Discrimination Pay Act (1974)
  69
anti-systemic movements 213

anti-war movements 4, 212
  Afghanistan 218
  First World War 49
  Iraq 210
  Vietnam 11
Association of Business and
  Professional Women 66
Association of Refugees and Asylum
  Seekers in Ireland 200
Attic Press 61, 62, 67, 70, 80, 81

Baile na hAbhann, Co. Galway 132
Ballybrado (Tipperary) 176
Belfast 113, 116, 118, 198
Belfast Agreement (1998) 7
Bennett, Louie 48, 52, 53
Bentham, Jeremy 107
Bewley, Victor 100
Biodynamic Association 175
black protest activity (1950s) 17
Boland, Eavan 80
Boole Library, UCC 61
Bove, Jose 169
Browne, Noel 100
Bush, George 210, 218, 219

Campaign Against a Racist
  Referendum 207
Campaign for an Irish Women's
  Centre 70
Campaign for Homosexual Equality
  (CHE) 96, 98, 103
Campaign for Homosexual Law
  Reform (CHLR) 95, 99–102
Carnsore Point protests (1979) 154,
  217

[*231*]

EU authorised representative for GPSR:
Easy Access System Europe, Mustamäe tee 50,
10621 Tallinn, Estonia
gpsr.requests@easproject.com

www.ingramcontent.com/pod-product-compliance
Lightning Source LLC
Chambersburg PA
CBHW061724270326
41928CB00011B/2106